Praise for **Radiating**
Wichita Women and the 1970s Feminist Movement

"Sixties' theories moved the '70s to action. It was a decade of great flux. I was new to Kansas, career, and motherhood in the mid-'70s. Now, I can read the stories of what else was going on while I was grading papers and changing diapers, because this volume gives a reader the trees and the forest. While certain buzzwords have largely faded from local discourse, the names of certain women have not. These were women active in all realms of society: politics, law, medicine, academics, business, religion, the arts. Their names show up over and over in these essays, some often enough that we feel we know them, cheer for them, want to thank them for their persistent efforts. Personal stories are political. They often began with one person imagining 'What if…?' This is a book that shows us some sample responses to that courageous question." —**Jeanine Hathaway, Author of forthcoming** *Ex-Nun Poems* **and Professor of Creative Writing at Seattle Pacific University**

"These stories from the heartland are perfect for Women's and Gender Studies classes because they allow readers to understand the people behind the political rhetoric – heartland women whose lives were forever empowered by the women's movement. The movement was not something restricted to coastal moments in front of TV screens. The Midwestern movement grew also from the yearning for freedom and opportunity felt by women at that time. Their achievements in the face of struggle are inspiring chronicles that belong to any true account of American history." —**Dorothy C. Miller, Ph.D., Director of Flora Stone Mather Center for Women, Case Western Reserve University**

"This compilation is an embarrassment of riches, private, political, funny, heart wrenching. Beneficiary of the generation this book represents, I offer to these writers, these movers and shakers, a favorite moment with my daughter, granddaughter to the revolution: 'Poor boys!' declared four-year-old Jade one day. 'They can only wear pants.' Only. Her sense of her own volition and options in the world are directly due to the blood, sweat, tears and words of her foremothers. Many thanks, from me and her." —**Antonya Nelson, Novelist of critically acclaimed book,** *Bound*

"Myrne Roe lived these exciting times, made herstory and now has recorded it in a very accessible and lively way." —**Gretchen Eick, Author of** *Dissent in Wichita: The Civil Rights Movement in the Midwest, 1954-72*

"*Radiating Like A Stone* is a thorough, comprehensive chronicle of the struggles, setbacks, advances and journeys of a community of Wichita women who found locations and relationships of support that empowered their resistance to oppression in the 1970s. As a relative newcomer to Kansas at a time when women's rights are again under attack, it is reassuring to me that these women were and are here and that we can resist in honor of our daughters, as we once resisted in honor of our mothers." **—Deborah S. Ballard-Reisch, Ph.D., Professor, Elliott School of Communication, Wichita State University**

"*Radiating Like a Stone* is a gold mine of Wichita history. This wide ranging compilation of memories of Wichita women who participated in the feminist movement circa 1970 does an excellent job of representing the organizational effort, galvanizing issues, reflections on daily life, and striking moments of enlightenment of that period. The electrifying drama that characterized the heady days of what used to be called women's liberation is here for the reader to enjoy as well as ponder, as is the courage and restless intellectual engagement of the women presented here. I could not put this book down." **—Deborah A. Gordon, Associate Professor of Women's Studies, Wichita State University**

"Wichita had a unique collection of talented women in the 70s in Wichita who were friends and mentors and made a huge contribution to the state. As Kansas women, these "Sunflower Sisters" stood on the shoulders of many before them. Kansas allowed women to vote in municipal elections early on, and then statewide suffrage was the law by 1912, almost a decade ahead of the country. Kansas women were the first in the country to be a dentist, a mayor, a black lawyer and a Pacific explorer. The first woman to argue before the Supreme Court was a Kansan, as was the first woman speaker at a Republican National Convention. Kansas elected the first woman sheriff, was the birthplace of the first woman player for the Harlem Globetrotters. Two Kansas Senators introduced the first Equal Rights Amendment in 1923. The legacy of the early Kansas women leaders was fulfilled in the '70s by the Wichita women whose views and accomplishment are captured in this book." **—Kathleen Sebelius, former Governor of Kansas**

Radiating Like a Stone

Wichita Women and the 1970s Feminist Movement

Compiled and edited by Myrne Roe

WATERMARK PRESS

Wichita

FIRST WATERMARK PRESS EDITION, 2011

Watermark Press
4701 East Douglas Avenue
Wichita, KS 67218-1012

The following works are reprinted with permission:
"Soccer by Moonlight" by Anita Skeen from *Moore Golden Apples:*
A Further Celebration and Women in Sport (Papier-Mache Press, 1986)
"On Vicki's Porch" by Anita Skeen from *Never the Whole Story* (Michigan State University Press, 2011)
"Confessions of Born-Again Feminist" by Linda Bell Gebert, *Equal Time*, 1977
"Untitled" by Mardy Murphy Previously published in the *Wichita Independent*, July 23, 1975
"Dick and Jane" by Ruth Ann Messner, *Equal Time*, September 1978
"The Long March to Equality Condensed" by Carolyn S. Russell, *Equal Time*, August 1978
"Weekend Was Eye-Opening; Needs Retelling in 2002" by Peg Vines
Previously published in a Special to *The Wichita Eagle* article, Sunday, July 14, 2002
"Confessions of a Born-Again Actress" by Myrna Paris, Marilynn Gump
Edited version of previously published article in *Equal Time*, August, 1978
"Thank You, Anita Hill" by Trix Niernberger
Excerpted from article originally published in *F5* on April 4, 2003
"Revisiting Domestic Violence: One Woman's Story" by Rachel
Excerpted from an article by Susan Melvin, D.O., published in the *California Family Physician*, November/December 1994
Photograph on page 165 is printed with permission by Trish Higgins.

Library of Congress Control Number
2011046754

Cover design by Beth Golay
Layout design by Kate Goad

ISBN: 978-0-615-53794-8

Printed in the United State of America.

10 9 8 7 6 5 4 2 1

This book is dedicated to my grandmothers, Jennie Stone Dorsey and Lena Ellis Richards, and to my mother, Ivah Dorsey Richards. Each illustrated how she could be a positive presence in the lives of others despite being directed into narrow roles of her time by patriarchal views. Each was a strong woman who did what she must while dreaming for more.

And to my younger sister, Jane Richards Hicks, who fought attitudes and events that would have crippled many women, but who became instead, a strong, caring and successful woman.

Table of Contents

Challenging Financial Status Quo...........................87

Removing Sexism From the Curriculum 103

Embracing Our Artistic Gifts 217

Facing Crimes of Violence Against Women 231

Foreword

In August 2009 Planned Parenthood and the National Organization for Women held a statewide meeting at Unity Church in Wichita. The purpose was to develop strategies for lobbying the Kansas Legislature in 2010. A friend and I decided to attend the morning session for reasons neither of us could explain. A way to remember days when we were embroiled in similar concerns? Curiosity about what younger advocates were saying about current women's rights issues? Might see some old friends? Maybe something we should be involved in again? After the meeting, we talked of how the women's movement 40 years ago had made countless positive differences in the lives of the younger attendees, of which they either did not seem to be aware or simply didn't care. As is almost always the case, the younger ones thought they were inventing something new and the older ones were certain they were not being accorded appropriate recognition for their past deeds!

That evening after the meeting, I recalled how many organizations feminist activists started in Wichita during the 1970s because of needs not addressed and services not provided to our mothers or to us. If the 1960s were the time for intellectual exploration of feminism, it was the next decade that formulated solutions. It was a frustrating but exciting and successful time fueled in our middle-American and mid-sized city, mostly known for making airplanes inside town and growing wheat outside of town. We weren't alone of course. The national movement was at its strongest, and many of its leaders came to Wichita to give and receive encouragement. We also had women from throughout Kansas and American history who had laid the groundwork upon which we could build.

Did we hate men? No. In fact, without the help of sympathetic men our task would have been much, much harder. We had husbands, boyfriends, sons and fathers, and we didn't dislike them all for our unequal state. Our anger was not personalized in that way. It was against the ignorant and narrow views of society about male and female roles perpetuated, in large part, by patriarchal religious views and by long-held tyranny of those who did not want to lose power, either because they were men or they were women who gained their status from the men with whom they lived or associated.

Did we include minority women among our mostly white, middle-class and educated group of activists, a large percentage whom were already in professional jobs or working toward getting them? Not always as much as we should have. We should have worked harder to include diversity as a goal in the movement. We failed to understand the conflicts felt by minority women, particularly Blacks who also were involved in the civil rights movement. Many of the women in the feminist movement were as well, but for black women the civil rights movement ran deeper and was far more personal. Homemakers were not as involved as they should have been either, especially early on. Later we woke up to the fact that those who chose homemaking had special concerns that needed to be addressed, too.

Did we change everything forever? Sexism certainly suffered a life-changing blow. We didn't, however, destroy it. Like racism and bigotry against gays and lesbians, sexism is a virus for which there has yet to be a cure. It's a sickness among those who simply cannot accept that human beings, if given equal opportunity to learn and hope and persevere, can reach their goals and contribute to society, making all our lives better.

The entries in this book tell the story of an extraordinary era in Wichita. The participants wanted to document what was gained 40 plus years ago so it won't be forgotten. History forgotten, after all, is history that will repeat itself. None of the women participants who remembered the shameful inequality that once existed wanted it to happen again.

In conclusion, I wish to note poet Anita Skeen's introduction in which she shares her Wichita experiences in the 1970s. Her poem, "On Vicki's Porch," is the source for the title of this anthology. It speaks to old friendships that bonded women both in the days spent struggling for equality and in the later days of reuniting. Together the friends bring warmth and light to each other. Indeed, they make the poet "radiate like a stone."

The following stories and poems you will read are bits and pieces of a local movement that changed the lives of women. May the young people who attended The Unity Church meeting that served as motivation for this anthology find ways to address the inequalities that still exist in our society. May they proceed with the same energy and determination that the writers in this anthology did. May each one radiate like a stone.

Myrne Roe

Introduction

Radiating Like a Stone: Three Poems in Context
Anita Skeen

When I sat down on the Friday of Thanksgiving weekend to find several poems for this anthology that I'd written while I was living in Wichita in the 1970s, I thought it would be a snap. I'd go back though my old notebooks and pull out several poems that spoke to the political and social events of the time, the community of women working and playing together, the gathering of friends. I knew I'd find many poems pondering the Flint Hills; the steel structures sprouting up from the prairie; oil wells to windmills to grain elevators; the long lonely ribbon of I-70 I seemed always to travel in winter and get stuck in some place like Hays or Colby during the worst snowstorm of the season; and the sky, everywhere the sky. I'd come from the hills of West Virginia to take my first academic tenure-track job (for which I later found out I was paid $6,200 and my two male colleagues hired the same year were paid $10,000 each). I had some adjusting to do.

But I'd forgotten how many poems I'd written about and for individual women in the community, and the number of poems I'd written in emotional states from outrage to disbelief at the patriarchal goings-on in the community as well as the nation. What I was most pleased to find, however, were those poems that took me back to soccer field and front porches, lunches at Dr. Redbird's, late night dancing at the Bus Station, and consciousness-raising groups where we sat on the orange shag carpet in a tiny living room and made plans to take on Anita Bryant, who was coming to Wichita to campaign against a ballot initiative to support gay and lesbian rights.

Robert Frost once wrote, "Poetry is news that stays news," and reading back through the poems I'd written during the 1970s and on into the first decade of the 21st century, I was never more convinced that he was right, for two reasons. First, when I read through the dedications I'd typed onto the poems from those Wichita years, the names string out like a list of inductees into a Wichita Women's Hall of Fame: Leigh Aaron-Leary, Sharon Werner, Lee Starkel, Beth Alexander, Susan Kraft, Cecelia Traugh, Cathy Burack, Mary Martha Stevens, Kay Closson, Jeanine Hathaway, P.J. Wyatt, Sally Kitch, Carol Konek, Carol Barrett, Marlene Hoagland, Pat Kelso, Karen Humphreys, Sue Nelson. These are only a few of the many women who impacted my life in the decade of the 1970s, and I include them here because I am sure their names will come up in other essays in this book, either as authors of the essays themselves, or as role models, mentors or colleagues mentioned by other authors. And there are many, many more that shaped my life but did not necessarily shape my poems.

Secondly, I am aware of how many of the issues that we came together as a community of Wichita women to work for or raise our voices in opposition to are still on the radar screen today. Our country is involved in another winless war, women are still battered by husbands and partners, doctors who perform abortions (still legal, for now) are gunned down in the vestibules of churches and in parking lots, gay and lesbian people do not have equal rights. All of these issues make front page news today, just as they did in the 1970s. Those of us who are poets are still writing about them because we believe that literature is not simply an imitation of life, as some critics say, but *a challenge to life*, that our voices, if heard only by a few, can record a moment or question a behavior that can change a life.

When I looked back on those poems I'd written nearly 40 years ago, I found myself in the room with those women; we were young and energized, and sometimes angry; we were going to make a difference. I happen to believe that all of us have, some in more visible and public ways than others, but all of us have left our mark, whether we stayed in Wichita or went to New York City or Boston, Bend, OR, or East Lansing, MI.

This commentary may seem pretty long-winded for a poet who promised the editor of this anthology she would "send a few poems," but as I tell my students, context is everything. The context in which I came of age as a writer, as a feminist, as a committed-to-social-justice adult was the Wichita women's community of the '70s and '80s.

I came in 1972. I left in 1990 to take a position in the Department of English at Michigan State University. Those 18 years spent among the vibrant and sometimes ferociously feminist women I knew taught me the strategies for making change, the creativity that comes in collaboration, the strength of community and perhaps, most importantly, I learned that friends who work together on behalf of social change and who sacrifice because it is the right thing to do will remain friends forever.

I still come back to Wichita once or twice a year. I stay in the homes of women who helped put the WSU women's studies program on the map, women who stood with me against discrimination in the workplace, women whom I stood with in picket lines, women who took me in when I had nowhere else to go. I have been friends with some of these women for more than 40 years, some fewer than 20. I will be friends with all of these women for the rest of my life.

Finally, I want to say a few words about the three poems I selected to include with this essay. I chose poems that had not been previously published because I wanted them to be fresh and new to readers. Many of the political poems and poems I wrote about women in the Wichita community were published in my first collection of oems, *Each Hand A Map* (Naiad Press). That book would never have been written, nor gone to press, without the unflagging support of the women I knew, particularly P.J. Wyatt and Kay Closson, who told me time after time, rejection letter after rejection letter, "Send those poems out again. Tomorrow." For once, I listened, and then there was a book.

Also, I wanted to include poems in this essay that celebrated women in community because, ultimately, that is what Wichita means to me. So the first poem I chose is a poem about a soccer team I played on, The Sizzlers, the oldest team in the league made up of professional women who wanted to be together more than we wanted to win, though we did want that too. The second poem is from a decade later and the third, a decade more, but each is important to this narrative, this progression. The second is the poem I wrote for the dedication of the Plaza of Heroines on the campus of Wichita State University. It is about a larger community of women than that soccer team, one that crosses geography and historical boundaries, but one that is centered, clearly, in Wichita. The final poem is one I wrote several years ago on a visit to Wichita. A group of those old friends I mentioned early in this essay gathered for an impromptu tea party on Vicki Stamp's front porch. I include this poem as a testament to the fact that community continues despite geography, despite life circumstance, despite aging. Women in sport, women in history, women in friendship. Women in Wichita, then and now.

Soccer by Moonlight
for Susie Massoth and The Sizzlers

They come to this schoolyard after work forgetting
patients, clients, students, and columns
of figures dead on the page. It is evening,

mid-November. Trees still argue
with stubborn leaves. Grass creeps back
into the earth for warmth.

On the bloodshot horizon, the curious eye
of the moon surfaces from sleep.
Again the blue team kicks off the ball.

In this strange light their feet
skate the silver pond of the ground.
The ball loops in the air.

To the east, legs tangle;
to the west, voices in shadow.
The ball scurries across the field, trailed

by two in blue, scoots just outside the posts
toward the ready shoe of the player whose leg leans
into it, a hammer swinging. The ball skids

through the goalie's outstretched arms, vanishes
in the net. The moon, buoyant overhead, lights
the night as the women embrace.

Fire Circle
for the dedication of the Plaza of Heroines at
Wichita State University

In our lives, for centuries, bricks
and stones:

stacked together they made a house
we made into a home. Laid out
around the fire, a hearth
we made the heart of that home.

Here we make a circle of bricks,
benches of granite, pavers of rock.
Each bears a woman's name,
each bares a woman's life.
Lives touch in this circle, women
who never met, never talked
across the back fence,
never exchanged recipes
or code words, never signed
petitions on neighboring lines.
Missouri borders Florida,
West Virginia's north of Canada.
Kansas is still the center of everything.

Chronology's gone out the window.
Here, time is a circle of heartbeats.

We come to this circumference
to kindle the fire. We light the names
with the sparks of our voices, sing
the syllables into flame. We fan
a prairie fire, the lives behind the names
blazing again in love and protest, art
and justice, nourishment and mystery,
the tongues visible for miles.

We warm our hearts beside this hearth.

On Vicki's Porch

We called it the *stoop*, a concrete
slab beneath the back door,
two steps down to the ground.
I sat there in the bee humming
thick of summer. Sniffing
the air for rain. Listening for tires
chewing up dirt. Watching
wooly worms hump across rocks.
My daddy painted the stoop green,
then, years later, brick red. In August
the stoop was a hot coal.

       This May we sit in wicker chairs
       on Vicki's curved porch, in the crook
       of its arm. This is the porch
       of Southern lore, Victorian veranda
       open to Lake Michigan, vacation
       folk from Chicago clinking cold drinks.
       But we're in Wichita, already a sea of heat.
       Old friends gather here for chat.
       Some crackers, a few glasses of wine,
       salted nuts, a bowl of fruit. One red apple
       on a glass plate, two strawberries touching.
       There's a tornado gusting from the west
       but we don't know it yet, one that will be
       headline news. The grass in the yard
       murmurs, talk of the entwined.

       Across the street, a dog hops on his igloo
       doghouse like a circus dog on a ball.
       But he's going nowhere, barking. A car
       goes by, honks the horn. *It's David*,
       someone says. Another says she's writing
       about hope, attempting to prove it doesn't exist.
       One of us has survived an aneurism.
       One this day gets a diagnosis: Parkinson's.
       One of us wants her life to change. Another
       believes it will. Two of us live four states away.

It's been years since we've all been together.
The porch shimmers, a constellation
harboring stars, a song learning its own notes.
The wind sings one tune we all know.

I sang to myself on the stoop.
I pulled my knee against my chest
and rocked, imagining the days
ahead, inventing words
I needed, letting warmth seep
up into my body, radiating like a stone.

Exploring Feminism

"In some fundamental way, I was awakened to the reality that my perspective alone was not enough. What I care about can't be just about me. Were that the case, what I care about would always be at the mercy of someone else. Perhaps this tiny epiphany that followed me along helped me realize how essential a feminist perspective would be in my life."

—Anna R. Anderson (A Feminist Perspective)

A Feminist Perspective

Anna R. Anderson

Throughout the '60s my primary interest as an activist of sorts was centered on civil rights and racial equality. Women's issues were tangentially in my brain, but having gone through my younger years always believing I could do anything, I gave little thought to what might one day be denied me on the basis of my gender. And so life went on into the early '70s when I took my first class with the word *women* in the title. It was Writing by Women taught by Dorothy Walters. In taking the course, my interest was in the writers – Flannery O'Connor, Willa Cather, Katherine Anne Porter – not in the fact that those writers were women. I expected nothing other than a good course in literature, and I was certainly not seeking a consciousness-raising experience. I guess that's why I didn't recognize it when it came.

A remark, an admonition from an instructor to a student, became a kind of mind worm that wriggled into my life. The remark came, not from Dorothy Walters, but from Carol Konek, who was addressing the class one day. A dialogue had developed between Carol and a young woman who related a situation, the particulars of which I do not recall other than the manner in which she finished, which was by calling some person from her story a son-of-a bitch.

"Never say that!" Carol quickly replied. Her manner was so strong that I remember feeling a little embarrassed for the student, and as well for myself, for *son-of-a-bitch* was an oft used word in my vocabulary. Carol explained that the name, though unintended, insulted the mother and not the son, the rightful target of the scorn.

Bah! I thought. My reaction was that she was over-reaching. And while I understood her point, I also knew that virtually no one who ever spat out the name or had been labeled as such, gave any thought to the literal meaning of the words. It is, after all, just a derogatory expression you pick up while building your lexicon of bad words. Let's not lose our sense of perspective here! But that was just it. It was all about perspective.

Why has that experience stayed with me after all these years? I don't worry myself over the mother of some jerk when he gets called a son-of-a-bitch. The insult that bothers Carol doesn't register with me in the same way. I think the memory sticks, because on that day I witnessed a concern so great. For Carol, any issue that would diminish women in someone's view had to be reckoned with. And reckoning meant speaking out, explaining, teaching, correcting, whatever it took to help people understand.

In some fundamental way, I was awakened to the reality that my perspective alone was not enough. What I care about can't be just about me. Were that the case, what I care about would always be at the mercy of someone else. Perhaps this tiny epiphany that followed me along helped me realize how essential a feminist perspective would be in my life.

Confessions of a Born-Again Feminist

Linda Bell Gebert

And they lived happily ever after. Raise your hands. How many of you bought it? Yeah, me too. Then, once upon a time, I began to doubt.

I realize now there were many signals along the way to liberation. They flash and burn from the inside out. The diary of this particular mad housewife concerns the nature of such fires. Coming of age in the 1950s, I was too indoctrinated by fairy tale beginnings and endings to recognize the clues for some time.

My upbringing was traditional and not unlike Joan Didion's who said in *A Book Of Common Prayer*, "As a child of a comfortable family in the temperate zone she had been, as a matter of course, provided with clean sheets, orthodontia, lamb chops, living grandparents, one brother named Dickie, ballet lessons and casual timely information about menstruation and the care of flat silver."

I abhor the notion that there is no sense of humor in the women's movement, so I decided to write it as satire. But as I began, I kept thinking, this is not so damn funny. This is life. This is my life. This is the reality of women's lives, and something is definitely out of kilter. But in the interest of levity, picture this scene: The school bus spews out a herd of children and within five minutes the dog has peanut butter in his fur, the couch is a trampoline, dirty socks are caught in the chandelier and the Red Cross, sensing the devastation, is knocking at the door.

I used to believe I could get sympathy from my mate or that it would help if I did. "What if?" I asked him. "What if someone came to your workplace and destroyed everything at the end of the day; how would you feel? Would the neighbors whisper, 'Gee, he's a lousy housekeeper, wonder what he does all day, watch soap operas?' "

Magazines of the day constantly told us how to improve our lives or keep our husbands interested. But did you ever hear of a husband wondering how to make things better by reading articles like "Putting the Zing Back in the Bedroom" or "How to Help Your Wife Live Longer?" No. It's apparent that husbands and wives live on different planets most of the time.

Discontent in the years B.F. (before feminism) was not always due to relationships with men. I recall one day when I was attending a coffee where the "girls" were planning a multiple choice: (a) bake sale (b) card party (c) garage sale to raise bucks for (a) church (b) PTA (c) ladies hospital auxiliary. Whatever the cause, it didn't feel like real friendships. It felt more like superficial relationships – doing what we thought we were supposed to be doing.

Women's conversations bored me. I bored myself when I was engaged in them. Did you ever edge over to the men's side of the room at a party in an attempt to catch a whiff of something more interesting? If it wasn't about sports, men's common denominator, it would occasionally be about politics or other worldly matters.

With women there was talk of childbirth, set in the framework of a contest of who suffered the most and the longest, not an inquiry into the treatment of female patients by male physicians and how to correct their stereotypical thinking. Like *I Love Lucy*, we weren't overtly pregnant, we just changed shape and knitted little things.

Another signal that my world wasn't quite right was my sense of melancholy and indulgence in an overabundance of daydreams of where I'd rather be. I played Joan Baez records while ironing. I wanted to be in Harvard Square singing folk songs. I mentally painted scenes of some lovely but rustic house in the woods where I would have a studio that people would seek out to visit. I would easily expound when people dropped by and asked my opinion on worldly matters. But the prevailing view was that I was lucky to have a husband; three healthy, bright children; a lovely house; and lots of clothes – lots of dirty clothes, lots and lots of dirty clothes. I had everything a "girl" could want.

I was well entrenched in marriage and motherhood when the modern women's movement started. My earliest memory of enlightenment was of sitting on the floor folding diapers while I read *The Feminine Mystique*. My personal frustration was beautifully articulated there. But upon closer reading it was apparent that Betty Friedan was speaking to women who were highly educated, preferably at prominent Eastern universities, and had important careers as neurosurgeons, physicists or college presidents. These were women who could afford maids and governesses, leaving them free to pursue careers. How did it apply to a wife in the Midwest who had not even finished college? I reluctantly returned the dream to the library. Chapter almost closed.

As fate would have it, due to health concerns, my husband's longtime secretary was suddenly out of commission. I was asked to "man" the front desk. I stayed on for some time and became the office manager.

With this new responsibility, a radical change had to occur at home. My own mindset had to shift, and everyone had to pitch in. It wasn't an easy transition. A few "traditional" roles shifted under considerable duress, (like a "strike" by Mom), but somehow it worked out. Doesn't it seem right that the people who make messes clean them up?

Real liberation has to take place within our own personas first. I was no longer paranoid about age and wrinkles (well, that's a stretch), but I did have much more important things to occupy my thoughts. I began to see that there's more to life than looking and smelling nice or having the cleanest house. Even projecting into the future, I wasn't looking forward to the empty nest, but I wasn't panicky about it, knowing that being a mother was surely not my only role.

Beyond the confines of home, it seems presumptuous to call one's self a feminist unless we take action on the system outside our homes as well. My commitments these days were not chosen for their social cachet. My friends were working toward important goals and learning to respect each other's accomplishments. I know now that when a woman falls in the forest she makes a sound whether a man is listening or not. Her sisters in the struggle are listening.

I began working as an artist. The best proof of my metamorphosis was when I overheard my daughter telling a friend: "My mom's not a housewife. She's an artist. She's going to have her own gallery, and we get to work there."

Hard-won civil rights decisions are being challenged and reversed all over the country. Some call it a backlash to "radical" feminism. Whatever the cause, it is a clear warning. Radical or moderate, feminists must emerge now from whatever closets they are hiding in, in numbers too big to be ignored. The call is out. Will you answer?

Epilogue

Reading back over that column these many years later, I realize I was a little Pollyanna about things, or maybe I wasn't ready to admit some truths to myself. For many reasons, I filed for divorce a year or so later. My personal liberation served my children well. There has been a generational shift. I now see that my son and my son-in-law are full participants in the needs of their families and households, far from the entitled men of the 1950s and '60s. My son told me he models his fathering by doing the exact opposite of what his father did. As for feminist women, we now may live very different lives than our mothers did.

A Reading Alphabet for Students of Feminism in Wichita, 1970-79

Sarah Bagby

A

Anthology: *I Hear My Sisters Saying: Poems by Twentieth Century Women*
ed. by Carol Konek and Dorothy Walters

B

(Raising) Babies: *Free to Be...You and Me* by Marlo Thomas

C

Christ: *Beyond God the Father* by Mary Daly

D

Disdain: *The Female Eunuch* by Germaine Greer

E

Evolving: *My Mother/My Self* by Nancy Friday

F

Fiction: *Fear of Flying* by Erica Jong
The Heart is a Lonely Hunter by Carson McCullers
The Awakening by Kate Chopin • *Wide Sargasso Sea* by Jean Rhys
The Left Hand of Darkness by Ursula K. LeGuin
The Yellow Wallpaper by Charlotte Perkins Gilman
Mrs. Bridge by Evan S. Connell
Little House Series by Laura Ingalls Wilder
The Women's Room by Marilyn French

G

Grief: *Their Eyes Were Watching God* by Zora Neale Hurston

H

Health: *Our Bodies, Ourselves* by the Boston Women's Health Collective

I

Inspiration: *The Second Sex* by Simone de Beauvoir
The Feminine Mystique by Betty Friedan

J

Journeys: *The Road from Coorain* by Jill Ker Conway
Out of Africa by Isak Dinesen

K

Kindred Spirits: *The Book of Lilith* by Kay Closson & Anita Skeen

L

Letters: *Anne Sexton: A Self Portrait in Letters*
ed. by Linda Grey Sexton and Lois Ames

M

Motherhood/Monologue: *I Stand Here Ironing* by Tillie Olson

N

Neighbors: Fiction by Sue Nelson
Sometimes the Coming of Babies by Jeanine Hathaway
Each Hand A Map by Anita Skeen
Poems by Linda Gebert • The work that became *Daddyboy* by Carol Konek
Essays by Sally Kitch, Deborah Soles, Ginette Adamson, Kathryn Griffith,
Bobbye Humphrey, Bernice Hutcherson, Annette TenElshof, Mira Merriman,
Jacqueline Snyder, Diane Quantic, Antoinette Tejeda,
Helen Throckmorton, and Rita Pratt
Drama by Joyce Cavarozzi and Betty Welsbacher

O

Outsiders: *If They Come in the Morning: Voices of Resistance* by Angela Y. Davis

P

Perfection: *Memoirs of an Ex-Prom Queen* by Alix Kates Shulman

Q

Quiet: *A Room of One's Own* by Virginia Woolf

R

Research: *Frankenstein and Vindication of the Rights of Women*
by Mary Wollstonecraft Shelley

S

Spirituality: *Diving Deep and Surfacing: Women Writers on Spiritual Quest*
by Carol P. Christ • *Gnostic Gospels* by Elaine Pagels
Women and World Religions by Denise Carmody

T
Tears: *The Bell Jar* by Sylvia Plath

U
Unknown: *Found Writings* by Women of the World

V
Violation: *Against Our Will* by Susan Brownmiller

W
Wonder: *I Know Why the Caged Bird Sings* by Maya Angelou

X
X Chromosome: *Ain't I a Woman* by Sojourner Truth

Y
Yield: *Harvest, The Girl* by Meridel LeSueur

Z
Zealot: *Ms. Magazine* and Gloria Steinem

Untitled

mardy murphy

at first we called it
Monday
and washed ourselves
except for one place
which we were saving

the next time it was
Tuesday when we swept
and ate the dust
rode brooms

Wednesday we kneaded
bread and watched the one place
we were saving rise

we said Grace for Thursday
but she never answered

on Friday we tried to iron out
everything except for one
wrinkle
which finally tore

so we mended it Saturday
with great stitches
and a needle from a mountain
peak

we had forgotten about the day
of rest when it came we were
not ready
and it creeped out of the place
we were saving and it trickled
blood

for a day which has no name
we said Grace
but she never answered

Becoming

Susan Nelson

1

It is 1937, and I am fives years old. Christmas is imminent, and I am focused with the intensity of a laser on what I know Santa Claus is going to leave under the tree for me. There could not be a worshipper more fervent. The gift I'm expecting is a cowboy suit that I saw in the window of Innes department store. It has chaps and a leather vest with fringe as soft as cat fur. There is a hat to match and a holster with a cap gun. Above all, the best thing of all – the final, delicious touch – is a pair of red cowboy boots!

On Christmas morning, I am raw from too much excitement and too little sleep. When I see the large, fancy box with the instantly recognizable Shirley Temple doll tucked into a froth of tissue paper, my mind refuses to accept what my eyes are seeing. I stare blankly. Whose gift is this? And where is my cowboy suit?

I am spiteful and merciless. I leave Shirley Temple in her box. No one, before this Christmas, has told me I can't be anything I want.

Miss Woodard's fourth grade class is standing in two lines on either side of the rows of desks. We are at war – partially for the winner of the math contest, partially for the much-sought-after favor of Miss Woodard, an idol for whom we would all drink castor oil if she said to. Howard and I, the best math students, have worked our way up and now stand head-to-head. The next mistake in a problem sends the loser over the cliff to second place.

I spot the error almost at once, and my eyes jump away. If Howard doesn't see it, I'll win. I look vaguely at the ceiling, at the flag in its stand next to the board, at George Washington sitting in his cloud. I look everywhere except at Howard, who finishes the problem and steps back. When he loses, he takes his medicine while I feign graciousness. But afterwards, when we're walking home, I hear him behind me, laughing with his friend Tim. He uses the world "fluke," which I don't know but think is something dirty.

Later, I make an A in geometry, but never take a math course after that. Miss Woodard is let go because she gets married.

2

Today I'm meeting my father at the Shrine Club to get a ride home, which I've done as long as I can remember. It's an old stone building downtown, and it smells like damp basements and old cigars and, sometimes, like moth balls. It's a "men's only" club, so I have to sit in the lobby while someone goes up the wide center stairs to tell my dad I'm here. He's stopped by after work to play cards, and I hear the familiar ripple of a deck being shuffled, hear the slap of its being cut and dropped back on the table, the even click of the deal.

My father doesn't come down right away, which means he's having good luck and will stay longer. So I go see what Tiny is doing. I find him cleaning up the coatroom, putting the stray coats in the lost-and-found, hanging up the familiar ones whose owners he knows.

I ask, "How about a lesson on the spoons? If you've got time."

"Can't today. I'm on my way to the dining room, got a banquet tonight."

"Later, man," I say, which is what Tiny always says. I go back upstairs to wait for my dad. I would never let him catch me talking to Tiny or playing the spoons. My father is from the South and calls the colored people Nigras. So does my mother, who is not ugly about anything else that I know of. I didn't have much of an opinion one way or the other, until I read a book about a girl my age that moved to the South from New York City.

When my father asks me what I was doing while I was waiting for him, I lie. Something I don't like to do, but it seems to me to be better than having him shout at me or having me tell him that I think he's a bigot. That's a new word I got from a magazine.

You have to be careful about words, because sometimes they are insulting or hurtful. I try to wait until I see them in a sentence or a paragraph so I won't make a mistake, but you can't always be sure. People say, "Sticks and stones will break my bones, but words will never hurt me." That's not true. Words are worse than sticks and stones – words are like fire. They can eat you up.

3

I remember a man comes to our door and tells us my brother is missing in action. The man is wearing his uniform and is very polite. After he leaves, my mother walks around and around the dining room table, circling the room like an animal making a nest. My father weeps, sitting on the bed in the back bedroom. I have never seen him cry. Everybody else is away somewhere. I'm alone with these stricken people, and I don't know what to do.

4

Usually the phone doesn't wake me, but this night it does. It's late, the middle of the night. I try to hear, try to stay awake but can't. I don't wake up again until my nieces, who have spent the night, start fighting. The four-year-old says someone called, and I guess it's true. We go into the kitchen. No one's there, but a note says, "Fix breakfast and get kids dressed. I'll call." I don't like this at all. My stomach says something serious is wrong, and I don't feel like breakfast. But I know Mom will expect me to do what she says, so I do. Norma keeps jumping around, but Janice, who's eight, is silent. I think she has the same sense of trouble that I do.

It's Saturday, so we settle down with our radio programs. There's no argument until we get to *Let's Pretend*, which is Norma's favorite show. She wants to sit next to the radio, but it's Janice's turn, and she won't move. So Norma conks her on the head. Janice, naturally, kicks her, and of course that's when Mom comes home. There's something in her face that silences all three of us. She pulls Norma onto her lap and puts an arm around Janice. "Your mom is in the hospital," she says. "She's had an accident. She's hurt, but she's all right. She'll be home tomorrow. We'll go see her this afternoon, if you promise to be quiet when we're there. Okay?"

The girls look at her. It's as if you can see them thinking, trying to figure out if they're getting the straight dope or some flimflam. I'm studying their faces, wondering what it is they know that I don't. I look back at Mom, and at first I don't recognize her expression – and then I do. It's anger – but an anger so deep, so intense it scares me. Mom sees me, and her face relaxes; she's herself again.

"You're missing *Let's Pretend*," she says matter-of-factly to the girls. "Let's go catch up."

How do you tell somebody about this? I mean, you start out saying, "My sister was beaten up by her husband. He almost killed her." And then what do you say? "Don't tell anyone?" My mother is trying to keep the girls from finding out what really happened, and I can understand that. She'd also like to keep me out of the whole mess, but that's not going to happen.

I already know things I wish I didn't know. I saw the pictures the photographer took, the ones the police said they had to have. I saw my sister, saw the stitches and the bruises. I heard the man in the ugly hat argue about bail – and I know what this is.

"Do you want the father of your grandchildren labeled a jailbird?" he asked. "Do you?" The scariest thing I know is that my mother has taken all my father's shotgun shells and hidden them somewhere in the basement.

Suddenly, as if a complicated knot has simply released itself, everything gets resolved. Alan's mother bailed him out, and he disappears.

My mother shakes her head and says, "She's lost her house, that poor woman!" Because Becca can barely move, my mom and I have to pack up the house they've rented. We take Janice along to help; she doesn't ask any questions, not about the cracks in the wood of the basement door or the blood that's turned brown on the stairs. Mom sends Janice and me to the kids' room to pack their toys and clothes. I hear her running water in the kitchen and know what she's cleaning up.

I'm used to Becca and the girls staying with us, and I understand that's what will happen now. That night, when I'm in bed upstairs, I open the vent so I can hear what's going on in the dining room. For a long time, it's silent except for my father turning the pages of the newspaper and my mom clattering dishes. Then I hear Becca come into the living room and slowly sit down; I can trace every move she makes, because her whole body is stiff, and she creaks when she turns her head or bends her knees.

Suddenly my mother just starts talking, as if we'd all been sitting here waiting for her to speak. "I know I've said something like this before, so you have every right not to believe me. But this time you can trust what I say." She pauses, then goes on. "You're going to need a place to stay, and you're welcome to be here as long as you need or want to be. But if you move in, and then go back to Alan, you can't come here anymore, because he's going to kill you and maybe your daughters too. And I can't be a party to that, can I?"

"You don't have to worry," Becca begins, but my mother stops her. "No. I don't want you telling me anything. You've made assurances before. What you do is up to you; it always has been. But what I'm saying is up to me. If you go back to him again, there'll be no place for you here."

I hear my mother stand up and put her book on the table.

"It's been a long day," she says. "Tomorrow we'll sort things out. It's going to be all right. Don't cry, shhhh." I close the vent, because I don't want to hear any more.

5

In ninth grade, I finally find my sport. Oh, I've paid my dues; I've stood alone on the gym floor, humiliated, the last person chosen for the baseball team. I've dangled help-lessly from a rope that refuses to be climbed. I've hacked and sneezed with the other two sissies too allergic to play soccer. It turns out, however, that I can play basketball. And I'm really good. I'm not a forward, casually flipping my hair back before I shoot a free throw; I'm a guard. I climb into the skin of the girl I'm guarding. I'm the shadow she can't shake off. I sense the moment when she's going to shoot, and as the ball leaves her hands, I lift it out of the air like a present she's handing me. I'm invincible.

It's a Friday afternoon in the school gym, which is lit brightly from the west win-dows and has the familiar rank odor of sweat, Pine Sol and Evening in Paris. We're the ninth grade team, and this is both the last game in the tournament and the last game we'll play together before we go to different high schools in the fall, which we all know but don't think about. What we think about now is becoming one body to face our opposition.

I'm feeling good up but not anxious. A little bit arrogant, maybe, but more like confident, expectant. A whistle blows, we huddle and the game begins. In the third quarter, we're down by six points. We haven't been that far behind all season, and it's jangling us. Our coach speaks calmly, then sends us out to score. My big chance comes when the girl I'm guarding gets the ball and is obviously going to shoot. I have to block her. As I swivel to take the jump, I go too far and crash into the unforgiving tile wall of the gym. From above, it looks like a ricochet on a pool table. My shoulder and elbow take the brunt of the hit, but my head gets a sharp tap and my left leg lies twisted under me when I land.

I am oblivious to my general pain, however, because I can focus on only one scene, frozen like an icicle spiked in my heart. As I hit the wall, a boy, someone I don't know, yelled in gloating sarcasm, "Well, Flash!" He doesn't have to say, "Serves you right." He doesn't have to say anything else at all.

6

This is my last Black lit class, and I'm trying to get through it without feeling sad. Vashti was a student in the third class I taught, polishing off her M.S. as if it had been a light snack before a real meal. When I finished grading the second paper she wrote for me, I called her in and said, "This class needs to be taught by someone really good – who happens to be black. How long have you taught? And when will you get your degree?" We've been team teaching the course since then, and I know what I need to do is leave it to her, but it's hard.

My husband says, "Tell her you get to come back for auld lang syne moments. Like when that guy called you a honky feminist goody two-shoes. That'll punch a hole in your nostalgia balloon." I tell him he just wishes he felt this strongly about any class he's teaching.

I start packing up my stuff, and Vashti and I arrange to meet the next day for lunch. When I leave the building, it's a bright Kansas day, and I go home, believing for the moment in literature, education and good will.

'70s Women's Studies Program
Widens Farm Girl's Life/Career Path

Ann T. Reed, As told to Elma Broadfoot

Ann Reed was fresh off a Kansas farm in 1973, when she enrolled at Wichita State University. She signed up for nursing classes thinking she "would be a good nurse, get married and have kids. That's what women did then: got married and had kids," Ann reflected. A couple years into college studies, she was introduced to a new academic field – women's studies. In the mid 1970s, WSU became one of a handful of universities to offer a women's studies program. At the time, one of the intended purposes of the program was "to deepen understanding of women's roles and continue to present and discover ways to help women to function as full human beings in today's society."

Ann's experience with the new program wasn't a bra-burning, women's libber, demonstrator kind of thing. "It was a very positive experience," Ann said. It was more of an opening to a variety of possibilities, to a wider life and career path. It was a reinforcement of the strong role models she saw in her mother and grandmothers, and a validation of her mother's dictum, 'You can do whatever you want to do.' "

Ann grew up outside Assaria, population 109, in a farm family with three siblings and surrounded by other farm families. In that setting, the woman's role was narrowly and clearly defined: stay home, take care of the kids, make meals for the family and farm workers, and drive the wheat truck. Ah, but there were some key exceptions; her grandmothers and her mother.

Her maternal grandmother, Evelyn Zaiss, was librarian for the Chapman grade school and public library. Her paternal grandmother, Margaret Reed, lived in Wichita and took charge of the social affairs of her husband. Her mother, Marie Reed, lived on the farm, was an involved community volunteer, and encouraged her daughters to experience a variety of activities, to open themselves to life's possibilities.

Armed with the core values of hard work and determination, Ann headed off to WSU. She declared a nursing major, but when she found herself "totally lost in chemistry class," she went in search of another major. Actually, she had eight different majors and graduated from WSU with a degree in general studies.

In her freshman year, before the women's studies program was established, Ann showed a willingness to stand up for her rights. She was living in the all-girls dorm, and her room had a radiator water leak that caused the tiles beneath it to float all over the room. She and her roommate had requested repairs numerous times, but to no avail. Then she and the other residents of the dorm received a bill for a broken front window that was to be repaired immediately. Well, this just didn't sit well with Ann, so she called the university president's office and asked for an appointment. She got it.

She visited with Dr. Clark Ahlberg, who shared some of his student university experiences, and then he made a phone call. The call started a chain-of-command process that resulted in Ann being on the bad side of the student housing resident director, but the repairs were made.

Her venture into the women's studies was circuitous and prompted by curiosity. She had taken English classes from Sally Kitch, an icon of the '70s Wichita women's movement, who happened to be a family friend. When Kitch began teaching women's studies courses, Ann signed up. "Frankly, I needed the hours," she admitted.

She heard women talking about the fact that their husbands wouldn't let them do certain things. "I thought, 'Why not? My mom says I can do anything I want to do,' " Ann recalled. This was also during the time that women decided to use the prefix Ms. rather than Miss or Mrs. "I'm not going to do that," she declared. "I rejected the Ms. title, but now I have MS," she said with an irreverent laugh.

The world of possibilities that opened to Ann included a year as the assistant residence hall director in an all-girls dorm at Oklahoma State, three years with the WSU alumni association and 16 years with Via Christi-St. Joseph Medical Center in various human resources employment roles. She had completed a master's degree in marriage and family studies at Friends University in the 1990s when she was diagnosed with Multiple Sclerosis. She's been an active community volunteer with the American Red Cross, the MS Society, College Hill United Methodist Church, Wichita Children's Home and Communities in Schools of Wichita. In the late '70s and into the '80s, she was awards coordinator for Kansas High School Activities Association state track meets at WSU.

Yes, she finds it ironic and satisfying that as a young woman she sought a career in nursing and then ended up in the health care field encouraging other young people. No, she never married and "settled down." She acknowledged that her children are the Lincoln Elementary School children she has met with over the past eight years who are her "lunch buddies," and the young people she interacted with in a puppet program she established at her church. "I was focused on what I was going to do with my life and on working and volunteering."

"My mom's funeral was the day before my 16th birthday and just before I went off to WSU. I would have loved to have talked to her about my studies and the issues of the day. She would have had good advice, I know, and she would have calmed my 'unsettledness'," Ann said. She leaned back in her burgundy recliner, strummed the arm of it with her fingers and recalled the memories of the three women life forces that had deepened her understanding of herself. Clearly, they had modeled a positive and enduring study of women who discovered ways to function as full human beings in their time and society.

Support: 34 Years of Feminist Growth and Friendship
Ruth E. Richards

It was 1975, time enough for the impact of *The Feminine Mystique* by Betty Friedan to have reached the plains and settled into a group of 10 Wichita women. Two of the 10 had already identified the malaise in their lives, so when a United Methodist friend announced that she was convening women to see if there was any interest in forming a feminist support group, the news spread like a chain reaction that only happens in tight-knit communities. One woman called another, and each reached out to talk to one or two friends whom they knew would be interested. More than 20 women showed up for that first meeting. It was an interesting mix. All were in their 30s. Most were married with children. A few were single and even fewer were single moms with children. Many were involved in the volunteer life in Wichita, either through their churches (several protestant denominations and Catholics were represented) or through the League of Women Voters or the Women's Political Caucus. About half of them worked outside the home.

That first assembly occurred in the evening for the benefit of the workingwomen and the moms who needed their husbands to watch the children. It was a crowded living room with all the chairs filled. Women also sat cross-legged or leaning back against the legs of friends. It was a large circle. After each woman introduced herself and told why she was there, Nancy*, the convener, quickly defined what a feminist support group would look like and what its activities might be. She talked about meeting once or twice monthly to talk about preset feminist topics chosen by the group and about the need for absolute confidentiality, not only outside the group, but also within the group. Talking about our sisters to other sisters was discouraged. The women talked about the importance of committing to the frequency of the meetings. They agreed that, for the time being, the support group would come ahead of family and other commitments.

It was quickly determined that 20 to 25 people were too many for the intimacy that most feminist support groups aim for, so the large group divided into two. Since about half of the women wanted to focus their discussions on topics of religion, they decided to continue to meet with Nancy as the convener. The other half wanted to be a feminist support group, meeting to discuss topics that were critical to their lives and to lend support to each other. In that first meeting they articulated that they were not a consciousness-raising group, since most felt they already were confirmed feminists. For the most part, the division occurred along church lines, with one group comprised of Methodists and the other from the Disciples of Christ.

The support group was the latter. There were 10 of us in Support, as we called ourselves. The oldest was 35 and the youngest 30. Seven knew each other from a small experimental Disciples of Christ church on Wichita's east side. The remaining were one Roman Catholic, one Mennonite and one United Methodist. Four were officers in Wichita's League of Women Voters and politically active. Only one of the women was single. She dropped out after only a couple of meetings.

Of the nine remaining, four were teachers and another two had been teachers but had stopped to raise their children. The teaching levels ranged from the first grade to the university level. One of the women was a lab technician; five were stay-at-home moms. There was a total of 19 children in the families of these 10 women, the oldest child being 12 when the group began and the youngest a newly adopted infant. Four of the women had adopted at least one child, so adoption and the subject of what it felt like not to be able to have children in a society that promoted family as the only norm was a lively one.

That first meeting was unruly with children playing outside and coming in to interrupt with questions or to gain mom's attention. It was in the midst of this chaos that the ground rules for the next four years were established:

– Complete confidentiality, even as husbands were concerned. No pillow talk. The confidentiality rule was to be repeated at every meeting as reinforcement.
– Openness and frankness, i.e., personal risk, an expectation from everyone. Silent observers were frowned upon because they build distrust.
– No children at the meetings.
– No husbands or children at home during the time the mom is hosting the meeting.
– No interruptions to answer the phone.
– No fancy snacks. Simply coffee and tea.
– Strict promptness in starting and ending each meeting.

Support quickly settled into meeting every other Saturday from 9 a.m. to noon with each of us signing up to host a given Saturday. We all thought that the frequency was necessary at the beginning until we had built trust and routine. We suspected that Support was going to be hard for families to get used to, particularly for the husbands who suddenly became the primary parent, and so the first several meetings dealt with the issues of getting away.

And getting away was hard to do. Some of the husbands never got used to it, even accusing the group of turning their wives against them and later helping to break up the marriage. Support group was a threat. One of the topics was how to enable one's husband to change and embrace the new social order of equal roles within the family. Other husbands acquiesced, thankful for the extra time to spend with the children and curious about the topics the women were discussing.

All were wary and uncomfortable about their wives discussing the personal details of their married lives and how they might compare to the other husbands. We all worked hard to make the husbands comfortable with Support and the changes that were bound to happen as a result of our discussions.

Other topics quickly followed as the tasks of picking the next session, deciding who was going to lead the discussion and what we needed to do to prepare became routine. No one was an expert; this was an experience-driven group. Most of the topics were new territory for all of us, but the meat of our discussions came from the content of our lives, our experiences. Sometimes appropriate books and magazine articles were discovered, and they were assigned as homework in order to expand our knowledge base and give us a particular point-of-view, a discussion starting point. Or someone would bring an article and we would discuss its content. The group resisted adopting other experts to replace the ones that had been in place for so long, telling us how to be good wives and mothers, how to keep the flame of romance burning bright within a marriage dampened with children and day-to-day responsibilities. In Support we were all experts.

Everything was discussed, and some of the more difficult topics were continued over a couple of sessions. Female sexuality lasted several Saturdays. It began with what we all called, "The Big O" or orgasm. When was our first? Did we regularly have them? When we didn't, why? And vice versa. Was the Big O necessary for a healthy and fulfilling sex life? How do we cue our partners on technique? At one point early in our discussion, Deborah pulled her body into an upright fetal position and exclaimed, her face bright red with embarrassment, "If my mother could only hear me now! I can't believe we're talking about this!" Masturbation was next. We were on a roll. We talked about our bodies and whether we liked them. What we would change, if we could.

A lively ongoing discussion occurred on the subject of how much we thought society had influenced our attitudes toward our physical selves. And, we talked about how our perceptions of ourselves were changing the way we were raising our daughters. An avid discussion occurred on the subject of Marlo Thomas' book, *Free to Be … You and Me* and whether complete individuality is possible or even healthy, and doesn't "free to be …" really mean free to be me and I don't care about you?

We talked about our husbands and whether we were happy. One of our more controversial topics was the subject of open marriage. Each partner could have other sexual relationships as long as the primary relationship was with the spouse. Two of the women were in such an arrangement. Several were shocked at the thought, and wondered if open marriage was even possible in a healthy marriage. Some came to the conclusion that an open marriage is for the convenience of the philandering partner and that the other partner acquiesces to the idea in order to keep the marriage together. In other words, there is no such thing as a truly open marriage.

We discussed the roles our mothers and fathers had in our lives and who had the most influence. That topic led directly into many discussions about our children and the ways we were raising them – whether it was nature or nurture, what roles sexist language and toys played in a child's development. The discussion about language had ramifications in the small church seven of the women attended. The minister was reluctant to change the language of the Bible and liturgy to be more inclusive, so an "Uppity Women Unite" pin began to make its way around the congregation as it was awarded to any liturgist who changed the language to be nonsexist. As the congregation changed and became more inclusive, eventually the minister changed.

Another discussion topic that lasted several sessions was about friendship, more specifically whether we had close women friends and what those friendships had meant to us as we were growing up. Shirley confessed she rarely made friends with other women, that she felt in competition with them, that they might even be considered the enemy. She went on to predict that she wouldn't last long with the group – that we would end up not liking her. It was a self-fulfilling prophecy.

For two years Support met every other Saturday. It was remarkable.

———————

Several marriages were already troubled, and they didn't last long after Support began meeting. By the time of the first reunion, 15 years later, only two were still married to their first husbands, and those two still are today. If asked whether Support was a significant factor in the others' divorces, I believe the women would say yes and no. Yes, in that they each became a stronger definition and more assured articulation of herself. That new definition would disrupt the status quo of any marriage, but they would also say no, because they had issues with their spouses before Support started, chiefly infidelity and alcoholism. These were not trivial issues, and it was only a matter of time. Support just made the women stronger to do what they had to do in order to get on with their own lives. Of the eight who divorced, three have remarried.

In 1979, Leigh moved to California. Support continued long distance. In 1980, Diane remarried, and the women became her family, acting as the mother of the bride since Diane's mother had died many years before. They planned and hosted the reception. In the late '80s Deborah decided to become a minister, and she and her family moved to Denver where she attended seminary. It was that decade the Group began a pattern of gathering only when one of the members would come back to Wichita for a visit. Eventually only four stayed in Wichita.

In September 1990, all eight women carpooled to Denver to Deborah's home for Support's 15-year reunion. They were beginning to enter their 50s and had all settled into their lives. Leigh's was the last divorce, happening two months prior to the Denver reunion, and by that time she was Support's first grandmother. The reunion was a multi-day sleepover for the nine, as rowdy as any teenage slumber party. There were picnics in the mountains, great communal meals, and plenty of wine and laughter.

A second reunion occurred in July 1995, when Charlotte came back to Wichita from California for a visit. Only Deborah was absent. Diane opened her home at Council Grove Lake, and the women sunbathed, cooked gourmet meals, drove into town to eat at Kansas' famous Hays House, napped and talked into the wee hours. Annette was in the middle of intense chemotherapy for her bone cancer and wore bright bandanas on her head. The youngest member had just turned 50. Most members of the group were in or entering menopause, and so health was a primary topic of conversation. After the fierce discussions on women's issues in the '70s, the women's conversations had centered on politics, the environment and world issues, so they laughed when they heard themselves talking animatedly about recipes and cooking, as well as the various health issues they all seemed to be having.

It was the last time the majority would be able to get together, but whenever any one of the group comes to Wichita, those who are there or near, gather to declare their sisterhood and catch up on the details of their lives. And in 1999, Annette tragically died of bone cancer that had started as breast cancer in 1984. The Support friends had supported her through the adoption of a child, a divorce, and the years of chemo, hair loss and suffering. Several drove to Arkansas to celebrate her courageous and determined life. Another memorial service was held in Wichita where Annette had taught school and made a tremendous impact.

Almost all are grandparents now. Some have white hair. Several have retired. They all have health issues. Two, Alison and Shirley, have fallen by the wayside – both had had a tenuous relationship with the group, due to the open marriage issue. The rest – Susan, Diane and Mary in Wichita, Leigh in Tulsa, Charlotte in California and Deborah in Montana – continue to communicate with each other by phone and email. And, when one comes to Wichita, the others gather to celebrate a remarkable friendship of support and love that has lasted 34 years! Longer than most of their marriages!

˙All names in this essay have been changed to protect the privacy of the included parties.

Late Bloomer
Lynn Kincheloe Stephan

On the most rudimentary level, I qualify to participate in this book; I'm a woman who lived in Wichita in the 70s. I was young, college-educated and, many would say, savvy and aware. Furthermore, I worked in a male-dominated world, which most would imagine automatically provided fodder for any story with a feminist focus. Yet somehow, some way, I was insulated from the problems women often faced, particularly at work. And today, embarrassing as it is to admit, as a result of my almost cocoon-like existence, the women's movement, including the definition of *feminist*, completely eluded me for nearly two decades.

When I look back at the 70s and what was obviously swirling around me – rallies on the nightly news, consciousness-raising groups and discussions of the shameful female experiences – my ignorance of the women's movement is astounding. I could have been a poster child for the era's moniker, "The Me Generation," because I was so absorbed in my career and disinterested in things political. I have no idea where my mind was or what I was thinking. I may have been reading *Love Story*, but I sure as hell wasn't reading Betty Friedan.

As a result of my oblivion to the realities of women, I feel very self-conscious being in the company of the women in this anthology, knowing that their stories are bound to focus on courage in the face of inequities, pain and disappointment. My story, on the other hand, centers on unanticipated workplace opportunity, acceptance and accomplishment – not exactly requisite obstacles if a woman is to be hailed a women's-movement heroine. Nevertheless, I can't change the past. My story is what it is. Fortunately, late in the 80s, the light finally dawned.

The Advertising Biz

My love and talent for the advertising business were a complete and total surprise. While I had written for my high school newspaper, worked on both my high school and college yearbooks, and even taken an introductory advertising class in college, I never considered advertising as a possible career. My plan was to teach English. After a couple of disillusioning years in the classroom – being told by the administration, for example, that it was necessary to pass failing students through the system – I answered an ad to write advertising copy for a small agency.

I was hired as the agency's lone copywriter, but it wasn't long till I was also serving as an account executive meeting with the agency's clients who were all male. While women's history is replete with stories about working women who were compromised by male coworkers, I never felt threatened or insulted. I worked with hundreds of men including suppliers, photographers, printers, artists, and radio and television owners. A couple of marketing directors were insatiable flirts, but they weren't intimidating. Rather I found their somewhat inappropriate and often immature remarks fun, funny and flattering. When it was time to get down to business, it was simple for me to deflect their comments. For me, sexual harassment was not an issue.

Then, as now, I viewed my clients as mentors. I was green as grass when I started in the advertising business. Yet if these men were unsure of my value to their businesses, I never saw it. Instead they provided me with necessary information on their industries and products. These owners and presidents of banks, furniture stores, restaurants, department stores, along with the agency owner (now my husband of more than 30 years) took me, a twenty-something novice, under their wings and taught me to fly. For over 20 years, I worked in advertising. I came to admire and appreciate my mentors, not only for their business acumen, but also for their interest in me and my growth.

While most of my female friends were isolated at home, cleaning and cooking and birthing babies, I was out and about, cavorting in the world of business. I was having a great time. The difficulty was finding common ground with my female friends who didn't work outside their homes. More often than not, I found myself sidling away from their talk of recipes and diaper rash to the male side of the room. While I no doubt inhibited their off-color jokes, I was welcome to listen in on their business conversations and occasionally chime in. Needless to say, the chasm between my women friends and me widened over the years, in time landing me on an island of isolation.

Finally, after 20 years, I began to notice assignments that had once primed the creative juices no longer did. Then one night, when my husband and I were visiting with a couple over drinks at a local club, I noticed their eyes. Both sets were glazed over. We, who seemed never to stop thinking or talking about the agency, had bored these poor people into zombies. That's when I realized the time had come for me to do something different. A few months later, I left the agency and enrolled at Wichita State University.

The Light Dawns

Initially, I had no idea what field to pursue for an advanced degree. Obviously, I looked at English and communications, even psychology. But the course descriptions I kept returning to were in women's studies. In the 1960s, when I was an undergraduate, women's studies did not exist. In 1972, WSU became the second university in the country to start such a department. By 1987, the program was strong and wildly popular, thanks to the unrelenting devotion of its founders: Sally Kitch, Dorothy Walters, Carol Konek and Annette TenElshof. My first semester, I took a full load of women's study classes.

There are no words to describe how exhilarating it was to go back to school as an adult with no motive other than to learn. There are no words to describe how exhilarating my first women's studies class was, since up until then, my understanding of my gender had been limited to the stereotypes and misinformation that culture and my mother and her mother, had innocently and not so innocently perpetuated. Most everything that semester was a revelation. First and foremost, I was stunned to learn about the women's consciousness-raising groups that had taken place in Wichita for years that I'd never known about. I was stunned to learn about the frequency of sexual harassment in the work place and the huge disparity in women's and men's wages. At the age of forty-five, I was embarrassed to learn how little I knew about my own gender, and how little understanding and compassion I'd had for women in general, which ultimately I discovered, also included me. After far too many years, my eyes and heart were beginning to open, thankfully for good.

End Note

No question, I had been a single-minded career woman who had focused on my professional life to the exclusion of everything else. My spiritual crisis took place one night at a Wichita club and led me to women's studies with eye-opening discoveries about myself, the women in my life, the women in this book, all women the world over. Looking back, I've realized that, with no female mentors, many years of working with men and constantly emulating them had begun atrophying the feminine part of me. I abandoned my coveted career and set out on a quest to find balance in my life.

There is another possibility for my '70s oblivion to the women's movement. "Perhaps," suggested my psychologist sister after reading this essay, "you were not consciously aware, because you were living it on an unconscious level, dealing with men on an equal playing field, earning fair wages, receiving recognition for your work – the things many women were striving for. Maybe it's because you were an example of a 'liberated' woman that the women's cause didn't resonate."

Perhaps.

Whatever the reason for my lack of awareness, having come close to forever remaining unknowing and unchanged, I can say with certainty, especially in the company of the women in this anthology, that a late bloomer can still become a rose.

Finding Myself in the 1970s
Elma Broadfoot

I strode into the late 1970s, a newly married workingwoman. My byline frequently appeared in the local newspaper telling stories of women who were once footnotes to the social and historical times, but were now thrust into the limelight by the women's movement. They were business owners, educators, artists, contractors and, yes, women working outside of the home. I thought I had a pretty good idea of who I was as a woman – independent, talented and free thinking – largely due to a college education at Sacred Heart College (now Newman University), an all-women's institution run by women leaders and educators. Plus, I had the example of my mother who worked nearly all of her life outside the home and had no qualms about telling anyone exactly what she thought.

When my husband, Fred, and I decided to start a family, we also decided that I would stay home as long as I personally could do it and our finances would allow. In retrospect, I probably should have gone back to work much earlier than I did. But, I'm getting ahead of myself. I got my first whack up the side of the head and up the side of my confidence when I made it known I would be staying home. I belonged to a women's communication group and while most of the women were supportive, one woman, who could kindly be described as a strident women's libber, declared that I was throwing my life away. Ah, the first of many shifts in my confidence.

However, it was through this same women's group that I attended a number of educational sessions on issues relevant to women and the women's movement. One session in particular had a direct and dramatic effect on my life. The speaker noted that gynecologists often gave women unnecessary D&Cs with the theory that the procedure didn't really hurt women. A few weeks later, I thought I was pregnant and went in search of an ob/gyn. Of course, there were no women ob/gyns at that time that I could find.

There I was in the usual uncomfortable and awkward position in the stirrups when the doctor asked, "How badly do you want to be pregnant?"

"Not badly enough to make it up," I responded. Next thing I knew he was talking to me about a D&C. "I didn't come here to hear that," I said, shaking with anger and confusion. Two weeks later I was in the offices of another ob/gyn who confirmed that I was indeed pregnant. The previous doctor had only done a physical exam and did not do a urine test. I was barely pregnant, but I was pregnant. Had I followed the advice of the first doctor we would not have had our first daughter, Stefanie.

I stayed home from 1972 through 1979 and felt very uncomfortable in the mother role. There weren't a lot of examples then of women choosing to leave a paid job to be at home rearing their children. I could look at how my mother did it, but the times were different then. The "how to do it" in the 1970s was being defined by the women's movement and each woman's experience. I found it agitating to be defined as Fred's wife and Stefanie and Stacie's mother, because that wasn't the sum of me. My confidence as a mother would shift with the simplest of things. (I see them as simple now, but they loomed large then). I would volunteer to bring cupcakes to the preschool Easter party. I'd show up with my pastel-colored frosted cupcakes, and then another mom would come in with perfectly shaped Easter bunny cakes. I'd take the girls to their school Halloween party with purchased costumes complete with plastic faces, and there would be kids in homemade Snow White and cowboy outfits.

Some women married and chose to hyphenate their married name to their maiden name. Out of some whacked sense of personal rebellion, I refused to sign my name as Mr. and Mrs. or Mrs. Fred Broadfoot and would only sign Elma Broadfoot. I struggled to find ways to find and assert myself. I began doing freelance writing so that I could do something outside the home, make a little money of my own, and prove to myself that I could still write and function in the working world. I'd pound on the electric keyboard late at night or when the girls were at school. Truth be told, I probably should have sought a full-time job outside the home sooner, because I think I would have been a better mother and wife if I had.

As it was, my inner turmoil was likely a perfect match to the turmoil of the times and of the women's movement. As the 1970s came to an end, I had taken a job outside the home and dealt with the guilt of making that decision due to the girl's first day care provider. After two weeks, my oldest daughter announced that all the day care lady did was talk on the phone all day and feed them peanut butter sandwiches with water for lunch. I promptly whisked them out of there and happily found a woman who fed them a four-course meal for lunch.

When my father died, my mother came to live with us and became a surrogate mother and, in many ways, wife to my family. When I married, my grandmother (my mother's mother) advised me, "Spoil your man." My response to that was, "Spoiling is a two-way street." Needless to say, spoiling wasn't something I took to, but my mother did. It took me awhile to undo some of what she did, but mostly, she made my life easier and allowed me to re-enter the working world.

I strode out of the 1970s with a different sense of myself. Initially, I had to psyche myself up and recharge my sense of confidence, talent and outlook. My independence was tempered by being a wife and mother. The women's movement brought a new and larger outlook to the slights toward women and the entitlement that men were awarded every day in every way. That aforementioned women's communication group was instrumental in keeping me in the loop during my stay-at-home days. I kept up on the changes in the communication field, got exposed to women's issues, took part in the Equal Rights Amendment state activities in the mid-70s, and kept informed of employment opportunities. One of the women in that group told me about a marketing position at Wichita Festival, Inc., producers of the annual Wichita River Festival, and encouraged me to apply. Her support and encouragement was key in getting me in front of the festival committee that hired me. The next year I was promoted to executive director.

In looking back, the impact of the local women's movement had a constant and positive effect on my life in the 1970s. I was fortunate to have some strong and positive role models that I believe ultimately led me to become the woman I am today.

My Feminist Heritage
Anne Welsbacher

As a callow youth, I didn't pay much attention to inequities borne by women and girls prior to the burgeoning feminist movement of the early 1970s. I knew people in the world were mistreated, but I scarcely noticed that I was among that population. There seemed nothing amiss about my need to memorize two sets of rules for playing basketball – the ones I used in girls' gym and the one played in the "real" games my father watched at Wichita State University.

When our family physician frowned at my request for birth control pills, insisting that I tell my parents before he would prescribe them, I blamed myself for my moral failings. I distinctly remember scoffing at the notion of changing the titles of "Miss" and "Mrs." to the more neutral "Ms." And I was decades away from realizing the profound hypocrisy of a peace-and-love generation that protested for equality for men of color and for young men shipping off to Vietnam, but that marginalized the women in its midst to pamphlet collating and objects of "free love."

When I was in grade school in the early- and mid-1960s, my mother and her best friend, Euny, embarked on a series of pioneering projects. In retrospect, I've learned the significance of their activities, but through my eyes at ages 10, 12, 14, my mom's work was abstract. She dashed in and out of the house, huddled with Euny and others over tables overloaded with papers, talked for hours on the phone, packed suitcases, went to the airport, got picked up at the airport, came home to relieve the baby sitter, went to the airport, and got picked up at the airport. She also performed the "usual" tasks of 1960s moms, attending PTA meetings, sewing dresses, throwing parties and preparing meals for frequently conflicting menu requests within the family.

By way of contrast, my father, while hardly a slug, lived by a considerably streamlined schedule. He taught most days from very early morning until late afternoon, ate dinner and often returned to the campus evenings, directing or performing in plays. Weekends there were year-round ball games, live or on TV depending on the season; odd jobs and shopping, often for electronic devices to accommodate his growing recording archives; and tech-dress rehearsals that ran late into the morning hours.

When Mom was out of town, Daddy's schedule varied slightly: Instead of sitting down to Mom's standard dinner fare – entrée, salad and dessert – he broiled steaks or took us to McDonald's. Otherwise, little changed except that the house was quieter. No phone calls jangled. No masses of paper weighted the table. No sewing projects spilled over the edges; nobody dashed through the house with some new armload of files or scurried off to meetings.

A family story has it that, when I was eight or so, I came home after a day at school involving a presentation about career options and was surprised and delighted to learn that some women stayed home all day. This was a revelation to me: "You mean," I asked my mother, "I don't have to have a job?"

I was so thoroughly indoctrinated with the notion that moms ran around doing things all the time, their frenzy interrupted only when they flew off on business to other places in then-still-exotic airplanes, that I had no idea that this was unusual, even radical and certainly uppity for a woman living in Kansas during the beginning of the women's movement. How could I have thought otherwise? In addition to my mother, who was creating the nation's first special music-education degree program, Euny was evolving into a national treasure in the exploding field of music education.

Sally and Marilyn (and Mom) were blowing away old notions about how to teach severely disabled kids at the nationally renowned Institute of Logopedics, now called Heartspring. Jo was teaching her sons to shop and cook "as soon as the youngest was tall enough to reach the stove top," after which she stopped doing either for them altogether.

Joyce was raising a son as a single mom, and working long hours to forge her own way in a world of academia still dominated by men. Marshall was raising his four kids alone (in between wives) – I barely knew their mother, though she lived in town and was devoted to them during their custodial visits.

Certainly I had friends with stay-at-home moms in families consisting of two parents, of differing genders, living under the same roof, but they were threads in a quilt dominated by larger patches of people who challenged that way of living. So how was I to know that the behavior of my mother and her friends was not the norm? That women could not necessarily do whatever they wanted, with men marching along beside them or – as was often the case in my own home – cheering them on from the sidelines?

Not long after I learned, in a fourth- or fifth-grade science class, that the universe is expanding and that life, therefore, was an existential paradox of ultimate meaninglessness, I hit another wall of competing realities. It plunged into our living room one day when I came home from junior high school and heard my mother in the kitchen, yelling into the telephone. Daddy was in the living room pretending to read. Mom slammed down the phone and stormed in.

American Express wouldn't issue her a credit card. The person on the other end of the phone apparently had suggested that Mom ask her husband to get one, and then, the person explained, Mom could use his card whenever she needed to. Mom was talking to Daddy, all right, but she was most decidedly not asking him to apply for an American Express credit card. He shook his head in annoyance. My father isn't as loud as my mother, but he shares her aversion to injustice – and pointed out the particular irony of this policy as it played out in our household. My father never flies and seldom travels, so unlike his enterprising wife, he had no real need for the convenience of a credit card at all, American Express or otherwise.

I don't remember how that issue was resolved. I think, but can't say for certain, that my folks boycotted American Express until the company was forced, not in small part by the growing power of feminists, to change its policies. But I do remember recalling that incident later, when I, by now in high school, had the aforementioned confrontation with my parents over my birth control pills request. My father was nonjudgmental, but – being a father – supremely sad. My mother's response was less complex, although it seemed more so to me at the time.

Mom was furious. Not at me – like my father, she didn't judge or lecture. No, her fury was directed unequivocally, and forever, at our doctor. Although she retained his services, she never forgave him. I didn't understand why. It hadn't occurred to me that our doctor could be wrong. It certainly hadn't occurred to me that my response to him had been colored by the way I, a girl, was treated in the 1970s. But my mother's angry responses – to our doctor, and to that person on the telephone – those large-looming figures of male dominance some 40 or 50 years ago, hammered the first crack of truth into my thick shell of ignorance.

My mother had taught me, with her own life, what it really meant to be a 20th-century woman in the most liberated country on the planet. Just as I blame her for my early naiveté in the Eden of my childhood home, where women behaved and were treated as equals, so too, I thank her for handing me the apple that fed my inevitable feminism during this awful, miraculous era in the history of American life.

Redefining Women's Work

" 'I'm sorry, Mrs. Johnston,' he said, continuing to shake his head. 'You can't take accounting.' Then he patted my hand and crossed the accounting class off my proposed schedule.
'Now let's find something else. You already have enough accounting to make you a nice
little bookkeeper'."

—Colleen Kelly Johnston (I Didn't Play With Dolls)

Ovarian Logic

Beth Alexander

On a frosted gray January day, as we traveled to Kansas City for an admissions interview for acceptance into medical school, I reviewed with my husband what questions I might possibly be asked by the three faculty on the interview team. I imagined questions like, "Why do you want to practice medicine?" "How do you think you can make a difference?" "Do you intend to practice in Kansas?" or even, "Do you think you can handle the pressure?" Instead, the questions were more pointed and personal:

"What will you do with your kids?"
"Does your husband know about this?"
"What did you do when you worked for Planned Parenthood?"

These were the *only* questions I was asked at my interview for becoming a medical student at University of Kansas School of Medicine in 1974. The school had just unveiled an accelerated three-year program (no vacations), with the last 18 months in a new Wichita campus, allowing the possibility of getting through faster and being away from home for much less time.

I decided, at the encouragement of my husband and friends, to try for a long-suppressed dream, although I thought the chances that I could get through prerequisites in physics and biochemistry were slim. I had taken those courses first in 1973 to avoid unnecessarily prolonging a futile effort. To my surprise, physics and biochemistry were actually interesting and not so difficult. I had gotten through the MCAT, all the prerequisite science courses and applied, offering a record that exceeded the requirements for most medical schools' admission standards. The dream was alive. The Wichita women's community was already planning my first office. The admissions interview was the last hurdle.

"What will you do with your kids?"
"Does your husband know about this?"
"What did you do when you worked for Planned Parenthood?"

Initially stunned at these questions, I realized that I had come equipped to answer them. My husband was out in the hallway, and I was not above offering him as Exhibit A, proof that this wasn't being done without verification of the seeming requirement for permission. The three questioners didn't push me into providing proof. I remained calm. As I reflect on this interview 35 years later, I find myself amazed that I wasn't furious about those questions being the exclusive focus of my interview. My

Wichita friends, with whom I shared the interview experience, carried the outrage for me.

"Of course, they all have wives, so they don't have to consider what they might do with their children," was the comment of one. "And wives never are asked for permission, only forgiveness."

"You could sue them, if they don't admit you," offered several others, who knew that my grades and tests scores were exceptional. "We'll testify that we need more women in medicine, someone who knows how to listen." Their faith in my ability, their sense of justice delayed for countless women for decades sustained me while I waited for the decision that would change my future.

The letter came in early March, when I was at home alone. All I remember was reading the opening sentence: "Congratulations. You are accepted into the entering class of July 1974 at the University of Kansas School of Medicine." I ran out into the street, caught up with the mail carrier and gave her a big hug.

"Thank you! You gave me the best news in the world." Spewing out the news, I again hugged her, kissed her on the cheek, and ran back to my house to call family and friends. Sue Eichler was my first call. I still have the acceptance letter. Years later, I now wish I knew the name of the letter carrier, another anonymous woman hero in my journey.

At 28, I was one of the oldest students admitted to the medical school, and as nearly as I could confirm, the first woman admitted with children. Patrick and Steve were three and five when I left for Kansas City that July. The first week I was in Kansas City, I cried every night, wondering what on earth I had done. Every week I studied hard Monday through Friday noon, left my books in Kansas City and returned home to Wichita for a long weekend with family and friends. It seemed much better than drawing out the studying for seven days and not spending time with my children. And I could move back to Wichita for clinical rotations in 18 months.

I dissected my cadaver, a woman who had died in her early 30s, as I listened to the breaking news of Nixon's impending impeachment and resignation announcement. The death of the woman so young seemed more tragic than the political drama. I wondered if she had children. I wondered if my children were okay without me. At times when I missed my kids more acutely, the echo of the questions from the admissions interview served as my motivation for refusing to abandon my opportunity.

"What will you do with your kids?"
"Does your husband know about this?"
"What did you do when you worked for Planned Parenthood?"

How dare they think that a woman with kids couldn't get through medical school. I was determined they would never ask this question again, so determined it seemed, that I compulsively over achieved to a level of academic work that I 'd never done before. I graduated three years later, ranked first in my class of 200 students. This feat was not because I was the smartest student in my class, but because I carried the outrage, the support and the excitement of friends in Wichita as well as the determination that there could be no doubt about the qualification of women to become physicians … even women with children.

There were other indignities in medical school that I sometimes ignored, sometimes complained about on my weekends back home and sometimes openly protested. There was a faculty member in ob/gyn who was known for following women up the narrow stairs in the hospital, lifting their skirts and fondling their buttocks. He called it "research."

There was the pathologist who railed that women in our class were only taking away seats from the men and that women would never practice medicine as intensively, as well or as long as the men in the class. He assumed we would just go have children and quit our professions. Once, I reminded him that I already had children, and he attempted to humiliate me in class by discussing the problems in society caused by women who abandon their children.

There were professors who interspersed pornographic pictures with science topics to entertain the male students in the class and to enjoy watching the women react. After some coaching from my Wichita consultants, the women medical students adopted a posture of silence as our first defense. It worked. Then there were those faculty who referred to women's thought processes as "ovarian logic." I concluded that indeed we were a threat and studied harder as both my defense and offense.

After graduation from medical school, the Wichita women's community came out in droves to support my beginning residency practice and later my private practice. Wichita had not had many women primary-care physicians, and whenever a woman opened a practice in the '70s, it was quickly filled. No need for advertising, other than word of mouth. We all wanted care providers who listened, who understood, and who could talk about contraceptive choices, menopause, sexuality and the challenges of motherhood. We dared to invite conversations about domestic violence, child abuse, infidelity, grief and aging. There was a growing belief that health meant more than the absence of illness.

The women's community in the '70s celebrated and supported our successes, forgave and commiserated with missteps and unfulfilled dreams, and grieved our losses. We watched Marilyn Harp tirelessly defend the poor and under-represented, and we cheered when she joined the National Board of Planned Parenthood. We celebrated when women's studies at WSU got stronger under the leadership of Dorothy Walters, Carol Konek, Sally Kitch and Annette TenElshof. Later, in the nineties, we bought pavers and benches for the Plaza of Heroines, populated by ordinary, memorable women.

The foundations built in the seventies carried us into the eighties when we laughed at Mary Estes and Yvonne Slingerland's annual Derby Day party; we went to poetry readings of Jeanine Hathaway, Anita Skeen and Lisel Mueller at the Kay Closson Women Writer's Series. We grieved Susan Kraft's, Kay Closson's and others' premature deaths. We watched in awe at Kate Snod grass's incredible acting in St. Joan. We discussed lines from *Crimes of the Heart*, directed by Joyce Cavarozzi that reminded us of our struggles:

"But, Babe, we've just got to learn how to get through these real bad days here."

And so we did, together.

I did not appreciate the strength of the women's community in Wichita until I accepted a job at Michigan State University. It took two years in Michigan for me to believe that the move might be okay. Before I left Wichita, I cried at the idea of leaving patients and friends. I cried frequently after I left, thinking I had made a horrible mistake, just as I did that first week in medical school. There was no women's community in Michigan that could touch the sisterhood in Wichita. I didn't know that until I didn't have it as a ready resource, comfort and fertilizer for ideas and growth.

Although separated by distance, those of us who took root in Wichita and now live in other places still return to Wichita, still remain connected. This book is yet another example. We are still friends and co-conspirators. And from the early outrage at interview questions in 1974, as an act of support and solidarity, I have held on to all that the Wichita women's community has meant to me in my personal and professional development. I would not have become who I am without my Great Plains sisters.

Division of Labor
Ruby Baresch

My mother was a whiz at arithmetic
out-ciphering the others at the blackboard
at the end of the fourth grade
she stayed home to help.
Her brothers went to high school, one to college
Years later we tried to convince her
that one-half times one-half equals one-fourth
but she remembered from arithmetic
that a number increases when multiplied.
                back in the horse and buggy days
                a farmer told his wife to pack her lunch
                the men were going to eat in the cafe.
you do see don't you that it isn't enough
to help with the housework
that if you did all the cooking and laundry
the structure would not support you
you would soon crumble you are starting to crumble now.

Original Sin
Emily Bonavia

I find I hope for someone
magically to materialize
and prepare my meal,
write those letters,
replace these screens,
clone me.
Then I remember:
I'm a woman
and get to do
it all myself.

Homemakers United 1978 - 1981;
Homemakers United and HERA 1978 -1982
Peg Roberts Browning

Changes in women's and homemakers' status seemed to come slowly, but are so obvious after 30 years that it is easy today to overlook their profundity. This is the story of a group of mainstream homemakers who did what we could to bring these changes. We were positioned in between the extreme factions of the day: not part of aggressive feminists who made men the enemy, nor part of the antifeminists who promoted the submission of women in marriage. Instead, our group tried to merge the benefits of women realizing their full potential while recognizing the essential value of marriage, home and family to a healthy society. Feminists have not yet achieved our ERA amendment to the Constitution, but some of the battles of that past era have been resolved to the great benefit of women. Ironically, issues in the arena of the home, such as housework and child care, are among those that remain unresolved.

The Homemakers United Committee was accepted in the late '70s as a project of Wichita's Commission on the Status of Women when it was evident that the cluster of problems so widely experienced by homemakers was not being adequately addressed elsewhere. Among these were:

(1) Homemakers are economically vulnerable. We think of the homemaker as a woman financially able to remain working in her own home. However, too often the well-being and goodwill of just one man separates that homemaker from women who have had to take low- paying jobs or go on welfare. If a homemaker becomes a widow or goes through a divorce, her standard of living can be deeply cut. Even her identity is in question when she is no longer linked to the status of her husband and his income. If her credit was merged with her husband's, it must be established all over again. She can find that homemaking skills do not transfer to well-paying jobs, and she is often unprepared by training or educational credentials to fulfill the requirements of better jobs.

(2) Homemakers' work is unvalued. The homemaker could not be defined by the Department of Labor as either employed or unemployed, so she was labeled "nonworking." The Gross National Product does not in any way include the value of work done by homemakers. Although perhaps explainable from the government's point of view, this has had the effect of equating the absence of specific dollar value with a lack of value. Society still has not found a good way of according economic recognition to women who combine the functions of home management, mothering and community volunteering even when they may be praised to the skies for these services. Social Security treats homemakers well, but not until they retire. Other than this, what the homemaker gets comes as a sort of gift, not as what is due to her as an essential component of the system.

(3) Homemakers have low self-esteem. In a culture that values success outside the home, she suffers from lack of self-worth. The National Organization for Women had been working to get employed women better pay, equal pay for equal work and access to jobs dominated by men. The enthusiasm was so great that NOW in the early '70s seemed to be saying that homemakers should stop taking a free ride and seek the recognition only a paycheck could bring. Homemakers felt devalued and, when asked if they worked, they started responding, "No. I'm just a housewife."

(4) Homemakers are disadvantaged in decision-making. The husband dominates in marriage, because he brings home the paycheck. Even if both spouses work, his pay is usually larger than hers; therefore, major financial decisions are mainly his to make.

(5) Homemakers can feel isolated. If there are very small children, young home-makers can find themselves isolated, lonely and at home full time, unless they can afford babysitters. It's even worse if new in a strange town.

Division Between Homemakers

Most active feminists were enthusiastically pushing an agenda for legislative and structural change at the 1977 Kansas Women's Conference. However, all efforts were for employed women, not for homemakers. Still, many mainstream homemakers were confident that society did value the homemakers' functions. They felt that re-dress of inequities was quite possible if homemakers organized themselves as a po-litical constituency, speaking out for their particular needs like other groups in our pluralistic society. The women who came to Homemakers United programs would mostly fit here.

There also was a clearly anti-feminist homemakers group that called itself "pro-family." These women threw their lot in with traditional women and counted on the privileges of "the pedestal" to maintain their lifestyle. They saw the women's equality movement as threatening and felt there was no way they would be helped by "all that freedom."

This faction at the 1977 conference was led largely by men and by the words of Phyllis Schlafly, head of Eagle Forum. She was formidable as she continuously railed against the ERA because, she said, it would bring unisex bathrooms, women in com-bat and gay marriage. Recently it has been pointed out that we are still hearing these anti-feminist arguments and that women are clearly not equal under the law in the Constitution of the United States.

The distinction between these two polarized groups became obvious in 1977. The pro-family traditionalists were in force at the Kansas Women's Weekend Conference, strongly resisting the feminists' statements of principle and legislation planned to help wage-earning women. The moderate, pro-feminist homemakers were not heard from on that occasion since they had not yet come together and organized on behalf of themselves. Unfortunately, this made the very conservative, pro-family, anti-fem-inist faction seem to represent all homemakers.

Organization

This was the background for the Commission on the Status of Women's approval of a series of programs for homemakers. The CSW believed that strong, feminist homemakers could be pivotal in generating a broad-based constituency for change. Programs for homemakers would be a place for them to come together. They would get information that would help them personally, and the programs would provide an avenue for their input.

The Steering Committee of Homemakers United, a sort of informal board, consisted of me as a CSW member and chair; Dorothy Hayes, also a CSW member and co-chair until her resignation; and Betty Foulston, Vicky Reiff, Fran Jackson, Janie Barrier Young, Dorothy Zimmerman, Jackie Nagel, Gail Skinner and Ann Peck. The group had eight meetings in members' homes prior to its first public meeting in April of 1978. In the preliminary meetings, the group formally assumed the name, Homemakers United, and made progress defining aims, deciding on programs and projects and developing an organizational structure.

As time went on, some of the original steering committee members went in other directions. They were replaced by Bonnie Till, JoAnn Ray, Jeanne Elmore, Kathryn Regier, Kathy Heinrichs, Jane Pelletier, Jo Chalfant, Ruth Luellen, Pat Argetsinger, Mary Oswald, Liz Sheffield and Kay Soltz. These outstanding women intellectually stimulated each other and contributed their most constructive ideas.

The monthly programs for homemakers, provided through the Commission on the Status of Women, were held first at the YWCA, but soon moved to the parlor of the First Presbyterian Church. Both of these locations had child care space. For the first seven programs, we tried various ways of providing child care, but we had to give this up when mothers failed to make care reservations and the numbers of little ones varied too much.

We had 25 programs in the three years between April of 1978 and the summer of 1981. Although getting publicity for our meetings remained a big problem, attendance averaged 21 homemakers. There were no formal memberships, but we considered someone a member if she attended three times.

We had several programs while under the city and the CSW show to assist attendees:

(1) Young homemakers felt isolated without babysitters. To help, one of our meetings compared the setup and rules for five different child care co-ops. Gail Skinner, recently from California, made herself available to help organize sitter co-ops, play groups and mother support groups.

(2) Homemakers were economically insecure. To help, they were given a brochure, "The New Volunteer," which included seeking volunteer activities to gain marketable skills. Using this method, along with adult education opportunities, she could sharpen her attractiveness as a potential job candidate later. A financially secure woman could use this same method to build her skills toward a career in volunteering. Further, Homemakers United strongly celebrated volunteering as bringing a dimension of caring and a quality of life that society would not otherwise have. Volunteers can do what government is not designed to do or cannot afford to do. When homemakers

can forego a paycheck and go the mother/volunteer route, they provide services for the common good of their communities that money cannot buy.

(3) Fundamentally, Homemakers United worked to recognize the social value of homemakers and to elevate the perceived status of this role. Women who suffered from low self-esteem and identified themselves as "just a housewife" were urged to consider their skilled homemaker functions as vital and easily justifying their remaining out of the job market. In every program, Homemakers United strongly promoted recognition that the job of mother and family supporter could often be more work and more important work than many full-time, paid jobs.

(4) A program on Life Planning and Time Management was presented by member Vicky Reiff, who had led career-development seminars. Women were urged to take themselves seriously, set up file folders, make lists of places she might like to work, and skills she might need if she wants to do paid work or should find herself in financial need. A woman needs to think in terms of stages in life: pre-family, parent/volunteer years, and either paid employment or responsible volunteer careers, post children. Life is not just happening to her; she is taking charge.

(5) Homemakers United urged women to build self-esteem by taking on the universal problem of sexism in language. In the 1920s the suffragists were content to get the vote for women and didn't make significant efforts to change the language. Today that is thought to have been a mistake. The CSW published a brochure called "Humanizing Language," which recommended avoidance of "mankind" and "man," and substituted terms that more clearly include women such as "humanity," "human beings" and "people." Today, these changes have been used to such an extent that the "man" and "mankind" of the 1970s are beginning to sound archaic and strange to a younger generation. "Humanizing Language" explains how everyday speech subconsciously teaches young children to accept the secondary status of women as not only normal and expected, but preeminently right and somehow the way things ought to be. As children become adults, what they read and hear continues to confirm the superiority of men over women.

(6) A popular program, Smoothing the Way to Equality, was led by Jo Chalfant. It was for those wishing to increase their status within marriage without threatening the stability of their marriages. The mainstream homemakers who came to Homemakers United meetings generally viewed their marriages positively. They wanted liberation from the old expectations of the 24-hour-a-day wife, mother, and servant-to-all, but they did not want to seriously offend or hurt their husbands and certainly did not want their efforts to end in divorce. They sought to smooth the way to establishing marriage as a legal and economic partnership in which the non-monetary contribution of the homemaker would be considered commensurate with the financial contribution of the breadwinner – with the specific roles played by each partner assumed to be a decision reached by both.

Although confrontations are sometimes unavoidable, a marriage or a friendship would not last if confrontation was too often the standard operating procedure. Similarly, for a wife to gain concessions by sending her husband on guilt trips would likely build a smoldering resentment. An easy-going partnership would tend to be the result of gradual accommodations by both spouses over time. In addition, the pair would notice that relating to a partner or a peer is much easier than to a person thought to be superior or inferior. This understanding on the part of women and men that both sexes are hurting is fundamental. It allows good will to replace anger, and people of good will can act in constructive ways. Empathy can be contagious and lead to smoother, more graceful interactions. This was the line of thinking that convinced us in HU that family relationships can be preserved and enhanced while moving toward equality. We concluded that we can be solid feminists and solidly married.

A New Beginning

Two and a half years later, in 1981, a new city commission came along that did not want to fund social causes. It seemed probable that Homemakers United and the Commission on the Status of Women would have their funding cut. By this time, we had an active and growing number of homemakers who were pro-feminist. It was with much appreciation for the sponsorship of the Commission on the Status of Women and funding by the City of Wichita that the Homemakers United group voted to leave the CSW and affiliate with the national Homemakers Equal Rights Association. Bonnie Till and I had gone to their annual meeting in Iowa the previous summer and found them to be very much like us. Our HU board voted Bonnie Till the first president of HERA and Kathy Regier as vice president, who would become the second president.

Our new organization started meetings in the fall of 1981 and continued to have monthly meetings with board meetings in between. Dues to HERA started at $10 per member, and HERA could take additional donations that would be tax deductible. Our local HERA had some well-known speakers and enthusiasm continued. However on June 30, 1982, at the end of the second year, feminists were crushed that the national Equal Rights Amendment had finally gone down in defeat. Some wondered if "rights" was the red-flag word, and whether just saying "Equality under the law ... " might have dampened objections and eased its passage. In any case, this defeat was a huge psychological blow to activists. HERA did not resume in September.

Perhaps that was the end of Homemakers United, but not necessarily. We believe there are a significant number of pro-feminist homemakers who would respond again to a perceived need or opportunity. Just in case there will someday be other pro-feminist homemaker organizations out there, like HERA, that may want to join together, I have turned over what might be relevant to Bonnie Till, whose enthusiasm and charisma has and would again serve HERA well.

Changing Women's Roles

Mary Ellen Conlee

Growing up in New England in a traditional family – Mom at home and Dad building his business, dinner at the table with my parents and sisters every night – who would have thought that I would find myself after college graduation living in Wichita, surrounded by a community of women who were making reality of the feminist literature of the '60s?

Throughout my life I found myself gravitating toward experiences where women were in the minority. In grade school it was baseball with the boys, in high school it was chemistry and in college I majored in economics. I've often wondered if we redefined women's roles or if in the '70s opportunity was there for those who took it. Where earlier most women were denied the opportunity, by the late '70s many realities converged and the doors cracked open. For those of us who stepped in, success was demonstrating that women could succeed in careers formerly dominated by men.

Maybe for me the seed was sown at those family dinners where we followed every step of our father's progress in building a successful business. I was the youngest of three girls, the last to spend summer vacations from college working in the office of our Dad's folding paper carton factory. There was never a thought that one of us could or would take over the family business, but we were an acceptable audience for the day's activities. During those summers, I learned to do cost accounting, went to lunches with my Dad and his customers, and watched how business was conducted. I heard his stories, read his *Harvard Business Review* and *Fortune* magazines, and somehow assumed – without a plan – that I would find fulfillment through interesting work.

In college, I started with idea of majoring in chemistry, but changed to economics – and yes, I was the only female econ. major in my class. I considered graduate studies at the Wharton School of Finance, but this was 1962 and a high school teaching career seemed more realistic. My next step was a master of education in history, followed by marriage to my college boyfriend and a high school teaching career. It was a good life. Our first son was born in 1970, followed by a second son in 1974. The right thing to do was to stay home as my mother had done. As much as I loved my family, I kept looking for that something else and soon found it by taking political science classes and teaching part time at Wichita State University.

Along the way, I found fascinating Wichita women: Helen Newkirk taking on the Housing and Urban Renewal battles at city hall; Ruth Luzzati breaking barriers as one of the first women in the Kansas House of Representatives; and Sally Kitch teaching women's studies at Wichita State University.

In the early 1970s, these women and others from the Wichita chapter of the League of Women Voters opened my eyes to the world of politics, and I was hooked. The research demands of academic political science didn't satisfy my more practical bent. I wanted to do politics. In 1978, I ran for the Kansas House of Representatives, but lost in the primary by a few hundred votes. Consequently, I judged my idea of elected politics as unrealistic. But Nancy Kassebaum had won her primary, so I took on the job of women's issues chairman for her U.S. Senate campaign. This was 1978, and no one on the campaign thought the title "women's issues *chairman*" was inappropriate, until I suggested the title change to chairperson.

Sometime later when visiting with Nancy in her Senate office, she told me that shortly after her successful election, a woman walked up to her in the grocery store and said, "Mary Ellen Conlee convinced me to vote for you. I hope she was right." By her actions and my evaluation during her tenure in the Senate, Nancy Kassebaum proved that I was right and proved that a woman could be an outstanding U.S. senator.

Recognizing that academic political science wasn't my cup of tea and that elected politics hadn't worked out, I was wondering what my next step toward that fulfilling work could possibly be. Then two Wichita lobbying jobs opened up in the fall of 1978. I really didn't know what a lobbyist did day-to-day, but with encouragement from those involved '70s Wichita women, I applied. For the job I didn't get – and not wanting to name names of the living – I was told that they were really looking for a bachelor who could go out drinking with legislators. Remembering that this was 1979 and many men were just beginning to internalize that women were equal in the workplace, my interviewer immediately corrected himself and said, "Of course, it will be an open application procedure." I did get a second interview, but not the job.

For the other lobbying position, I came in second, but the man that they offered it to first, turned it down. Thanks to City Commissioner Bob Brown and City Manager Gene Denton, I was offered the governmental relations manager position with the City of Wichita. In the interview Gene Denton asked me why I thought that a woman, who was also identified as a Republican, could do the job. I answered: "I had the same concerns, so I went to Rep. Ruth Luzzatti and Sen. Wes Sowers to see what they thought." Luzzati was a Democrat House member, and Sowers was a somewhat stern, older Republican gentleman who chaired the Senate Public Health Committee.

I told Denton that Ruth said, "Go for it. Of course you can do it, and I'll help you with the Democrats." Sen. Sowers said, "I work closely with Judith Runnels who lobbies for the Kansas State Nurses. She does her job well, and she is clearly a Democrat, so why couldn't a Republican woman become a successful lobbyist as well?" Denton told me a couple of years later that he was fully aware that his question could be considered inappropriate, but he hired me because of the way that I answered it. He knew that in the real world of politics, one had to be able to handle the inappropriate along with the appropriate. I later saw a copy of my human resources' evaluation. Written in the corner was: "Not qualified, but we need to interview because of political pressure." In addition to being a woman, my 10 years of teaching experience was evaluated as unrelated. In reality, that experience was very valuable. It honed my skills at taking complex information and turning it into a story for elected officials, most of whom are generalists.

Bob Brown told me that he supported my application and had no problem with appointing a woman lobbyist. In fact a few years earlier, as a member of the Kansas

Truckers Association Board of Directors, he had made the motion to promote Mary Turkington from secretary to executive director and lead lobbyist for the organization. Those who know Kansas legislative politics know that she broke the glass ceiling for women lobbyists in Kansas in the early 1970s.

When I arrived in Topeka in January 1979 there were only three other women employed as lobbyists – Turkington represented the truckers, Judith Runnels represented the nurses and Kathleen Sebelius represented the trial lawyers. We were joined by a handful of women volunteers who represented the League of Women Voters and the Women's Political Caucus. At that time there were about 100 registered lobbyists. Today, among the 200 or so lobbyists that are actively involved on a day-to-day basis, at least one-third are women.

The Kansas Legislature has seen a similar increase in the numbers of elected women. When Ruth Luzzatti began her service in 1974, there were four women in the House of Representatives and one, Sen. Jan Meyers, in the Senate. To this day, insiders still repeat the story of how Luzzatti decided to run for office. She had attended a big Wichita rally in support of a constitutional amendment for women's rights in the early 1970s. Speakers were challenging women to run for office. As Ruth told the story she said, "Like a sinner at a revival, I stood up and said I would run for the Kansas House of Representatives."

By 1979, my first year as a lobbyist for the City of Wichita, there were 13 women in the House and still just one in the Senate. By 1989 there were 34 women in the House and nine in the Senate; by 2008, 35 in the House and 12 in the Senate. While there hasn't yet been a woman president of the Senate or speaker of the House, two Republican women – Shelia Frahm (1993-94) and Lana Oleen (2001-2004) – served as majority leaders in the Senate. Democrat Donna Whiteman (1991) and Republican Sherri Weber (2005-06) served as majority leaders in the House. While women have chaired many committees, only one, Rochelle Chronister, has chaired the most prized committee appointment, The Ways and Means or Appropriations Committee.

Clearly women have become influential in the Kansas political arena over the 30 years I have been active in politics. Changes are evident. I remember the small, symbolic battles like Sen. Norma Daniels' struggle with her Senate colleagues insisting that the Senate open a woman's restroom to match the existing men's lounge and restroom. More significantly, I remember how the rise of women in Kansas politics mirrored the opening of the political system to include a broader dialogue with less backroom politics. I believe most women seek more openness in government, but at the same time have learned how to impact backroom politics when necessary and do deals to be successful – a skill less natural for most women of my generation.

Over the years of my journey, I have found that the most successful women who choose the challenge of working in the political arena share several characteristics. They tend to enjoy working with both men and women on an equal basis. They work hard and are detail oriented. And they step up to help other women, often acknowledging the importance of their women mentors who preceded them.

In my early years, both Representatives Luzzatti (D) and Jo Ann Pottorff (R) offered to help ease my way into a world dominated by men. At the same time, I built relationships with male colleagues and checked to be sure that my approach in meetings with a room full of men was understood, heard and effective. On one such occasion, while representing Wichita, I calmly challenged a dominate speaker who was clearly providing incorrect information. After the meeting, I asked a male colleague if I handled the situation appropriately. He smiled and said, "You were one mean SOB," and I understood that as a high male compliment.

In January 1979, when I faced that first legislative session, Jim McKinney, a WSU political science professor and friend, provided advice that has guided me ever since: "Lobbying is a relationship game." And he added, "It will take three to five years to be really good at it, so do your best, relax a little and give it time."

At the end of my third legislative session, I was observing a conference committee deliberation on water issues. Committee Chair Sen. Norman Garr turned to me and then to my League of Municipalities colleague, Chris McKenzie, after each point was established and asked us, "Does that work for you?" As I left that meeting, I turned to Chris and said, "Jim McKinney was right. It took three years, but now I feel like I may actually be doing this job right."

Now 30 years later, I own Conlee Consulting Group, Inc. and have impacted public policy on behalf of many different clients many times and in many ways. The ground-breaking feminist literature of the '60s, the women who stood up for women's rights in the '70s, and the men who said, "Why not a woman?" all helped open the doors. It was then up to each individual woman who walked through those doors to define women's work by one success after another. In the final analysis, gender has little to do with it, which was the message of the vibrant, active women who stepped up in Wichita in the 1970s, changing attitudes and giving support to each other. The rest is history.

From Girl to Feminist

Carolyn Patton Conley

Believing that "who you are now" depends on "where you were when," I began my narrative in the 1960s, because my experiences in that decade influenced what I became during the 1970s. My original plan was to be an executive secretary and follow in the footsteps of my aunt who worked for the Ford Motor Co. in Detroit. Toward that end I took typing, shorthand and bookkeeping in high school. I was very good at shorthand and bookkeeping, but my typing was not quite so good. I needed another plan.

Fortunately, my second-year bookkeeping teacher recognized where my talents lay and encouraged me to go to college, major in accounting and become a CPA, which would allow me to earn as much as $400 a month. I had no idea what a CPA was, but if it paid $400, I'd give it a try. What he failed to tell me was that during the 1960s, girls weren't supposed to major in accounting. (Yes, we were called girls then.)

I enrolled at the University of Wichita, as it was called at that time, and found I really did enjoy accounting. I also found almost all of my classmates were male. I made a lot of friends with the guys in my classes and seemed to have the respect of the business faculty, until my junior year when I took a production management class from a person who wasn't as impressed as the accounting professors had been. He announced to the class on the first day, "Gentleman, we seem to have a female in our midst this semester. I can assure you I will do everything I can do to make sure she doesn't stay."

Midway through the semester, he was asked a question about what the numbers on a graph in the text meant. He blew them off as meaningless until I pointed out the mathematical relationship that existed from one number to the next. He was clearly surprised and said to the class, "Well, Gentleman, it seems the female has something between her ears besides cotton." That was the only positive remark he ever made in my direction, but I did receive a B for the class. The rest of my classes were positive experiences. I had a lot of male friends, a good relationship with the rest of the College of Business and the highest GPA in my class. My femaleness was never an issue, with the exception of that one professor.

When it came time for on-campus job interviews, I was a bit surprised. I can only assume that the interview schedules listed the students by last name only because at the beginning of every campus interview I had, the prospective employer would look at me and say, "Nobody told us you were a girl. We don't hire girls."

My response was always the same. "It appears I may have some trouble finding a job, but since we both have nothing else scheduled for this time, would you at least allow me to practice interviewing for a job?" They couldn't very easily refuse, and at the end of each session, the interviewer would tell me that maybe they needed to rethink their policy about hiring girls. Even though I knew I was a minority in the business college, it was still a surprise to look back at the line of graduates in 1966 and realize that I was the only female in the class. Everyone behind me had on slacks; I wore the only dress.

In the meantime, I decided that if I was going to have to compete with these men, I'd better get a master's degree in accounting before leaving school. I started the master's program while still finishing my bachelor's degree and, as a result, received my B.B.A. in accounting in the spring of 1966 and my M.A. in accounting the following spring. I also passed the CPA exam while still in school, something I had been told would be almost impossible without practical experience.

I received two job offers before I finished graduate school, one here in Wichita and one in Kansas City. My plans for marriage and children were discussed almost as much as my education and experience. Before finally accepting the offer in Wichita, I learned from the guys being made offers that their bachelor degrees were worth $25 a month more than my master's degree. When I questioned the personnel manager about the fairness of this, he tried to convince me I was mistaken, but finally agreed that if I had passed the CPA exam, I would get the $25. The test results came in the next week, so my M.A. and CPA exams gained me as much as their bachelor degrees without a CPA exam.

I worked my way through the end of the 1960s and into the 1970s. I was well aware of the inequity. The guys I was hired in with were assigned mentors; I was on my own. The guys were told that the day after April 15 (tax day) was a holiday; no one told me, so I went to work. After working on an inventory until 3 a.m., I was back at work at 8 a.m.; the guys I had worked with the night before stayed home.

There was a big party at the end of tax season for the CPAs, unless you were a woman. Women CPAs attended the secretaries' party. All the CPAs in town met regularly for lunch in the Men's Grill at Innes. Every month I would be met by the hostess who told me I could not enter. Every month I had to wave my boss over to tell her I was one of the group.

One job took six weeks in an office beyond the west edge of town. After a few days, I was told I was no longer welcome to eat lunch with my fellow workers and the client's executives. I was given the choice of bringing my lunch to eat in the break room with the client's secretaries or going out alone. I was told every day just before lunch which restaurant the men were going to. I was expected to find a different place to eat – anywhere as long as it wasn't the same restaurant they had chosen. The list went on and on until I finally decided to become self-employed.

Women in Energy

Donna Dilsaver

Women have been managing energy from the first time humans learned to harness fire, bank it and use it to their advantage. Those with knowledge who believe in technology have been, and are, engaged in the struggle to improve the lot of every human being. Historians have long tracked and documented the use of energy and its parallel to our rising expectations for comfort and wealth. That simple reality was jolted in the 1970s. Up to that point, the electrification of the United States was applauded as the technical accomplishment of the 20th Century. Natural gas was piped to most major cities, reducing coal and wood burning, and fueling the industrial, commercial and service expansion of a growing world economy.

Gasoline for independent transportation gave new freedom for moving out of cities and into the suburbs. Supplemental energy was available in even remote areas. An abundant energy supply offered the least of developed countries hope for development to remove the drudgery of their lives, provide safe drinking water, adequate food supply and hope for a different future. Technology for future development was on the horizon in most independent and university laboratories.

Then came October 1973.

The Organization of Petroleum Exporting Countries cut back 5 percent on the oil supply they exported to the United States. The act sent drivers to waiting lines at service stations. It cut back industrial plants' output and commercial building. It sent engineers to drawing boards to recalculate energy production and distribution, and scientists to look for additional domestic oil resources and to research for alternate energy sources. Environmentalists, more and more interested in alternative energy sources, entered the discussion.

As public focus changed, so did public surveys. The Westinghouse Co., a major supplier of energy equipment, began tracking women's perceptions and attitudes about energy. They found that when provided with the same science/technical information as men, their survey answers were the same as men.

As a member of the Atomic Industrial Forum, an industrial group based in Washington, D.C., Westinghouse began searching for effective ways to communicate with women about energy issues. The outgrowth was the formation of Nuclear Energy Women. In 1977, the nation was divided into 15 regions designed to provide programs at a local level to women's groups. I was appointed Region V chairman, which consisted of Kansas, Missouri, Oklahoma and Arkansas. I had the support of KG&E going into the task, but there were no other names in the energy industry provided. I began calling on CEOs of electric companies involved in the operation or construction of nuclear-powered generating facilities in the area and getting names of professional staff members who would be available to serve on committees and become involved in the educational effort.

One of the first calls was to the president of Kansas Power and Light in Topeka. I asked for five minutes of his time and rehearsed my presentation to just that on my drive from Wichita. His secretary greeted me with many questions as to the purpose of taking up my boss' time. He came out of his office, offered me a cup of coffee and invited me into his office. A half hour later, he followed me to the elevator and said, "Yes, I'll give you the help you've asked for, because I think you just might be able to pull this off."

That was the beginning of my calls to every electric, gas, gasoline and pipeline company in my region. I had asked company presidents for members I could appoint to the board of directors who could speak for company policy. Initially, invitations for membership were sent to professional women's organizations, then branched out to include individual members in the community, volunteer groups and eventually to women in the general public. Public Service of Oklahoma in Tulsa signed up 70 members, because once they started inviting women to join, they could not find an appropriate cutoff. Their company, along with many others, found they needed to promote women and give them professional status.

In each state, women were promoted, as they would never have been without the public focus we encouraged. Our members learned that we needed to expand the base to include all forms of energy, including but not limited to nuclear information. In 1979, Women in Energy was started in Wichita and was Region V based, but soon it branched out to include other states too.

Energy issues were expanded in the educational programs. Women were provided statistics from national organizations, industrial reports, commercial applications and everyday usage documents. Frequently they were asked to list five of the most essential energy-consuming items and rank their use in their households.

We taught women how to pump gas for their vehicles; read their electric and gas meters; calculate water usage; caulk windows; measure and increase insulation in their homes; walk more than ride on short trips; and check their offices and homes for energy conservation. They became involved. The program worked. When given the same opportunity and information, women could handle, not only their own, but also executive decisions.

To prove the point, Women in Energy gave Woman of Achievement awards to leaders in their fields: Mary Hudson who started her own service station chain from Kansas City; Margaret Bush Wilson, president of the NAACP who steered her organization to a nationally recognized energy policy; June Brooks, Brooks Oil, who was the first "land man" in the oil patch and appointed to energy policy boards by four U.S. Presidents; Gov. Dixy Lee Ray, the first woman to be appointed chair of the Atomic Energy Commission; and Hazel O'Leary who became the first woman to serve as secretary of the Department of Energy.

The list goes on. Glass ceilings were shattered. The success of the effort not only opened doors for women, but acknowledged the talent and contribution they continue to make in energy management, development, research and political decisions to advance the improved human condition in every part of the world.

I was once asked by a VP at Arkansas Power and Light, on an elevator ride in his office building, why there were Women in Energy but no Men in Energy groups?

I responded, "Oh, but there are. They are called Investor Owned Utilities." The timely closing of the elevator door ended the discussion.

In recent years, that has changed. Women have taken their rightful positions in the management of utilities and energy. No longer is there the need to "educate women" about energy. We are an enlightened population regarding energy and energy issues. And much of the enlightenment began in Wichita.

Notes on Law School in Two Parts
Nola Tedesco Foulston

I.

I graduated from Fort Hays State University in 1972, with degrees in speech communication and English literature. I was accepted at the University of Kansas Graduate School in theater. While I still had the practice of law in sight, I attended KU in the fall of '72 and enjoyed all those moments of playing make believe and honing my drama queen skills.

With my higher education completed in 1973, I was anxious to tackle the world and begin the search for my first paying real-life job. I placed my resume with headhunters, and right out of the chute, I was contacted for a wonderful opportunity to work with a regional arts council that specialized in booking cultural events. I was offered a position as a booking agent that was right down my alley, since it supported my interest in the arts and in law. While the location was far from New York, it was a chance to begin a career that I hoped would lead me back to the Big Apple and a career in theater management and contract law.

The greatest disappointment came when I traveled out of state to find living accommodations. There had been a slight "change of plans" I was told. Unfortunately, they had decided to hire a man for the position, and all they could offer me was a position as his secretary for half of the pay they had promised. Flames shot from my eyes and some tears. I was humiliated, angered and forlorn as I crawled back to Kansas. I felt like I had been stood up for the prom. While wounded, I still had the sense that there needed to be some retribution exacted. I brought my case to my professors at the university who felt my disappointment and encouraged me to explore alternatives.

Now, thinking clearly, I took action. I wanted to learn more about the protection of women from discrimination in employment so I went right to the source – The Kansas Commission on Civil Rights. My zeal and adamant belief that someone needed to right these wrongs must have been quite impressive and persuasive; the very next day, I received a call from the state director who asked me to join the staff as a civil rights investigator. Not a bad day for a little irate Italian girl from New York.

In September of 1973, I proudly started my work in Topeka, surrounded by like-minded and dedicated workers. I was assigned to a team and began my statewide travels as a field investigator. My parents expressed sincere concern with my employment. Around the nation, not all were accepting of the changes, and violence against civil rights worke ◆ was still a reality.

Kansas was not immune. After some threatening actions against investigators, the Kansas Civil Rights Commission seals were removed from our cars. I never felt threatened. In fact, I was always welcomed. Since I didn't have the appearance of a civil rights worker, my investigations were generally successful. In 1954, Kansas' capitol city had been the focus of the U.S. Supreme Court in the landmark civil rights case of *Brown v. Board of Education of Topeka*. In the intervening years, and despite a national education program, conflicts over civil rights continued to impact America.

We all should recall that in 1960, the early days of the civil rights movement, four young men who were college freshmen quietly sat down at the F.W. Woolworth "white only" lunch counter in Greensboro, NC. This act of determination set in motion the waves of civil rights protests that changed our nation. In Kansas two years earlier, although it did not receive as much publicity, black students held a protest against Dockums Drug Store and its "white only" lunch counter practices. The Wichitans won their battle when the practice ended due to their sit-in.

In Topeka, Maynard's Restaurant – famous for its cinnamon rolls and lunchtime fare – catered to the lunch crowd in the downtown area. On any given day, its premises would be filled with attorneys and lawmakers who conducted their business over a Reuben sandwich. It was so busy that Mr. Maynard carved out a *pied de terre* for the male professionals and advised other customers, specifically women, that their presence was prohibited. Posted outside the infamous lunchroom was a large sign: "Ladies, please let the men have this room during lunch hours." Obviously there was a concern that women, with their idle chatter, would disturb the men who were conducting legal business.

Talk about waving the red flag. This sign and Maynard's became a rallying point in 1973 for the young women in law in Topeka. They felt that they should have the same opportunities as the men to further their professional careers. If it meant breaking Mr. Maynard's rule, then so be it. The women, en force, took seats in the male-only lunch area. They were refused service, subjected to slurs and told to leave the restaurant. Undaunted, they returned again and again, only to be treated in the same manner. Seeking their remedy, a civil rights complaint of discrimination in accommodation was filed by the women who had been refused service at a public restaurant. I was assigned the case.

I worked diligently on my assignment and met with the women many times. I went to the lunchroom, and I saw the sign. My next job was to see Mr. Maynard and get his side of the story. "Women are nuisances, and the men need a place of their own," he said. He had the right as a restaurant owner to rule his premises. He refused to budge and would not follow the law.

In the face of litigation, Mr. Maynard took the last stand and closed his restaurant rather than allow women to eat lunch in the private dining room. There were lots of unhappy patrons, who for years had enjoyed the food and society of this Topeka dining establishment. Time would march on, and Maynard's restaurant would fade away and be forgotten except by those who loved the cinnamon rolls and the young women of law who took a stand.

II.

Who says that independent women don't have a sense of humor? In our domestic relations class at Washburn University School of Law, Prof. John Howe always exaggerated the whining women who found themselves in divorce court. Not to be outdone, I went to a farm, purchased a piglet, dressed him in swaddling and took him to class.

Together with my female companions, we prepared "adoption papers" for "Little John Howe" and presented him to our professor. Taking it in stride, John Howe held the pig close, soothed his ruffled snout and took him home to his farm, where he was the big pig in the house. The news reported that "women law students ham it up!"

Notes After Law School in Three Parts

I.

Fresh out of law school in 1976, degree and license in hand, I became an assistant district attorney in Wichita.

An older man stopped me outside the courtroom and told me that his wife had also studied the law; however, she had the good sense to stay home and raise a family.

"How unfortunate," I replied.

II.

You could more easily move a mountain than be a woman and a trial attorney. No problem. Take the cases the men don't want to try and work twice as hard at half the pay to accomplish your goals. Sharon Werner and I, the only women in an all-male bastion, did just that. With support from our women colleagues in the Bar, we advanced the notion of vertical prosecution of sexual assault and child abuse cases. The local headline read: "They Are Not Women; They Are Attorneys."

III.

In the years that have passed since my graduation, women have advanced in great numbers to pursue their juris doctorate degrees. Most law school classes are equally divided between men and women. Prof. Linda Elrod penned a journal article about the history of women in law and commented on my career and that of my contemporary colleagues in the '70s. She called us "trailblazers." It was more like taking a machete to a jungle and hacking our way to the top, but I would do it again in a heartbeat!

I Didn't Play With Dolls
Colleen Kelly Johnston

I love math. I have made my living with mathematics and statistics, working with Fern Van Gieson in a political survey business and by myself in my family's law firm as business manager. In the 1970s, after decades of put downs by male teachers and other men, I finally made peace with my abilities, thanks to the patience of three Wichita State University professors, all male. I have always been good with numbers. In grade school, I made straight A's, annoying the boys in my classes. Girls were supposed to play with dolls and learn how to cook. While I had a dollhouse and a lovely Princess Elizabeth doll, they were in virtually unblemished condition when I left home.

In high school, I took all the math courses offered. Although I liked algebra far better than geometry, I did learn how to measure the height of a tree based on the Pythagorean Theory, a feat I have never found necessary to use in any practical way. When I was preparing for graduation, my math teacher informed me there was no place in the math world of the 1950s for women, unless I was willing to use my mathematical brain in theoretical physics, and that would be a struggle. Sister Mary Alberta's cautions would not deter me. My mother's, however, hit home with a vengeance. If I were determined to have a career instead of marrying a nice Catholic boy and raising a family, I had a choice. I could go, all expenses paid, to a solid Catholic girl's college near Chicago and take the standard liberal arts courses.

On the other hand, my parents would acquiesce to my attending the University of Wichita – the precursor of Wichita State University – but I had to agree to study medical technology, the only possible career available to women at that time except for nursing and teaching. In addition, I had to pledge a sorority; my mother considered me inept at social graces and dating. I would also continue to live at home. I began college at WU in the fall of 1951. To fulfill Mother's mandate, my class schedule held the full complement of freshman requirements – English, history, algebra, chemistry – plus six hours of biology and beginning med tech courses. Epsilon Kappa Rho took me as a pledge. At the end of the fall semester, I achieved full membership in the sorority and got the only D in my life in chemistry.

That D shook me up; to say nothing of the effect it had on my parents. Colleen was fallible. It could not be allowed. I was ordered to take the course over. It was taught by the same teacher and his lab-rat assistant, but I got a B the second time. I also sneaked in accounting and applied geometry, which was slightly more useful than regular geometry.

The summer after my first year, Mother got me a job as a nurses' assistant at St. Francis Hospital. It was a miserable experience. Sister Blondina, in charge of the floor nurses, set out to give me a taste of every disease and injury patient. I gave potassium permanganate baths to skin patients that turned my hands purple. In July, she assigned me to work weekend nights in the emergency room, taking care of all the knifing victims. The result of Mother's intercession with Sister Blondina convinced me that under no circumstances would I become a nurse.

Math was my only way out. The fall semester of that year, I continued to enroll in liberal arts requirements. I also received permission to squeeze in a second accounting class. By this time, I was determined to find a career other than medical technology. Med Tech was not my way to a rich and satisfying life, which also in my dreams did not include a man and children. If I wanted to take the educational direction of my choosing, I had to get a job and pay the cost of my own tuition and books.

At the end of my second fall semester, I was making A's and B's in accounting and math, A's in my liberal arts classes and C's in biology and other science requirements. I had also stashed away enough money to pay for my summer classes in geology and Latin American history. I loved geology, particularly memorizing geological periods, ages of rock layers, and the stratigraphy of how the rock lay and was laid down. It was so simple. Numbers clicked with me. However, my expected A in geometry did not appear. Instead, I got a B. When I confronted my geometry teacher, a very nice, elderly, practicing geologist, he told me that his lab assistant – read the first three letters of assistant – would not allow an A because of my ineptitude in the required laboratory work. Therefore the B. Prof. Cullen, however, took the time to talk to me about my gift for analytical work and practical applications, rather than identifying the data itself. I should have absorbed this more than I did, because it became one of the best pieces of advice I have ever been given.

During that past spring and summer of 1956, I met and eloped with a young man, James Johnston, headed for the University of Kansas and law school. As a result, my own education halted. While my husband worked part time and went to classes, I worked as an assistant purchasing agent, then as a teacher in a one-room country school. Later, when he graduated and began practicing law. And between our children's births, I worked as a bookkeeper for an accounting firm, a chain of grocery stores and a manufacturing firm, therefore utilizing the two semesters of accounting I had taken. In 1962, I knew the firm I worked for did not employ pregnant women. I was able to work until I could no longer keep from showing before the office manager fired me.

In 1972, life had stabilized enough – our youngest began kindergarten – I was able to find a few hours a day to get back into college. With six children, there was little possibility I had the time it would take for me to qualify for a degree in physics or math. Even though I might have succeeded, teaching would have been the only career open, and I had no desire to teach.

Accounting seemed the way to go, so I declared a major in accounting and went for my appointment with my academic adviser, who happened to be the chair of the accounting department. He looked over my record from past years, then at my proposal to take the third course in accounting. He began shaking his head and then looked up at me.

"I'm sorry, Mrs. Johnston," he said, continuing to shake his head. "You can't take any more accounting." Then he patted my hand and crossed the accounting class off my proposed schedule. "Now let's find something else. You already have enough accounting to make you a nice little bookkeeper." Furious does not come close to describing my anger. He was preventing me from taking more courses in the field I had already been using to help support my family. I was getting tired of being told I could not do something because I was a woman. Unfortunately, the head of the department had the last say then. My degree hopes had to turn in another direction.

Several years later, when the accounting department was directed by another man, I received permission to continue my accounting goal. It was difficult to get back to, and I struggled with the work along with family responsibilities. I knew my grade was not going to be what I wanted, but I kept up with the assignments. The mid-term exam was in the form of a word problem. It seemed inexplicably simple. "Given certain stock information, accounting data and production levels for two companies, tell which of the two companies would be a better investment opportunity."

The problem solution outlined itself in my mind so clearly I spent most of the semester break worrying about what I was missing. Finally I remembered a class I had taken in archeology where the answer to the final paper was so simple I didn't trust my own presumption. As a result, I got a C on the paper, and the single word "stratigraphy" emblazoned in red across the first page. Then, Professor Cullen's comments on my geology grade reasserted itself. I wrote the answer to the investment problem in my best analytical prose and handed in the paper.

When classes resumed, Dr. Cho appeared at his desk looking very unhappy. "This was not well done," he said, holding up and rattling a stack of papers to the entire class. "If you were to get a semester's grade based on this work, most of you would get, at best, a D."

My heart sunk. Dr. Cho began calling out names and taking papers around the room.

"Brown. You should be ashamed."

"Mr. Jones, even your father wouldn't hire you with this kind of work product."

"Tsk. Tsk. Terrible."

The castigation continued, each sentence seemingly worse than the last. My name was not called, and he was getting closer to the bottom of the stack. He went to his desk in front of the classroom. "This work does not qualify for third-year accounting students. Most of you will get a D for the semester if you don't begin paying attention." He waved one paper up in the air. "This is what you should have handed in, a perfect example of the application of accounting data to a problem. Instead, many of you handed me pages of solved problems proving nothing. The problems you solved were supposed to bring you to a logical conclusion. Instead, only Mrs. Johnston achieved a perfect paper. Exactly what I was looking for." He smiled in my direction. "I congratulate you. Now, I'm going to pass her paper around, and I suggest you all look it over carefully if you wish to end the semester with a grade above a C." He handed my paper off to the man in the farthest row from me and turned back to his book. "Why don't we see why the rest of you missed the simple solution to this simple problem?"

On Being a Somebody

Myrne Roe

The women's movement in Wichita in 1970 promised a way to meet my life goal. I had spent many hours since junior high trying to figure out how to be somebody. It was Dad's plan. He had made it clear I probably would never achieve such a lofty aim, but should try for his sake. His formula for my success included riding a bicycle so "you can get a pair of legs on you," and dating boys whose fathers were somebodies since "the acorn doesn't fall far from the tree."

Females, according to him and backed up by males and females on both sides of the family, could not be somebodies without the help of men who had money. He didn't have money, so he bullied his skinny oldest daughter to go for it. The message was clear: If no one with money wanted to marry me, then I should be a teacher. Mother said to listen to Father, I suspect, because when he was instructing me, she didn't have to listen to him. I think both of them failed to have the life they wanted. She was limited by her prescribed role as a woman who married in the 1930s; he – in large part – by an undiagnosed bipolar disease.

Ah, but the feminists at Wichita State in the 1970s, where I was teaching part time and working on my master's degree, had a different view. They dared to believe that success could be ours without having to marry into it. They all wanted to be somebodies too, but it was on their terms and their abilities they chose to reach that goal. Actually, I had wanted to be a lawyer, but when my male debate coach in college made it clear that was not an option (as in laughing at me for suggesting it), that was all there was to that. Awfully easy to get discouraged when what you want is met with derision.

From listening to women at WSU, it was becoming clear that to achieve I needed a chance to earn respect, to be taken seriously. I wanted to accomplish something positive, something that helped others, made things better. Something that got me my somebody card. I was already a wife who married for love, not money, and a mother and a teacher. For many women teaching is their way to become a somebody. For me, it was fulfilling someone else's aspirations instead of my own.

So, I became a volunteer preacher in the church of women's liberation. I sermonized about feminism. I published sermons to grow my flock by writing a feminist column, "Kindly Call Me Ms." for three Wichita weekly newspapers: *The New Newspaper*, *The Prairie Journal*, and finally, *The Wichita Independent*.

I wrote, *Several of My Sisters*, a reader's theater show – even wrote some songs for it. I performed in it with some of my students at a national women's conference at Wichita State. The only lines I recall from the show were these lyrics: "There are three choices for me. I can be a teacher, a nurse, or a secretary. Wait, I have a choice of four. What fun! I can be a nun."

I also wrote and performed a one-woman show, *What Do You Want to Be When You Grow Up, Little Girl?* My main memory of that show occurred when I was invited to perform it by a woman faculty member at a church-related college in Eastern Kansas. The college administration was very concerned about the evil of women's lib, and she thought her students needed to hear another side. I performed the show in front of a packed house of females. During Q and A, the enthusiastic crowd was instructed by the male college president, who interrupted our discussion, to leave the auditorium. Apparently, they shouldn't be exposed to such heresy. Some left. Most stayed.

Actually, the college president and I had some things in common. We were both preachers. He spread the word about how woman should always submit to narrow and patriarchal dictates. I wanted to spread the word that it was both unjust and unforgivable to continue to deny more than 50 percent of the human race the right to make their own decisions.

I taught the first women's studies course in Leadership Techniques for Women (preaching) at WSU. I led a successful campaign to change our public library's policy of requiring a married woman to get her husband's written permission before she got a library card. (That took some preaching to achieve.) Gave speeches (even more preaching) and served on more committees and boards than I can recall (which also, at times, involved preaching). I would continue to preach in the church of women's liberation while searching for a career that fit.

In 1973, I took a part-time position as director of Planned Parenthood, thinking this was my ticket to a new career. The position was attractive, because it focused on helping women and was far from all the traditional roles I'd been advised to pursue. It wasn't long into my 40- to 50-hour per week "part-time" job when my life fell apart, and my whole goal-driven plan to achieve was blown to hell. Depression had been my on-again, off-again companion since I was 12 years old. This time was different. I didn't want to live. The pain was too great. I had a psychotic break, along with three suicide attempts and three hospital psych-ward stays.

My male doctors had been giving me Valium at such a rate for so long that I had plenty to make three attempts, and if some nurse on the ward hadn't found the other bottle in my purse, I could have made it four. Even so, I knew that if I wanted to try again, chances were some friendly doctor would give me more pills. My doctors were not only pushing an addictive drug that made me a depressed zombie, they were also giving me lousy advice. Two propositioned me. (Gee, Dad, you may have been right; if I'd taken one of those big-time, well-to-do doctors up on that prescription for recovery, it could have given me a shot at somebody credentials.)

One told me to grow up. Another explained I hadn't really wanted to kill myself, that I just wanted attention. One thought the cure was having a baby and learning to be a good wife. Finally, I found a doctor at Prairie View in Newton, a man. He started me on my journey to recovery.

And, I found politics. I had volunteered in the 1972 McGovern campaign, and the local coordinator of that campaign had been given the same position two years later in the Bill Roy Senate race against Bob Dole. The coordinator asked me if I would be his secretary. I said no, but I'd be the office manager. I thought manager would look better on my resume. Damn. I was good at the political stuff. I could organize press conferences and big fundraisers. Furthermore, I had some good ideas about strategy. Not bad at writing political speeches either. From there I worked in a city commission race. I thought this is it, my ticket to somebody-land. Of course, the campaigns where I was honing my organizational, management and political skills were all losing ones.

When a former high school debate student of mine, Dan Glickman, asked me to run his campaign for Congress, I figured I'd try a political job one more time. If he lost, then I'd read the tea leaves and find another career choice. He won. I became his chief aide. I was somebody. Not important, rich or famous, but I was enjoying my work, good at it and respected for the job I was doing. I had my spouse's help with parenting. I had the joy of being given an opportunity and making the best of it – just like a guy.

Okay, it wasn't all roses. I ran into some not very enthusiastic men who didn't much care for me doing what I was doing. My favorite example of sexist attitudes toward me since I was in a "man's profession," was the campaign volunteer who was supposed to be raising money, but who decided instead to usurp my role as campaign manager in the congressional race. He'd come into headquarters and tell the staff what they should be doing.

Fortunately, they knew to enlighten me and not follow his edicts. He annoyed them a great deal, however. He also – on two occasions – acted as spokesperson for the candidate, which he wasn't supposed to do. I was given the task of explaining his job role and mine and getting him to concentrate on fundraising. I set up a meeting. I was feeling that I was firmly, but nicely, making my case when he interrupted me to ask, "Has anyone ever told you that you have great legs?" (Thanks, Dad. I rode that bike all over town. Got the great legs. See what else I got for my trouble?)

The fact is, however, my career happened because three male candidates and a male campaign coordinator discovered I had a good head for politics. Of course, women were rarely in a position to help me in the same way, but I give those four men much credit for giving me a chance to prove myself on my own terms.

My work for a congressman introduced me to many influential folks, and when I decided to move on, it was that experience and those contacts that got me a job as executive director of university communications at WSU. Talk about needing political skills. The joke among my friends on campus when I decided four years later to leave WSU and return to my old congressional staff job was: "Myrne is leaving politics to go back to work for the Congressman." Later my credentials and contacts allowed me to move into my final job at *The Wichita Eagle* as an editorial writer and syndicated columnist.

Well, maybe I'm not the somebody that Dad had in mind, but at least the choice eventually was mine to pursue careers doing what I wanted to do. Now retired, I have the good feeling that I've done my jobs well. Women have come a long way since I grew up with the prevailing notions of my parent's time. We haven't come far enough, though. Guess, then, being a preacher will continue to be part of my life. That's how this book came about. It's one big sermon about the glory and rightness of women's equality in the face of those wrong-headed people who opposed change at every turn. It's the story of those who helped us, of our own growth as citizens and leaders, as well as mothers and wives and partners.

Sadly, there are still men and women who want to paste on all those torn-off calendar pages and return us to a time when women had far fewer choices and far less control over their own lives. This book brings together women somebodies to tell those stories so that we don't ever have to go backward to the 1970s again. We must keep preaching the truth about equal rights. That was the truth that set us free, and we need to ensure our daughters and all future daughters are free too.

Twice as Good Just to Be Equal

Carolyn S. Russell

It was June 1973, and I was in Anniston, AL, standing in line with other Army trainees at Fort McClellan. We were waiting to complete our official Army records. I had already grown used to waiting, and I'd only been in the Army three days.

I leaned against the wall, and someone behind me snapped, "Private Russell, that wall will hold itself up just fine without you helping it." I stood up straight, embarrassed, which was the corporal's point. But the really terrifying thing was hearing *Private* Russell for the first time. In my heart, I knew I was at least a captain. What had I gotten myself into? At 25, I was the oldest of 36 women in Bravo Company, 2nd Platoon, where our eight weeks of basic training in the Women's Army Corps was about to begin. When we finished our Army schools after basic, we would no longer be WACs, but soldiers in the regular Army.

Just three months before I enlisted, virtually all military occupational specialties (MOSs), other than combat roles, were opened to women. The draft was ending and the new, all-volunteer Army beginning. Women were only two percent of the troops, and new recruiting campaigns were aimed to change that. New opportunities in non-traditional job fields was a key recruiting message. I took my Army qualifying tests the same week I was divorced. It was an unhappy time. I wanted to erase my pain and thought this was a path. I would travel, do new things and get the GI Bill for college later. I could choose a guaranteed duty station or a guaranteed MOS. I dreamed of being stationed in Germany, but didn't want the Army to pick my job.

I really wanted to become an Army photographer, but if I did, I'd start my enlistment as a private. On the other hand, since I was already an LPN, the medical corps promised a Specialist 5 rank after basic, with a guaranteed promotion to Spec 6 within 18 months. That was appealing, pragmatic and logical. So I chose photography. My plan was to graduate at the top of my still photography class after basic. If I made it, I'd be quickly promoted to Spec 4 in less than six months, and that would at least be a decent head start. But first there was basic, and the worst eight weeks of my life were before me.

Now at Ft. McClellan, we went next to the barracks to settle in. No privacy – only wall lockers separating all 36 of us – and no air conditioning in the sweltering Alabama summer. I wrote to my family in Wichita: "So far it's been a bummer, but I guess I expected that. ... Lights are out at 8:30 p.m. this week, and we get up at 4:30 a.m. ... I'm sure part of this eight weeks is necessary, but a lot of it is a bunch of crap. ... Let me explain something – when I called the other night I really couldn't talk freely ... the drill sergeant and cadre walk around and can listen to everything you say. So obviously you can't talk about how absolutely lousy everything is."

We were taught military customs and courtesy, how to salute, how to march, and most importantly, how to starch and iron the very odd and ugly trainee uniforms – light blue cotton shirts, very thick cotton shorts and A skirts, worn over the shorts.

"Dear family … We spend more time ironing than anything else … besides ironing everything for morning inspection, you have to take your skirts off and iron them every time you come back to the bay (barracks), which is three or four times a day. You also get to wear black anklets with your granny-type black shoes. One of the marching songs we sing goes: "Joined the Army to see the world, all I see are ugly girls …""

We finally got our real Army uniforms, marched to our graduation and in the parade that followed. Mom and Dad went home a few days later, and I flew to Ft. Monmouth, NJ, and the signal corps post and training center. That's where I met my classmate and friend, Darla, who helped keep me sane and laughing. I finally had some privacy, though not much – still a big barracks room, but partitioned into tiny cubicles. Several times in the next several months, there would be shakedown inspections – mostly an excuse to find women in bed together and boot them out of the service.

I had a few weeks while waiting for my school to start. That's when I got my picture in the post newspaper while working on detail – in the latrine. Everything was being converted for women soldiers, so they covered the urinals with wooden enclosures and we got orders to paint them. It was a striking photo op.

Meanwhile, my 12-week still photography school was finally underway, five days a week, eight hours a day. There were three women in our class of about 30. Each student was outfitted with a large 35-pound metal case, which we lugged around for every assignment. Inside was a 4x5 Speed Graphic, a tripod, flash bracket, bulbs and other gear. No light meter, no strobe. We were among the first women ever to be in the course, and Mr. G, the civilian course director, was delighted with that. Some of the Army instructors didn't want us there, thank you – but many were good teachers and mostly fair. While many assignments were measured by a point system, a few were judged subjectively. I took a big hit on a composition assignment I'd done well, while the same instructors gave high marks to a male student with marginal work.

"Dearest family…I just reread your letter, Mom, and it makes me feel so much closer to you all to have mail. I do hope you'll keep it up … We changed phases and instructors today, thank God. Things should really get interesting now. We'll be going up in a helicopter four times to shoot aerial & will be going off-post for picture stories … Maybe these instructors will be fairer than I felt the others were. "

We learned field photography, studio lighting, darkroom skills and action work. I loved using a view camera for architectural work and the excitement of shooting from an open helicopter door, leaning out for perfectly vertical shots, secured only with a shoulder and belt harness. Flying over the Naval Air Station at Lakehurst, NJ, was eerie. We could actually see the imprint of the Hindenburg, which crashed and burned below us in 1937.

In spite of the two unfair sergeants, I did graduate first in class. The women in our company cheered when it was announced, and cheered again when I was promoted twice in seven days – the reward for the number one spot.

My next stop was Germany. When I arrived at Coleman Barracks – the name of the entire installation – near Mannheim, I was delivered by jeep to the women's barracks. It was a new building, with bathroom and showers on the main floor only, and a small kitchen and break area above that. My room was on the second floor. When I opened the door, a woman in fatigues was waxing the floor with a big electric buffer we'd all learned to use by now.

"Hi," she said. "Please try not to step on the floor. I'm getting ready for inspection."

I tiptoed in with a duffel bag containing all my belongings, and did my best to comply.

What had my recruiter told me? "As a Spec 4, you'll get a private room on post, permission to live off-post in an apartment." *Dammit. Dammit. Dammit. He was such a liar.*

My new roommate's bed was covered with a lot of unfamiliar OD (olive drab) green stuff, though I recognized a gas mask from basic training. She stopped battling the buffer, apologized and smiled. I was still reeling from exhaustion and my two-to-a-room status.

I asked, "What is all of this on your bed?"

"It's my TA-50," she said.

"What's TA-50?"

"It's the gear you take with you to the field."

"What's 'the field?' "

"It's when we go into the woods, live in tents and do mock war exercises."

I really, really hated the recruiter now.

The next day, it was time to go to work. The photo lab was in the basement, down sharp, metal-edged concrete steps. The building itself was harsh, gray and depressing, like all the others here, where Third Reich troops and pilots had made ready for war. There were still Luftwaffe airplanes in secret underground hangers here, I was told, probably surrounded by mines. The area was off-limits. Across the street, where Field Marshall Hermann Goring had held forth in his Officer's Club, there was now U.S. Army NCO Club. A mile away Gen. George Patton was critically injured in a jeep accident in December 1945, dying 12 days later in the American Army hospital in Heidelberg – just seven months after victory in Europe. Nearby Mannheim was a major industrial center for the Nazis. The city center was destroyed by Allied bombings, leaving only a landmark water tower, *der Wasserturm*, still standing.

On my way downstairs, I was nervous but excited, eager to meet my fellow soldiers and get to work. I followed my escort into the photo lab. Army greens perfect, new Specialist 4 rank on each arm, brass and shoes shining. I was the first woman photographer assigned to any Signal Corps unit in Europe. That could mean I was the first in Europe, period, but I've never known for sure. The Pfc. introduced me to the five men in the room. They had heard that I was coming, and they had never worked with a woman photographer.

After quick introductions, a mousy Spec 5 could barely wait. "We're glad you're here," he said. "We need someone to type captions."

Think fast, Russell. "I'm sorry, but I don't know how to type," I lied.

He was shocked, crestfallen. I read his mind: "They send us a woman, and she has a gender defect. Oh great."

The next day, the (thank God soon-to-be leaving) senior NCO, an unseemly person, wanted to show me his portfolio. He was smug, but not too bright. As he opened the four-inch thick binder, he glanced surreptitiously in my direction, watching for my reaction. He explained all about the studio lighting, the film he used, where and when he had shot each image. I didn't care. His stupid portfolio was filled with photographs of nude or nearly nude women – and nothing else. I concentrated on being expressionless, though I wanted to stomp on his crummy little book and tell him he was a pig. After several pages I said, "I don't know what to say," which was true and ended the thing.

Several weeks later we got a new NCO, and the sleazy sergeant was gone. Staff Sgt. Mitchell was a lanky Vietnam veteran who walked with a slight limp. His chopper was shot down in Nam, breaking his hip, legs and other bones. He was in the hospital for five months afterward. Mitch was likable, professional, fair and competent, and made great smoked ribs at our company cookout. I liked him a lot.

Meanwhile, it wasn't long before headquarters senior staff was requesting me for photo assignments. I wrote home that "I didn't get to go to Bertchesgarten last weekend for the 3-day pass. At the last minute the brigade commander, Col. Blair, requested me and me only to shoot his farewell party. Good for the ego, but hell on your plans! I also shot the main events at the change of command ceremonies."

We had a pretty good team in the photo lab, and most of the guys were fun to work with. I shot portraits mostly on location. The work ranged from decorations and promotions ceremonies, to re-enlistments and training exercises. We covered headquarters and four other battalions in other towns. We were also an Army Aviation post and had the luxury of going to these shoots via helicopters. I also had aerial photo assignments, and the pilots sometimes gave me a chance to photograph castles on the way.

One day, while on one of these assignments – in Darmstadt, I believe – a staff car pulled up a few yards away. The driver walked up to me and said, "Gen. Bailey would like to speak with you."

Holy crap.

The woman in the back seat motioned for me to come to the car. I snapped to, camera over my shoulder, and quickstepped there. It really was her – Brig. Gen. Mildred Bailey, director of the now-transitioning Women's Army Corps, only the second woman to become a general officer. She had served the country since 1942. She was on a tour of Army installations in Europe and wanted to meet women soldiers who had once been denied most Army specialties, including mine.

"How's it going, Specialist?" she asked. Basically, it was going lousy most of time, but not bad when I was on assignment.

"I'm doing fine, General," I said.

"Have you faced any difficulties as a woman photographer?"

"Yes, Ma'am," I said boldly. "They expect us to be twice as good just to be equal to the men. But fortunately, Ma'am, that's not a problem." The general grinned. I watched as her car drove away. And then I went back to work.

Work Options for Women
Margaret Simmons, Interviewed by Marietta Anderson

Q. *Margaret, tell me about Work Options for Women, and your role in it.*

A. In about 1977, Pat and Jerry Irish came to town. Pat was a dynamo. Pat brought a lot of far-reaching ideas from San Francisco, and she really wanted to make a big difference in Wichita. She decided that probably the YWCA was the place to go, so they listened to her, took her suggestions and they started Work Options for Women. She talked them into doing two funded director kinds of positions, to be split among four people. She was really talking about job sharing or flex time, that kind of thing. I've been told that she, Leigh Aaron-Leary and Karla Langton worked together on Work Options for Women in the beginning.

Q. *Did the YWCA board accept Pat's proposal?*

A. I assume so. I don't have any documentation for that. Space was allocated in the former YWCA facility on North Market. You know we got in big trouble with the Y, and I will get to that. Pat's West Coast ideas kind of collided with Midwestern values. The board was mostly older women, cautious. I was on that board for a while.

I need to tell you a little about my background and why Pat decided I would be good for a position with the program. I grew up in New Gottland, KS, and was married during World War II, ended up in Wichita and I worked for a lawyer for more years than I want to remember. In the 1960s, I began questioning the Vietnam War, questioned a whole lot of things, and the women's movement was beginning. My son had long hair. And all these things made me think about the world and what I wanted to do about all the things happening. I decided I wanted to do something. I didn't want to go to college, because I wanted to get more involved, and I knew how long college would take.

Q. *Where did you begin?*

A. First I was elected to the first Citizen Participation Organization. It was an advisory group to the city commission. I was vice chair. It was a lot stronger organization when it first started, because we had representatives who went downtown and met with the commission, and these people really had some clout. It was a wonderful training ground. It taught me politics and showed me how officials operate. It didn't take too long before the developers took notice, and they were not happy with citizen input. The next election saw some significant changes. The CPO council, made up of members from all kinds of organizations, had met, as I said, with the commission every month and that was eliminated.

Then I worked for two campaigns for city commission. Both the candidates were elected, and one appointed me to what was called the "Manpower Area Planning Council."

Q. *Were you volunteering in other roles?*

A. Yes. I was on the board of the Women's Political Caucus and on the board of United Methodist Urban Ministry. I organized the committee on the Commission on the Status of Women in the West Heights United Methodist Church. I was a founder of the Women's Equality Coalition and also was active in the Democratic Party.

I went over to the Y one day and asked Pat, "What kinds of things can I do?"

She said, "How would you like to be a co-director here?"

I said "Sure. I never had to go before the board. That was it."

Q. *What year was that?*

A. This was 1977. A lot happened that year. That was the Women's Weekend when we discovered, "Hey, everybody isn't on our side." I also did write the person in charge of the Manpower Planning Council to see if it was proper for me to serve on the council, because I worked at Work Options. I thought there might be a conflict of interest. The council was funding Work Options. There was no conflict, as long as I didn't vote on anything directly affecting my job.

As it turned out, there were three directors. We didn't fill the fourth position. Leigh Aaron-Leary, Pat Irish and I were the three. We all had contacts. Pat talked to construction people and other blue-collar representatives. Leigh worked with university people. I did a lot of organizing of workshops, tried to get young people interested in job opportunities – that kind of thing.

Q. *What did the workshops consist of?*

A. I was chair of WomenArt/WomenFair for two years, 1979 and 1980. I organized workshops there. I was always able to take one area of my life and use it to complement the other. So, I wrote some things for workshops for West Heights Methodist Church, making sure they were included in WomenArt/WomenFair. We did a thing for the United Brethren Women who came to town and wanted a workshop on women. We also talked to the youth group at West Heights about the work opportunities besides going into secretarial work or teaching.

Q. *Alternative, nontraditional jobs and roles?*

A. Yes. I did not do a lot of the presentations. I pulled stuff together. We also had job development at work options. At one time, we had 15 employees, and they called around to various businesses and got job listings. We compiled those for women to look through. In the beginning, this was targeted only to women. We were growing like crazy. We were taking over all the rooms at the Y, and Pat just moved into those rooms. The director of the Y wanted more control over the program. The director subsequently fired us.

Q. *What happened then?*

A. When the staff heard of the firing, they loaded all their files into their cars and took them out of the Y. We appealed. After a long time, we were reinstated. More time passed, and the Y board decided to drop our program.

Q. *Was that the end for Work Option's for Women?*

A. Yeah, I think so. The city commission wasn't sure whether they were going to keep us. So we were both homeless and possibly without funds. When we left, Inter-Faith Ministries decided they would take us in under their umbrella. I don't know if you remember that dumpy, little place on North Market. It was just a storefront with a wood stove, but we managed to keep going.

We had lost our funding, and Pat did not have a salary. Jerry got another job, and they started talking about moving. Leigh went back to school. I took over as a volunteer director. We were running programs that 400 women a month were attending or using. They were taking training, and we were helped by our six volunteers in Service to America workers. They were wonderful. One of them was Peggy Jarman, now Peggy Bowman. I was their supervisor.

My 1980 February calendar shows how busy we were. I had sat in a lawyer's office for so many years, and I had all this pent-up energy. This year, and the following year, we finally got some funding and moved to Waco and 13th. We opened up classes, so we had a few young men. It was a shock to me to find out that many didn't know how to read. We also had women who would be dropped off by their husbands, and they'd never see their husbands again. We had to refer them to other services and resources.

When Pat first came here, I think the concept was aimed at middle-class women who wanted flex time, job sharing and that kind of thing. We found out that there was a whole different group of people who needed our resources. It was a survival thing for lots of women.

Q. *It sounds like in the process of creating workshops and opportunities for people, more and more people came out looking for help.*

A. Yes, I think that's right. I always remember the class we had on teaching people how to lift heavy objects, how to access alternative jobs and so on. One of the programs that really helped was Jimmy Carter's quota system.

In order to get certain federally funded jobs, you had to have so many jobs filled by women. So we worked with some of those companies. You'd see women out there on road projects wearing the gear; that's what we did. I remember one young woman who came dancing out of one of our workshops, saying, "We're never going to be pregnant and barefoot again."

The last grant we got was supposed to fund exploring how to get additional funding for women to explore alternative kinds of jobs. Many of them, however, also needed transportation. We were trying to identify child care needs. And, then job training.

Q. *Your three major need areas were transportation, jobs and child care?*

A. Yes. Workshops related to these were how to manage money, how to get good nutrition.

Q. *Do you have any of the old materials from the workshops?*

A. No, not much. What I do have is the information from WomenArt/WomenFair. I have a letter from Barbara Jordan, who taught at the LBJ School of Public Affairs, declining our invitation to speak at the event, and a letter from Kansas Representative Martha Keyes, who also could not attend. I also have a piece from *The Wichita Eagle*, written by reporter Cheryl Pilate, about Work Options. Now, we are at the point where John Carlin called me and wanted me to run for the state legislature. That was 1980, during the Reagan sweep. In 1981, all the job training funds went away.

Q. *What did you do in the '80s then?*

A. I taught businesswomen to network with each other. We still had workshops. Pizza Hut was always good about sending women to our workshops. Carol Konek did some workshops, as I remember. We involved the community as much as we could. We couldn't pay our presenters. In 1982, I decided I was pretty tired of this, so I told the board I wanted to look for something else. It was about this time that Myrne Roe called me and asked if I wanted to work for Rep. Dan Glickman's re-election campaign.

I said yes. I always treasured my time at Work Options. I think we made a difference. I think about my granddaughter, actually. She is a single mom, went through Wichita State University and graduated summa cum laude. She bought a house not very long ago, has a good job. Her daughter is 12 years old, and she has done this all on her own. She had no help from anybody. That couldn't have happened in 1970.

Q. *She had a pretty good role model in her grandmother, didn't she? Those folks are pretty important people in our lives. Not just organizations, but individuals.*

A. Yeah, I guess you're right. We had a great group, especially the Women's Equality Coalition. They were wonderful resources, a great support group. It is surprising to me that few of us have died. We are a long-lived bunch. I think maybe they're out there still working.

Q. *What have we missed in our discussion?*

A. I think we've missed the energy the three of us – Pat, Leigh and I – demonstrated. We just took out into the community. We had a plan and held community meetings with such groups as Church Women United, Wichita City Commissioners, Bureau of Apprenticeship and Training. We tried to work with schools. To have an apprenticeship in electrical, you have to have a certain background in math. The schools didn't teach it.

Q. *What about public school vocational training?*

A. There was a little bit. They had started that school, but nothing much. Brown bag lunches brought some of these people together, every week on Wednesday, with resource people from inside and outside the community.

Q. *What else might you have done?*

A. I would have lobbied the city, especially, to change the bus routes and worked harder with the Child Care Association to get places for care that young women needed for their children. I would have continued to expand job opportunities. It is very gratifying to think I was part of Work Options. Pat Irish was the kind of person who inspired a lot of enthusiasm.

Q. *Where did your talent lie?*

A. In drawing things together, to integrate everything. But now, I really enjoy taking it easy, gardening, spending time with children, grandchildren.

Experiencing the World of "Real Men's Work"

Margot Brown Skinner, Interviewed by Katie Pott

Q. *What was your work experience?*

A. After graduating from college, I came home and worked at Excel (Packing Co.) in the office, answering phones, then later in billing. After marrying and having a child, I stayed home until Mary was in school. I was a single mom then. At that time an Excel employee I knew asked me if I would come and work in sales. I sold boxed meat -- beef. I just talked on the phone to my customers – chain grocery stores and chain restaurants.

Q. *What were the pressures you felt in your work?*

A. It was a perishable product, and you had to sell every day to meet the inventory. You take the inventory which is how many cattle they are going to kill that day, you figure out what percentage of the inventory is to be made into specific cuts, how many sales you're going to make that day, and that's what you sell. You have to sell every day and get rid of the product or it will spoil.

Q. *If you didn't sell that inventory would you be fired?*

A. No, you just get it done … I suppose I would be fired, but I was very good at what I did.

Q. *How many other sales people were there?*

A. Oh, about 10.

Q. *Were you all in one big room?*

A. Except for me, the only woman. We were all in one big room all the time, but I was on the other side of the room. I was never with them.

Q. *Did they put you over there?*

A. Yes, they put me there. I mean they discriminated against me. One day I went to work, and nobody was there. Just happened that there was a big "sales meeting" in Arizona. Actually, they were there playing golf and having fun.

Q. *And they hadn't said anything to you?*
A. No, they really didn't.

Q. *Did they ever have conversations with you? Did they talk to you at all?*

A. Well yeah, they had to talk to me. But I sold Holsteins mostly. The other sales-people weren't very nice; they wouldn't help me.

Q. *What do you mean? How could they have helped you?*

A. We were all responsible for selling all the beef – all kinds and all cuts. They wouldn't help selling the Holsteins.

Q. *Why wouldn't they sell it?*

A. Because they didn't want to. I guess they wanted me to look bad.

Q. *Is it harder to sell?*

A. Well it's a different kind of product. It's lean and high yielding. It's not like for nice tablecloth (restaurants). It's from the forequarters; they grind it for fast food places, for hamburgers, and then they sell off the good part for steaks, but it is a different kind of product.

Q. *Were you good at selling it?*

A. Yeah, my customers liked me a lot.

Q. *You were working in the 1970s?*

A. Yes.

Q. *You mentioned a paper that said: "If it was easy, women and children could do it." What was the paper?*

A. Every morning [the company] would issue a daily sales notice telling what we were long on and what needed to be sold and any price changes. At this particular time, it was a really bad market. On the bottom of the paper it said, "If it were easy women, and children could sell it." Oh, that made me mad! I was, after all, the only woman salesperson.

Two Situations Remain in My Memory

Donna E. Sweet

As a woman who is considered successful by many, I have never really felt being female was a hindrance. Rather, I think most of the time it has worked to my advantage. With that said, things were not always smooth in my early years as a female medical student and resident. I started medical school in 1976, a year when women were just showing up in larger numbers. But larger numbers then meant less than 10 percent of the entering class was female, and less than 5 percent of the graduating class that year was female (compared to approximately 50 percent now).

I came to Wichita for the last half of medical school, the clinical years, in January 1978 and stayed on to complete my residency and ultimately join the faculty at The University of Kansas School of Medicine-Wichita. Thinking back to my difficulties throughout medical school and my residency, two situations remain in my memory as significant occurrences.

The surgery rotation, I recall, was the most difficult for women to be accepted, into because it was a previously male-dominated area. It had to do with wearing "scrubs" and having changing rooms and lockers to store our personal items. The surgery lounge was male only, and the nurse's surgery lounge was female only. We were the first female surgeons/surgery residents. There was no place for female students on surgery to change. Initially, we were told to use the nurse's lounge, but interestingly, the nurses did not want us in their lounge. As a result, the surgery administration found, literally, a closet and made it the female surgery students' changing area. It was not up to par with the surgeons' lounge where the male medical students went. That lounge had coffee, food and other things available for them. The "girls" lounge had a door, light bulb and four walls – not much else.

The other memorable incident occurred when I was a first-year medical resident in 1979. Grand rounds, on this particular day, was dermatology. The male dermatologist giving the lecture started the presentation with a "skin" picture. It was a scantily clad woman in a bikini. Between slides of true skin pathology/disease, he had interspersed soft-porn "girlie" shots. After the third or fourth one, a fellow female resident was so incensed she slammed her notebook together and stomped out. There were two or three other women there (me included) who didn't know quite what to do. We sat through the rest of the lecture (which we probably shouldn't have done), but supported our peer in her complaint to the administration. To my knowledge, the dermatologist did not show those pictures again.

A Different View of the Room

Jill S. Docking

Why would I agree to write an article on life in Wichita in the 1970s when I was attending college in Lawrence at the time and had never lived here? It is because I want to pay tribute to those Wichita women of the '70s who danced so hard on the glass ceiling that all I had to do, when my time came, was kick aside the pieces of shattered glass.

The female mentors and role models who mattered most in my life were my mother, Margery Sadowsky, and my mother-in-law, Meredith Docking. If Meredith and Margery had something in common, it was the disparity between their public images and their private lives. Both women were a beautiful, Donna-Reed-like "homemaker" (as we called them then) prototype, wrapped around steely determination and political acumen. Publicly, they may have referred disapprovingly to women of the 1970s as "bra-burning feminists," but I can tell you from my own experience that in private they were saying to me, "You must demand more – you must become equal."

Thus after college, when my husband Tom and I moved to Wichita, I already had some understanding of the need to overcome any inequality I might face. In 1982, Tom ran for lieutenant governor of Kansas, and my world turned upside down. I went from being a stay-at-home mom (as we had come to be called) to becoming deeply involved in politics. It was a world filled with talented, accomplished, professional women – women like Jo Androes, Myrne Roe, Pat Lehman, Margalee Wright and Colleen Johnston. The list could go on and on.

They were a revelation, and if I had ever had any doubt of the ability of women to compete alongside men, it vanished as my world filled up with the power of these capable women. Younger by a generation or two, I stood back to observe as they plowed through the "old boy network" without a whine or a look back. In those days, it was common for women who were perceived as a threat to men to have their womanhood or their personalities impugned openly. Yet these successful women developed the ability to compartmentalize the hurt and ugliness on the political battlefield for the sake of forging ahead and getting the job done. They were truly trailblazers, changing the rules by which the game is played, and when I ran for the US Senate, in 1996, these champions had paved the way for me. Politics was my first venue, but the business world was a natural second act, and I became a financial advisor.

As a woman who has had a wonderful life balancing family, business and politics, I am glad to have the opportunity to thank all the women who made this life possible. What a joy it is to see young women today and to know that they can accomplish what their female forbearers would have seen as impossible – becoming scientists, doctors and engineers, business leaders and university presidents, or even governors and US Secretaries of State and Speaker of the US House of Representatives. As today's young women struggle to make their own balance of challenges and opportunities, I offer words of encouragement and support. But I also smile a little, as I remember a time not so long ago, when they would not have had to "worry their pretty little heads" about making such a choice.

Another Day
Another 59¢

Challenging Financial Status Quo

"... the chairman of our department told me that he was giving one of my colleague a somewhat higher raise than he was giving me because he had four children. I said fine. I imagined small incremental differences. When I found out that the man's raise was a third more that mine, and that a new young single male with no children who had been hired at about the same time I was and was given a higher salary than mine, I was stunned."

—Dorothy K. Billings (Wichita State University and Equal Pay)

Pot Holder Payoff

Elma Broadfoot

So there I was eight months pregnant and still working, but only for a couple more weeks. Fred and I were sitting in the home mortgage office finalizing the papers on our house. The mortgage agent directed all his explanations to Fred and not once even looked at, or acknowledged, me. At the end of the session, he reached into a drawer and handed me two pot holders, "for the lady of the house." Fred grabbed me as fast as he could and nearly shoved me out the door.

"What are you doing?" I yelled.

"Getting you out of there before you kill that guy," he said. I wouldn't have killed him, but I would have let him know exactly what I thought of him.

My Money and Hot Air Balloons

Liz Hicks

The first time I saw a "59 Cent" button, I thought it was a fundraising gimmick and carefully avoided the woman wearing it. But as the evening wore on and I didn't see anyone handing her checks, I approached her and asked what it meant.

"Women in the U.S. only earn 59 cents to the dollar men make," she responded.

"Pardon me," I said, "but I can think of women who earn a lot of money, such as movie stars and heiresses."

She replied, "Yes, and when you add them to all the women who can only bring home a pittance, you get the average wage of women, which is 59 percent of what men earn."

I didn't exactly disbelieve her, but the number seemed awfully low. And I wasn't ready to buy her idea that Americans had economic disparity problem based on gender. Sure, the catechism classes had said that the poor would always be with us. But most of us had the American opportunity to rise above our beginnings. We had free public schools. We had a capitalistic society, so we could choose our own work. Besides, I had chosen a field that was mostly occupied by men. I was told that my pharmacy license would assure me the same earning opportunities as my male counterparts. Surely other women could also find better employment? Was the problem in the overall roles of work, or was it in the individual's personal decisions?

My mother had worked outside our home many of my growing-up years. She taught school. Of my seven aunts, some had been full-time homemakers, some had been career women and some did what was needed at the time. I had to concede that none of them made a fortune as a nurse, secretary, attorney (self-taught), saleswoman or teacher. But then neither did my uncles as office manager, attorney (university), railroad man, salesman, or guard. Neither did my dad did as a pharmacist.

I was proud of my career decision. I would earn a decent living and have a middle-class life to prove it. Then came the day my husband Frank and I went to the bank to inquire about a home mortgage. We filled out the paperwork, and the loan officer was friendly. He crossed out part of what we wrote and looked up.

He said, "Based on this information, we can approve a small loan." He pointed to the page and showed us Frank's income. Frank and I looked at each other in confusion.

I asked, "Why did you cross off my income?"

He replied, "We never consider the woman's income. You might have a baby."

Still confused, I responded, "We do have a baby. Do you need to see her?"

He smiled. "No, but you might have another one. Then you would stay home and not have any income, so we never figure it into our data."

Frank caught on faster than I did. He stood, pounded the desk, and yelled, "My wife was head of her class. There is no better pharmacist in Wichita than she is. You don't deserve to have her choose to use your bank!" And we marched out.

I am fortunate to have many supporters. My parents always told me I could be whatever I wanted, and they helped me through college. My husband treated me as though I was the best of the best. And at work, my employer was also my mentor. He wanted to provide me more benefits, so he offered to set up a retirement plan in which he and I would contribute. His insurance agent came to present the plan. I studied the proposal and said, "I don't think this is a very good plan. I could earn more with ordinary passbook savings than by contributing to this. Is this what you sold Tom?"

The agent shook his head and gave me highest compliment. "You think like a man!" Then he pulled out another proposal. This one had a much higher return on the investment. I asked him why he hadn't shown it to me first. He replied that his company said that women preferred the other one. I asked if he showed women both of them to choose between. He said I was the first woman to challenge him. And he didn't even realize that he was cheating all the other women he had sold policies.

Like most of us, I was raised to consider the difference between right and wrong. I was also full of a sense of fairness. I usually asked if something was fair, rather than if something was wrong. I felt better able to judge fairness. And selling women lousy insurance policies seemed distinctly unfair. But I couldn't help his previous customers, and I could help myself, so I signed for the better policy.

When Frank and I married, he already had a bank account and some charge accounts. We added my name to those. And when we opened new accounts, we listed both names. So when I saw a public service announcement on television from the Wichita Commission on the Status of Women, asking women if we had a credit rating, I felt smug. Of course I had a credit rating. I paid taxes. I paid bills. I paid loans. But I called the phone number and gave my name. Nothing came up. With joint accounts, the first name (the husband's) was the only one that counted.

After Frank and I quit fuming, I followed the instructions to create my own accounts. I opened some store charge accounts. Then I went to the bank. This time I went to the branch where Frank and I were on a friendly basis with the cashiers and the branch manager. I explained that I needed to open a separate account to establish credit in my name. The manager agreed that this was a good idea and started the paperwork for a checking account and a savings account. But he paused at the small loan idea. He suggested that we up the amount from $500 to $1,000. He pointed out that the credit rating goes up when the amount paid off is in the four digits and that $1,000 is as good as $9,000 as far as the ratings go. I agreed and said, "I'm going to put the loan into the savings account and pay it off in six months."

"Whoa," he said. "Don't let the suits downtown hear that, or you'll never get any money!" He paused, thinking. "Would you let me handle this my way?" Then he called the main bank. "Hey, Joe. I've got a regular customer here. She and her husband have several accounts with us. She wants to buy a fur coat (What would my animal rights friends think of that lie?), and she wants to take out the loan by herself. Can I okay that over here?" So I got my loan and paid it off. I was on my way to my middle-class dream.

I saw a class listed in the Free University catalog that intrigued me: Hot Air Ballooning. Diana Forshee taught the class, and at the last session, she mentioned some of the organizations ballooners can join, including the "99s," the female pilots' organization. A man (someone we would later call a male chauvinist) made a put-down remark about women flying high. I felt Diana stiffen before she continued the class. Later I asked her what she felt about women's rights.

"I'm president of the Wichita chapter of NOW. Does that tell you anything? We're meeting next week. Want to come?"

By now I had learned that even those of us women privileged enough to have higher education and supportive families still faced an endemic economic unfairness in Wichita. I joined the chapter and moved from just trying to get a fair shake for me to trying to get a fair shake for all women.

Equal Credit Opportunity for Women
Texanita Randle

As a member of the Wichita Commission on the Status of Women, my focus was women and the Equal Credit Opportunity Act. I remember the day in 1975, when 86,000 plus Wichita Municipal Water Utility bills were delivered to my house. Throughout the day, people gathered in my living room and attached a notice to each water bill. The next day, the bills were taken back to the water department to be mailed. The content of the notice explained that the Equal Credit Opportunity Act became effective Oct. 28, 1975, and as a result, "It shall be unlawful for any creditor to discriminate against any applicant on the basis of sex or marital status with respect to any aspect of a credit transaction." The information mailed to households in Wichita was the culmination of a major project of the commission and had the potential to reach thousands of women.

Another service of the commission was a speakers' bureau covering topics important to women. I gave speeches to educate women about the credit act. As I spoke to various groups, my purpose was to inform women about their right to obtain credit, and the steps to take in order to be considered creditworthy. I explained that to qualify for credit, one must first have the ability to pay (source of income) and second, a credit history of prompt payment.

To establish a record of prompt payment, the procedure was the same for men and women:
   1) Open a savings or checking account in one's own name
   2) Establish a file at the local credit bureau
   3) Obtain a loan at a bank with no co-signer
   4) Obtain retail credit in one's own name

My personal experiences provided insight into the problems women faced in 1975, when they tried to obtain credit in their own names.

First, I opened a savings account in my own name. Later, I obtained a loan of $1,000 from the bank to purchase a painting. I repaid the loan in three months to develop a history of prompt payment.

Next, I applied for a credit account at Dillard's in my name based on my employment. Three different times I received a credit card from Dillard's, but each time the actual account was in my husband's name. The third time, I wrote a letter explaining that the Equal Credit Opportunity Act guaranteed that I could obtain credit in my name and that I was contacting my lawyer. Within one week, I received a Dillard's credit account in my own name.

As I spoke to groups in Wichita, women repeatedly informed me of situations in which they were denied credit even though the Act had been enacted into law. For example, a high school teacher was required to have her 70-year-old father co-sign her loan in order to purchase an automobile. Another was a woman who applied for and was denied a mortgage loan with her husband based on the supposition that she might become pregnant and quit her job. Yet another example was a married executive woman who was required to reapply for her credit card in her husband's name, even though his salary was much less than hers. The Act was the law in 1976, but discrimination continued.

The Equal Credit Opportunity Act did provide a legal process through the federal courts when credit was denied. Women in Kansas could file complaints with the Kansas Commission on Civil Rights. It has taken years, but the law now prevents creditors from discriminating against applicants for a credit transaction on the basis of sex or marital status.

Yes, the law has helped women just as it was intended to do.

Equal Pay
Ruby Baresch

Equal pay for equal work is fair, but

you can't mess with language
says the professor

you can't mess with sports
says the coach

you can't mess with family
says the husband

Ah, but we can.
We did.

Wichita State University and Equal Pay

Dorothy K. Billings

When women whom I knew in the English department at Wichita State University decided to start a women's studies program in the early 1970s, several women in other fields were asked to join the effort by developing courses that focused on women. I was in the anthropology department; other fields included philosophy, psychology, history and communications. We all gladly agreed.

The developing issues of the women's movement were not issues about which I was able to take leadership. I think I was considered recalcitrant, at least. It was students who made me understand what was going on. Judith Eisenberg, a graduate student in anthropology pointed out to me that my own role in the anthropology department was not related to seniority and merit, as I had naively assumed, but it appeared, to gender. Undergraduate Elizabeth Searle founded Associated Women for Action, Resources and Education and gave several women faculty certificates to honor us because women, she pointed out, never got the honors.

Soon after two of my male colleagues and I had completed our doctoral dissertations in 1971, the chairman of our department told me that he was giving one of my colleagues a somewhat higher raise than he was giving me because he had four children. I said fine. I imagined small incremental differences. When I found out that their raises were a third more than mine and that a new young single male with no children had been hired at about the same time I was (1968) received a higher salary than mine, I was stunned.

By any criteria that anthropologists use to evaluate other anthropologists, my credentials were clearly beyond theirs. One need go no further than research credentials: I had anthropological fieldwork, the *sine qua non* of an anthropologist, and they did not. I had publications in a major refereed journal, and except for the single young male, they had no publications. I had presented papers to our national organization and had attended international conferences, and they had not. I had taught anthropology in New York, Minneapolis and Sydney. They had not. I went to see the dean of Liberal Arts and Sciences, who agreed to raise me to almost the same salary the men had. However, when the dust settled, the dean told me that my department was so angry with what he had done that he could not do it.

With the encouragement of Dean of Women Annette TenElshof, who had been instrumental in establishing the way for women's studies, I decided to lead a class action suit on behalf of the women faculty. Because it seemed so easy to distinguish my record from that of my male colleagues, the other women faculty thought my name should be at the head of the list. In order to follow proper procedures, I first filed a complaint with the new affirmative action officer, who found against me while privately sympathizing. My next stop was the Kansas Civil Rights Commission. This group had no one in it with a college degree. It took them a while to produce a document more muddled than the one WSU had produced. My next step was the federal level of appeal, the Equal Employment Opportunity Commission.

In 1973, I filed my complaint as a class action. I was finally contacted by an EEOC official in 1978. He came to WSU for two days and interviewed faculty and administrators. He told me it would take another five years to maintain the class action. I did not want to go on alone, as if I were the only one affected, but we were all tired of the case and the other women really didn't want to continue. So I went on alone. It did not take long for EEOC to send me the official's findings. In a statement dated June 7, 1978, he found that I had been discriminated against on three grounds:

1)Evidence was introduced and corroborated indicating that Charging Party was victimized by an official maintaining a stereotyped expectation of female behavior not relevant to the salary process.

2)An examination of Respondent's defense disclosed an inconsistent and selective application of their (the university's) criteria.

3)A comparative analysis of credentials disclosed evidence of Charging Party superiority in discipline-related accomplishments prior to and as of the date of filing.

The official thought my case was very strong, and he sent it to the U.S. Department of Justice. He asked them to provide a lawyer for me and, in any case, a Right-to-Sue letter which permitted me to pursue a legal remedy. In 1981, I sought the intervention of my congressman, Rep. Dan Glickman, in prying the letter out of the Department of Justice. Six weeks later, I got the certified letter giving me the Right-to-Sue within 90 days. My lawyer, Jim Phillips, filed the case about 80 days later.

The trial began early in January 1984 in front of Judge Patrick Kelly. A year earlier, he had decided to dismiss 11 years of the case because he said Mr. Phillips should have filed the case 90 days from my phone call to Rep. Glickman (of uncertain date) rather than from the date specified in the certified letter from the Department of Justice (of recorded date).

Mr. Phillips busied himself taking depositions from anthropology faculty, various administrators and my expert witness, a Pacific scholar at the University of Kansas. He countered the rumor that the University of Sydney, which awarded me my Ph.D., was a foreign-degree mill. That university boasts one of the oldest anthropology departments in the world -- and was founded and carried on by some of the great names of Pacific anthropology. My expert witness testified for $1,000. The trial lasted about a week. I found out what depositions were for (which had seemed unnecessary to me, because why would people lie?). One witness after another wiggled out of what they had said. Attorney Phillips held their feet to the fire by quoting back to them their depositions.

Particularly remarkable was the wobble of my expert witness, who suddenly was willing to say that it did not really matter whether or not scholars had publications. Jim Phillips read back to him his strong statements to the contrary from his earlier deposition, and he admitted that what he had said earlier was true. Five students testified that I was a good teacher. My long-time colleagues who stood by me and testified for me were psychologist Dr. Gary Greenberg, philosopher Dr. Jay Mandt and chemist Dr. Anneke Allen. They were all leaders of the American Association of University

Professors at local and state levels. Dr. Dorothy Walters, chair of women's studies, testified for me. She sat through the whole trial with her friend Gina Barnett, who became the trial hostess. She welcomed my supporters at the door of the courtroom and told them where we were in the trial.

I was very moved when some of my friends from the Black Historical Society Board came to give support. Dr. Deema DeSilva, director of student support services who had developed and taught a course in intercultural relations in the anthropology department with me in 1981, was asked by the Board of Regents attorney, rather sarcastically, if she had had any trouble with me.

Dr. DeSilva, who projects the grace and calm of her Sri Lankan background answered, "None whatsoever."

During the trial, I was very curious to see what evidence the university would present to justify paying me less than the male faculty (quite a bit less by 1984). I naively assumed that there was some reason, some evidence, some argument. The anthropology faculty gave general statements about what faculty do. Only one said anything about me, and he quoted the negative opinion of a blowhard male in math who found that I had not agreed with him on a committee. The vice president was the only serious witness for the university. He presented statistics about how salaries were determined using nine criteria without ever mentioning me or any other individuals. The categories he used did not reflect the three contracted for in university documents: research, teaching, service. Our rebuttal witness was Jeneva Brewer, a long-time teacher of statistics in the mathematics department. She said statistics could be used to show anything.

Judge Kelly ruled against me. He said he was astonished to find out how little we were all paid, and he felt glad to find out what a fine group of faculty members WSU had. He was sorry we were all paid so little.

Later the vice president wrote the anthropology department and said how proud he was of how we had all (including me) behaved. The position of college affirmative action officer, Dr. Allen, was eliminated, as was the human rights commission of which she had been chair. My dean, who had by then moved on, wrote me a letter and encouraged me to go on doing productive work. We have remained friends. The student newspaper, *The Sunflower*, and *The Wichita Eagle* were remarkably supportive of me.

After the trial, as Jim Phillips (now my husband) and I were walking down the back stairs of the courthouse to face a sea of news people, I told Jim that I was about to cry like a girl and that I could not go out there. I asked him to say something funny.

He gave me a big smile and said, "What are you worried about? They sent Lenin to Siberia for five years!" After that I was ready for the press. When the news people put a microphone in my face and asked me what I thought, I said: "I think I finally believe in sex discrimination."

That's what I got out of this effort: I learned that even in a university full of learned people, there is sex discrimination. I haven't looked at the budget to see what other people's salaries are since 1984. I have done what I could, and I don't want to know. I have continued to publish my research and work with anthropologists internationally. I thought I wouldn't stay forever at WSU, but in many ways I liked the place and the people.

When I am tempted to think that the whole effort was a waste of time, I'm comforted by a quote from a speech by Jill Ruckelshaus to the National Women's Political Caucus in 1995: "I have the certain knowledge that at the end of [my] days [I] will be able to look back and say that, once in [my] life [I] gave everything [I)] had for justice."

Removing Sexism From the Curriculum

"My daughter came home from kindergarten complaining, "I'm not allowed to play with the big blocks. Only boys can."
—Gloria Bonwell (Teaching Sexism in the Seventies)

"One of the things I think is essential to real success in teaching is a human value system that genuinely respects individuals, a value system in which one feels neither superior nor inferior, but alive in a shared world."
—Dr. Geraldine Hammond, WSU English Professor, *Equal Time*, March, 1978

Fundraising for Female Athletes
in the Bad Old Days
Bonnie Bing Honeyman

The decision to be a teacher came when I was 5 years old, and to teach physical education when I was 12. That's exactly what I did, starting in 1970. With such a long-term plan in place, it was a jolt to my life when I decided to quit teaching in 1976. I was leaving a system that had competitive sports for boys, but not for girls; a principal who called me "Body Bing;" and a yearly pay increase of a whopping $200 for completing my master's degree. Further, I had a new job that would make me aware of what the world was like outside a junior high school gym. I was the new assistant to the women's athletic director at Wichita State University. My job was to educate the public that we did, indeed, have women athletes at WSU, and to raise money for scholarships.

During my first week on the job, I was told by an administrator not to call on the community for scholarship dollars, because those individuals and companies had been tapped for large contributions for the men's athletic department. I could see from that moment that my work was cut out for me, both on and off campus. I didn't formally call those on the "don't call" list, but it wasn't my fault if I happened to end up in a buffet line at a party by someone on the list, or chat it up with the president of a company at a WSU women's basketball game.

When asked what I had been up to lately, I had to tell them. It would have been impolite to hold back all the information I had about the wonderful women athletes who were representing Wichita State. By the end of the semester, I had talked to and had donations from nearly every person and company on the list. Even so, it became evident that businessmen weren't used to a woman walking into their offices and asking for money to support a women's athletic program, especially when there was a men's program. When I was hired, I was told that I was one of only three people in the United States raising money specifically for women athletes. Remember, this is when there was football at WSU and the men's and women's programs were completely separate.

Natasha Fife was the women's athletic director and is now in the WSU Athletic Hall of Fame, deservedly so. We always shouted and laughed when we got a check, whether it was $100 or $1,000. But it was slow going, especially at first. "I didn't even know they had any girl athletes out there," was the common comment when I started into my spiel.

On one of my first calls, I made my plea for funds and was glad the businessman seemed to be listening and not making some of the remarks I'd already heard many times, such as: "Won't this take money from the men's program?" or "Women won't bring in any money. No one wants to see women play sports."

When I stopped long enough to draw a breath, he said, "You're really serious about all this, aren't you?" Hell yes I was serious. It was time to get serious. Title IX was so new it hadn't forced administrators to make changes that would eventually be made.

Some days went well. Some presented frustration that made me wonder if I should have stayed in the gym. Then a female athlete, or one our coaches, would thank me for looking far and wide for the needed dollars, and I would be ready to start in again the next day.

One event stands out that made me realize I couldn't trust my instincts. After I called on a guy at a huge corporation who would be able to secure a large donation for the program, I felt good. He seemed convinced that a women's athletics program was valuable to the lives of these women and that it would take money to build a strong program. He was a gentleman and sure enough the department received a hefty check.

Then I talked to a friend of mine who said the guy had called him and said that I showed up for the appointment wearing a very short skirt and low-cut blouse. He said that I had crossed and uncrossed my legs the whole time I was giving my pitch. *What?* As I told my friend, I was wearing a navy blue, pinstripe pants suit and a white shirt almost buttoned up to the collar.

"He was going to see what he wanted to see and say what he wanted to say, because it made a better story," was my friend's response. So it didn't matter how professional I was, or how conservatively I dressed, some businessmen would still "see what they wanted to see?"

I remember calling on a businessman who was celebrating New Year's Eve a day early in his office. I was hoping for an end-of-year donation. He and another businessman who happened to be there during my appointment started laughing and giving me suggestions as to how I should be raising money. They suggested getting "female midgets and have them wrestle." As I left, they said I should be the referee and wear short shorts.

Today, more than three decades later, a lot of women are calling on men in the business world. And men are calling on women. Who knows how many people are out there gathering dollars for women athletes? Thankfully, Title IX made a difference. Now women have scholarships; women are bringing in the fans; women get to travel to compete. Every time I go to a women's volleyball or basketball game and see a crowd cheering, I smile – because there was a time hardly a dozen people showed up to watch a game. It even makes me happy to have to park far from the entrance.

Currently, I am a mentor for a terrific young woman who is on a full basketball scholarship at Wichita State. She's a freshman who is in total disbelief when I tell her how things used to be. Progress? Yes. Still room for improvement? Absolutely.

Teaching Sexism in the Seventies

Gloria Bonwell

The thump-thump of the washing machine drowned out the rest of the world in the '60s and '70s. The Vietnam War. The end of legally segregated schools. The rise of feminism. The end of poisonous pesticides like DDT. Elvis. The washer and dryer ran constantly to provide clean covers for the bottoms of four babies. My uterus was working its way back to post post-partum position. I faced menopause fearlessly. Finally potty trained, my children started school. I began to notice the world without dirty diapers.

My daughter came home from kindergarten complaining. "I'm not allowed to play with the big blocks. Only the boys can."

"That's the way it is." I heard myself say. Then I said, "I'll talk to the teacher."

The teacher said, "The boys are more active than the girls, and playing with the big blocks helps keep them in control."

But my daughters would not let me accept simple answers. In junior high, I was asked to persuade the principal to allow girls to visit the vo-tech schools like the boys did. My request caused consternation. To my amazement, however, the girls were invited to go for a visit. By bus. Segregated from the boys.

My next visit to the junior high administration was prompted by a ruling that forbid girls from taking photography because of dark-room behavior of the boys. I was told, "One boy kissed a girl on the leg during a dark room exercise. We can't have girls in there."

"I don't think it's fair," I said. "Why weren't the boys disciplined?"

"We'll look into it." A standard response, and there was no change.

My daughter was a discipline problem in home-ec class, a subject required for girls. Several times the school called to inform me that she had been removed from class. I would call my husband for his support as we faced the male-dominated junior high school administrators. I dressed for the occasion by putting on hose and a skirt. Together, my husband and I would argue to reinstate our daughter.

High school challenges were next. When my daughter enrolled at North High, the principal told me she could take chemistry if she desired, but the class would be difficult.

"Only boys, mostly the football team, take chemistry. The teacher doesn't like girls, so your daughter will have to work extra hard to get through it." My daughter is now an accomplished physician, still blazing her way through sexism.

Cheerleading was one of the few athletic programs offered girls. Volleyball required busing the girls to a nearby elementary school gym because the boys' team used the high school facilities. When my daughter decided she wanted to be a cheerleader, I called the school and asked the athletic director how cheerleaders were chosen. He told me the teachers decided. I thanked him. When my husband came home from the office that night, he informed me that the athletic director had called him and asked him to control his wife.

Bill told him, "Hell, I've been married over 20 years, and I've tried."

While my children were in junior high school, I noticed that with one or two exceptions on the elementary level, all secondary administrators were male; assistant principals were mostly former coaches, large and intimidating. I thought, naively, that I could be a caring-mother-solution to discipline problems if I were a junior high assistant principal. I enrolled in the master's program in education administration at Wichita State University, along with two nuns and a bunch of former male coaches with losing teams.

Classes in women's studies were offered, and I eagerly registered for a graduate-level seminar on women's issues. My concerns about sexism in the Wichita schools were authenticated. I was right! For a class assignment, I researched and documented my findings on sexist hiring practices in the Wichita school system. There were no women in secondary administration, two in elementary, none in upper administration, no female bandleaders and zero in powerful or decision-making positions. My teachers asked me to present my paper at a hearing in Kansas City on the implementation of Title IX. I agreed. Quivering and weak voiced, I summed up my findings for the hearing officers, Jill Ruckelshaus and Casper Weinberg. They asked for a copy of the main reference source for my paper, a brochure entitled Superintendent's Committees. As president of the secondary schools PTA, I had been given a copy.

The following week I was informed that, because of the significance of sexist practices by the school system shown in my report, the U.S. Department of Health, Education and Welfare would treat the findings as a formal complaint. Within a few years, women were moving into higher administration. Academic and athletic opportunities for female students increased. And copies of the brochure, Superintendent's Committees, disappeared.

Wichita State Women's Athletics:
It Was Years Before the Dream Came True
Natasha Matson Fife

A few years ago my husband and I decided to attend a women's basketball game. It was my first time back on the Wichita State University campus for an athletic event since I retired. Thinking we had plenty of time to find a place to park and get good seats to watch the game, we left our house 15 minutes before tip-off. When we arrived at Henry Levitt Arena, we quickly realized we would not be able to park as close as we originally thought. In fact, we were going to have to park close to Duerksen Fine Arts Building. When we entered the arena, we were surprised it also took us some time to finally find two seats – all the way up to the 32nd row. As I scanned the arena, looking in amazement at all the people who had come out to support women's athletics, tears began to surface. It was then that I understood that a dream three women had more than 40 years ago had finally come true. Levitt Arena was sold out to watch the Lady Shockers play Southwest Missouri State!

For me the dream began 1968 when Yvonne Slingerland, Sue Bair and I noticed our physical education majors wanted to compete. To provide these women that opportunity, we decided we needed team sports. This became the inaugural "seasons" for women's volleyball, basketball, softball and field hockey. The university didn't have a budget for women's athletics, so the full-time teachers also became full-time coaches. Even though we had little coaching experience, I became the volleyball and basketball coach, Yvonne became the field hockey coach and Sue the softball coach. We had no money to hire assistants so we asked (conned, begged, pleaded) other physical education majors to fill those roles. We also didn't have all of the basic necessities such as equipment, travel expenses, meal expenses, transportation, etc.

Being new to the world of athletic competition, we had no idea what to expect. But we had a dream and the interest and desire of young women to compete at the intercollegiate level, and that's all we needed to forge ahead. As momentum for women's intercollegiate athletics began to slowly gain speed across Kansas, a meeting was held with interested colleges and universities to discuss forming leagues. It was decided to separate the state into regions, and teams would compete within that region regardless of size. This meeting also resulted in the decision *not* to award scholarships to women.

Now that WSU had a structure for women's competition, we turned our attention to acquiring the necessities to run an athletic program. With no real budget to speak of, Henrion Gymnasium, which the physical education department used for classes, became our practice facilities. The opportunity to use Levitt Arena was nonexistent; it was only for male athletes. Our student athletes took on the responsibility for team uniforms. They went to the campus bookstore and finally decided on black shorts and T-shirts. They would *iron on* numbers. There was no "need" to purchase specialized athletic shoes; they could use the shoes they wore in their physical education classes. With a competitive schedule in hand, our women began practicing in the east/west wing of Henrion. The north/south wing was reserved for competitive events, because there was spectator seating in the balcony.

When competition began, the fan base consisted of parents, grandparents, friends of the athletes and any student walking by who decided to look inside. Needless to say, a seat much closer than the thirty-second row was always available. Admission was free. Eventually this program won over the fans, physical education staff and student government. Armed with information about other programs across the state, I approached Dr. Robert Holmer, physical education department chair, about funding. He agreed to include some funding from the recreation budget if I would approach the Student Government Association for additional funding. SGA was in favor of it; the women's athletic budget was set at $1,500. Even with a budget, we had to continue to drive our personal vehicles and pay for our gas. The athletes were given 50 cents for meals to use on road trips.

Once statewide competition began, the coaches continued to teach full time *and* maintain all other faculty commitments required by the university. Since the larger schools had more students to draw from and could gain an advantage over the smaller schools, the conferences were changed to have larger schools compete against each other and small colleges compete against each other. All competitive events were held in state, because the available funds did not allow out-of-state travel.

At a regional physical education conference held in Kansas City, there was a discussion to develop a national association to govern women's athletics. Sue Bair returned to campus with the details, and the Association of Intercollegiate Athletics for Women became a reality. The women in Kansas involved in women's athletics founded the Kansas AIAW. Since we were changing women's intercollegiate athletics for the state, our main objective remained to offer no scholarships to current athletes. The rationale for this was simple. We wanted to "keep women's athletics clean." We didn't want to fall into the same pit as men's athletics had. AIAW continued to govern until after Title IX.

Judy Akers, Kansas State University, can be credited with going to the state Legislature to lobby for a bill to fund women's athletics. Title IX was in the works in Washington, which helped the bill in Kansas to pass, but it didn't happen overnight. Those involved in women's athletics in Kansas continued operating programs with limited resources, but also thought about what opportunities women athletes could have in the near future.

When Title IX passed in 1972, individuals once again met to discuss the future path for women's athletics. With Title IX and state funding, the WSU women's athletic department became an integral department. Our budget grew from $1,500 to $50,000. This increased budget would include funding a women's athletic director, a secretary and part-time coaches who would coach two sports. At this point, there were several coaches who coached one sport and one coach who volunteered. The department began with volleyball, softball, basketball, gymnastics, and track and field. Since we had an official department, we needed a trainer. Rex Schott was hired part time and worked from the current athletic building below the football stadium. Previously Rex had been the men's trainer. Our first offices were on Harvard Street by the university police office. We would move two more times, once to another house and then to office space on the ground floor below the apartment building on Hillside just south of Seventeenth and Hillside. And so our first women's athletics department began. This caused many sleepless nights for men's athletics. They strongly believed that the women were going to take away all their funds, demand use of Levitt Arena and use the locker rooms.

Over the course of several months, the problem of practice time allocated between the men's and women's basketball teams in Levitt was resolved. The women practiced in the early morning hours before classes; the men had the court from 3 p.m. until the coaches decided it was time to call it quits. There was also an issue regarding volleyball matches in the arena, which even during the best negotiating sessions was like trying to kill an alligator. At the heart of the matter was concern about securing the volleyball nets to the floor. The men's athletic department thought that having a means to secure the net to the floor could cause a male basketball player to fall and get hurt. This was an interesting rationale since the arena already was rented out (with approval from the men's athletic director) to a circus and concerts, both of which I'm sure required some way to secure the equipment they needed to the arena floor.

Even with Title IX now a law, the women's athletic department continued to struggle securing funds from the state and other sources. I don't think there was a president of a university who would allow funding for women's intercollegiate athletics to invade deeply into the budget of men's athletics. But the costs associated with utilities, arena cleanup and our office space came from somewhere. I firmly believe that President Clark Ahlberg was trying to find a way to include appropriate funding for women's athletics in the university budget, but he had to keep it under the radar.

As WSU women's athletic director, my major goal was to have full-time coaches for each sport offered. To accomplish this, the program needed to raise additional funds. I hired Bonnie Bing as the women's assistant athletic director; her major responsibility was to raise money. She and I thought we were in heaven when she brought $500 into my office.

I also hired Steve Shaad as sports information director. He was a young man interested in women's athletics who worked for a part-time salary while working full-time hours. Steve was instrumental in having the first-ever home volleyball game televised. He also developed a rapport with the newspaper and radio and television stations, and they slowly began to promote women's athletics.

Larry Thye was hired as the part-time basketball coach, and he continued to work part time in the physical education department. Sue Bair continued as the softball coach and full-time physical education assistant professor. Janet Kohl Pew was hired as the volleyball/assistant track coach, and Mary Ellen Warren as a part-time gymnastics coach. What these individuals brought to the success of women's athletics cannot be stressed enough. Without their dedication, progress would have moved at a much slower rate.

During this time, the women's basketball games were played in Levitt Arena. Fans would only fill the first two rows in one middle section. We still played volleyball in Henrion since the equipment was much easier to set up there. I think admission was $1. Only recently did the women's volleyball team begin to play at Koch Arena. They played most of their matches at the Heskett Center after it was built.

Fundraising continued. Bonnie saw in a flyer that Kathy Rigby, Olympic gymnast, was available to perform in various cities. It was arranged to have her perform in Levitt Arena. Press releases were sent to the media and area public schools. Both Bonnie and I thought this would give us some additional revenue, but no one involved with women's athletics really knew what to expect. On the afternoon of the event, yellow school buses ended up filling the parking lot. It was almost a capacity crowd that afternoon. After the event, the arena floor was filled with future gymnasts who wanted an autograph.

The first time we played the University of Kansas here, Lynette Woodard, a former standout basketball player from North High, played for KU. Bonnie and I were taking tickets (which we did at all home games), and we looked up and saw that the line of people waiting to get a ticket went out the door and down the sidewalk. We had to delay the game about 20 minutes to allow for the huge crowd.

At budget time, I would complete the paperwork, adding additional revenue. I remember being called into President Ahlberg's office to review a budget and was told the additional revenue was not approved, and therefore, our budget was not approved. I was told that the department was overspending. When I tried to explain that I had included additional revenue, a short explanation on the budget process followed. The need and the ability to acquire additional revenue through the state and other sources was holding us back from moving toward the goal of full-time coaches, proper budget, better schedules and better salaries for the coaches.

I filed a grievance within the university; it was time the powers-to-be realized the true nature of inequality on the part of women athletes. Comments from a few of the committee members hearing the grievance were beyond understanding:

"Why can't women sleep two to a bed? After all, men are bigger and need one bed."

"Why do women need more for food? Women are not as big as men".

At the time we were traveling in private vehicles or a 15-passenger van. So the question arose, "Why do women need to take a bus?"

"Why do women need a better schedule/conference?"

At this time, I can't remember what decision the committee sent to the president. It seems that shortly after a meeting with President Ahlberg, we discussed the possibility of combining the women's and men's athletic departments, since women were still struggling to obtain the funding necessary to build a women's program. Bonnie and Athletic Director Ted Bredehoft were contacting the same businesses and individuals for financial support. Most of the time additional funding was secured for the men, but donors were still warming up the idea that women could be competitive and deserved to have their program funded.

It wasn't until the daughters of the mostly male donors began to have athletic opportunities at the high school level that they began to see the importance of funding women's athletic programs at all levels. However, fundraising continued to haunt the women's athletic program at WSU. The prevailing wisdom was that it would be better if one person were making contact with donors for both departments, so the programs were combined. This was a hard thing to swallow, since most of the women's coaches would be fired. But I could see that in order for women's athletics to continue to grow it was the correct thing to do. A few of the larger institutions had already combined their departments, and the conference was the same for both women and men. That meant NCAA was in control.

After the departments merged, the women's athletic department, as I expected, lost personnel. Bonnie went to work for *The Wichita Eagle*, Rex to a physical therapy company and Steve to a baseball team. I became an assistant athletic director and worked in the ticket office for a year; then I returned to the Department of Physical Education to again teach.

Not one coach, staff person, athlete or fan could say the struggle or setbacks were not worth the fight. We continued on, regardless of discouragement, because we could see the light at the end of the tunnel. The dream we had in 1968 would continue on and on and on and on, because eventually, there was that light where we had hoped it would be.

The Uneven Playing Field:
A Young Woman's Athletic Experiences
in Wichita Prior to Title IX, June 23, 1972
Pamela D. Kingsbury

My family revered learning and the importance of a college education. They placed great emphasis on reading as the basis of an informed and productive life. In addition, they appreciated the importance of sports to create a healthy body and to teach social and behavioral skills. My maternal grandfather and grandmother and my parents played golf. My mother, in addition to golf, played tennis as a child and a young woman. In high school, my father was on both the swim and track teams, and in college he was a low and high hurdler destined for the Olympics, until he pulled his hamstring. Not only did my parents participate in sports, but also they were avid major league baseball and college football fans. I grew up playing sports with the neighborhood boys. Our mainstays – football and baseball – were played across our front lawn and that of a neighbor's. In the evenings, I shot baskets and played imaginary basketball games with the family Pekingese, Gung Ho.

On reflection, my junior high days in the mid-'50s seem like a mythic Stone Age. It was the first time competitive sports were permitted in the school system, but only for boys. The boys competed in baseball and basketball with other junior high teams, while the girls were relegated to playing baseball, basketball and volleyball during gym classes. Why were girls not permitted to compete competitively against other schools? The answer, repeated *ad infinitum*, was that girls must save their bodies for marriage, childbirth and child rearing. We now know that this is a specious argument. But in the 1950s, it was taken quite seriously.

After a particularly heated game of pickup basketball with the boys after school, I was told by the female assistant principal that I should not be playing for those very reasons. My frustration at hearing this mantra once too often got the best of me. I told the assistant principal that she had no right to dictate to me how I spent my childhood and adult life. My fondest junior high school memory pertaining to sports was when the boys' gym teacher, Mr. Jackson, called me into his office. He told me I was the best athlete in the school and that he was very sorry he was not permitted to let me play on the boys' baseball and basketball teams.

The other galling aspect to girls' baseball and basketball is that they were quite different games from the ones the boys played. Girls' basketball consisted of six players not the five required for boys' basketball. There were three forwards and three guards, and no player was permitted to cross the center court line. The basketball could only be dribbled three times by a player. Any more dribbling would be exhausting for girls. The three guards were responsible for guarding the opposing team's three forwards and for getting the ball to their three forwards who did all the shooting. What a frustrating, unnatural mess it was. Girls' baseball, known as softball, was played and still is played with a much larger ball, and the pitcher is required to throw her pitches underhand and not over hand like male pitchers do.

Outside the public school system, there were other avenues for competitive sports for girls. These included amateur competition in golf, tennis and swimming at the local, state and national level sponsored by such organizations as the United States Golf Association and the American Lawn Tennis Association. For swimming, there was the Wichita Swim Club, founded in 1955, and the American Athletic Union, a national organization. Unfortunately, baseball and basketball did not have such national organizations. Although my family were avid golfers, and despite the fact that family members encouraged me to play golf as well as tennis, I was totally disinterested. It was baseball and basketball or nothing for me.

Things changed radically when Vince Norman, the children's director at First Presbyterian Church, came to the house to ask my mother if I could try out for the church softball team, part of a citywide women's church league. Mother agreed, and I was accepted as the youngest and tallest team member. We played other Wichita church teams and teams in small towns surrounding Wichita. On many occasions, after concluding our game in the early evening in a small town, we would go square dancing.

In the winter months, I played on the First Presbyterian basketball team. I was ecstatic; I could compete in my two favorite sports. The composition of both the softball and basketball teams was a cross section of Wichita society and consisted of high school students, University of Wichita students who were majoring in physical education, physical education teachers working in the Wichita school system, housewives, and others who were employed in businesses and the aerospace industries. Both the softball and basketball leagues represented teams from a cross section of Wichita's churches consisting of the old established churches, the African-American and the evangelical churches. My experiences on and off the ball diamond and the basketball court provided me learning experiences and lifelong friendships that I could not have had elsewhere.

During the time I played in the church softball and basketball leagues, I learned of the women's industrial league in basketball and softball. Sponsored by local businesses, such as Steffens Dairy and Ideal Body Works, these leagues competed against teams in Wichita, around the state and in national tournaments. The industrial leagues were composed of women who worked in Wichita industries, physical education teachers or housewives. Although I was asked to try out for one of the industrial league softball teams, as were several of my teammates on the First Presbyterian team, I declined as my sports' interests were changing.

Gradually I became interested in golf. The turning point was the Wichita Open played at the Wichita Country Club in 1954. For years I had been a devoted sports fan of Mildred Didrickson Zaharias, fondly know as "the Babe." She was an athletic phenomenon in basketball, softball, track and field, and golf. I was fortunate enough to monitor the Babe's gallery, selling tickets and keeping the gallery quiet and under control. In an age when women were taught to swing at the ball in a ladylike fashion, the Babe pulled up her skirt and attacked the ball with a powerful swing. On the first tee, she sailed her drive over the tall row of trees in the left rough, landing the ball in the valley less than 100 yards from the green. She hit the ball with gusto and verve. I was impressed and excited that a woman could hit the ball as well as or better than a man.

Just as impressive as the Babe's game was her gallery. Around noon men in hats, suits and ties and women in dresses and high heels crawled under the wooden fence separating the golf course from the street. These were businessmen and women spending their lunch hour watching the Babe play golf. My duty was to charge them an entrance fee but, of course, I did not charge them admission. In fact, I encouraged them to watch the Babe for the duration of their lunch hour. The Babe finished fourth in the Wichita Open and received the paltry sum of $500 for her effort.

The following year, the USGA Woman's National Open was played at the Wichita Country Club, but Babe was not a participant. She was in a Texas hospital dying of cancer. I followed another up and coming young golfer with the most perfect golf swing, a balance between a hitter and swinger. Her name was Mickey Wright. After watching Mickey for the four days of the tournament, I told my Mother that I wanted to play golf. I stopped playing softball and basketball and devoted myself entirely to golf. To this day, I continue to play golf -- but on a limited basis.

Today, I am extremely pleased that the women professional golfers receive generous prize money in comparison to what they received when the Ladies Professional Golf Association was in its infancy, although it is nowhere equal to their male counterparts. Furthermore, when I listen to an LPGA commercial during a nationally televised women's golf tournament, I am thrilled to hear the girls and women say they hit the golf ball like a *woman*!

Every Moment a Teachable Moment

Joyce Markley

The elimination of a gender basis for toys, in order that Cindy's children could be whoever they want to be, has been enlightening to her mother, Lillian. Thus armed, Lillian has taken a big step away from the traditions prescribed for many 62-year-old women in the 1970s. Cindy's husband had been "gently" trained in the philosophy too, and was not surprised when he heard the story of Gama, who came to sit with four-year-old grandson, Tommy.

That day when Tommy said, "Let's play house, Gama. I'll be the Dad. You be the Mom," Gama was ready for it.

Gama, the Mom, at one point said to Tommy, the Dad: "Don't forget the doctor's appointment at two o'clock. The twins need to get their shots. And I work until four o'clock, so can you pick them up at the baby-sitter's? Okay?"

"Okay. I won't forget." Dad immediately proceeds to load the similarly clad dolls in his blue pedal car, trying to be careful, but still one twin falls from his loaded arms.

"Oops! Dropped one! Sorry, Billy." Dad pats the head. "Sorry, Billy. C'mere. Sit down here. C'mere, Barbie. You sit here, too." And then Dad proceeds to career around the room several times with lots of gear shifting, screeching tires and squeals and such, and stops the car on a dime.

And, Gama says, "Now, I'll be the doctor. Over here." And it was agreed.

The little Dad said, "Doctor, my babies have to get their shots."

"Oh, yes. I'm glad you're taking good care of their health. Yes, indeed. My records show it is time for their shots."

(But, Tommy wants to jump out of character long enough to help give the shots; he decided that after locating the syringe for the doctor.)

The babies were well inoculated by the end of the doctor's visit.

One has to start somewhere.

———————

Frankie's kindergarten class has been assigned to the various play stations. Frankie's group of four children is playing with the puppets. Alecia has a dog puppet. Frankie, playing with a boy puppet, is talking to Todd's puppet when the Mama puppet tells Todd's puppet to do the dishes.

"No, that's a girl's job," Todd's boy puppet answers.

And soon they all get out of hand as Mama puppet and child puppet start hitting each other, and they boisterously laugh, disturbing the entire class as all four get into the free-for-all. At this point, the teacher has to make a decision. This is the optimum teachable moment. But, it wasn't an easy decision.

She is conflicted because of the pressure of the predetermined district schedule for keeping students up with other schools in math scores, and math was scheduled in her next slot. She had always been very diligent about reaching goals, especially those from the district and state. But, oh, how social issues can affect classroom behavior as well as impacting life at home and lives in the future. So she determines that social learning is very needed at this time.

She asks the students to gather around to sit in a circle for a "confab." The topic is generated by asking questions: How many of us have seen moms working somewhere besides home, so they can use the money to help the family? How many of you have seen dads do housework? Everyone is working really hard and trying to do lots of good things. Well, when you children learn all you are learning now, and even more later, and you get strong, and even stronger later, you can do anything you would like to do – any job at all.

The teacher asks for a show of hands as she names careers that interest them. They raise their hands many times, but they look at each other, boys and girls, wondering if any are going to laugh at the girl who thinks she could be a police sergeant. The students raise their hands on almost every choice – some, very confident, raise hands quickly; some hesitantly – because they've been conditioned somewhere, sometime, to divide skills by gender, or were told they weren't smart enough, or were told some other disparaging indoctrination over their few short years, by some, or many, people in their lives. The teacher then reads a short and colorful book about power called *I Thought I Could. And I Did!*

It wasn't long before the children joined in on that and repeated the refrain at the end of each chapter; it became a mantra: "I thought I could. And I did!"

Someone has to start somewhere.

Oh, my, how Don Quixote tries to right all the wrongs of society, gets depressed at all the injustices and wants to fix them. He dies trying. Cervantes' words describing *Don Quixote de La Mancha* were:

> "All he reads oppresses him … fills him with indignation at man's murderous ways toward man. He broods … and broods … and finally from so much brooding his brains dry up. He lays down the melancholy burden of sanity and conceives the strangest project ever imagined … to become a knight-errant and sally forth into the world to right all wrongs. No longer shall he be plain Alonso Quijana … but a dauntless knight known as … Quixote de La Mancha."

Don Quixote sees a tired and depressed woman, and tells her that she is beautiful so many times that at last she believes it enough to have happiness in her heart. She sees herself as Dulcinea, just as he had called her.

So, beautiful women of the world, those who keep fighting for right, don't give up if your goal has only been partially accomplished. To give up, to become lukewarm, to be "too busy" to champion women's issues in the further decades of 2000 – because it is now better than the problems back in the decade of the 1970s and a whole lot better than in our grandmothers' times – is to lose passion for that which helps *all* people. To push for equalizing the gender issues of talent and equal pay for it, is to push the demand for fair benefits for more than half the world's population and their offspring. Women have strength of conviction. Those who want human rights need us the world over. We are the fighting women – the ones who believe in life lived to fullness, liberty to be oneself and the pursuit of happiness as defined in each individual heart.

Someone, somewhere has to start.

Dick and Jane

Ruth Ann Messner

Title IX of the Education Amendment of 1972 says: "No person … shall, on the basis of sex, be excluded from participation in, be denied the benefits of, or be subjected to discrimination under any education program or activity receiving federal financial assistance … " September marks the beginning of another time-block of institutional learning, building onto the layers of knowledge, opinions and evaluation in today's students.

Since the passage of the Education Amendments of 1972, educators have been forced to take a long, hard look at Title IX as it relates to sex-role stereotyping in school textbooks and the ensuing implications to learning. A wide variety of textbooks and curricula were found to be sex-biased in one way or another, perpetuating misconceptions about the limitations of women and men. As a result, school authorities reportedly have taken steps to create sex equality by collecting data on content, illustrations and language, and establishing in-service education programs for teachers to help them deal with discriminatory practices.

Rita Younglund, fourth grade teacher at Kistler Elementary School, is optimistic about the Title IX implementation in the Wichita Public School system. "The law is with us," she said. "Teachers cannot sit back and say, 'I am going to do nothing about it.' Of course, we've got a long way to go, and the problem is not solved. But Title IX applies to all federally funded schools, and it is being taken seriously in Wichita. The administration cares."

Younglund said that all Wichita schools have had workshops, faculty meetings and in-service workdays so teachers would receive information about the law, the implementation and be given a chance to look at their own attitudes. Each principal made a report on the activities within the buildings and submitted it to the administration for review. "It's definitely a change – like going from one subject matter you are familiar with to another," Younglund said. "But now Title IX is an ongoing concept in the schools and is constantly emphasized."

Teachers are very aware of it in placement and hiring practices. "Awareness is the key word – not only of teachers but parents. Each of us must be aware of past practices and stereotypical behavior that we have all been guilty of. When we are aware, we can do something about it. Of course, you run into individual personalities and individual levels of awareness. I think it is very difficult for any of us to change life-long patterns overnight, but I am convinced that changes are being made – slowly. Personally, I cleaned up my own attitude. Years ago I used to refer to children as either *fluffies'* or *'tuffies*. Now I have some checklists to follow. Also, I had the good luck of going through a training program at Wichita State University concerning Title IX implementation.

"The changes were subtle at first. I let boys and girls run errands, carry boxes and run the projector. I encouraged boys to learn how to arrange flowers in a vase. Also, we talk about stereotyping and what it means openly in the classroom. I help the children become aware, so they can make their own evaluations. One thing I like to do is have them watch television commercials; they come back with some very good examples of stereotyping." Younglund said that textbooks, now chosen by a committee that must consider Title IX criteria, are definitely improving, but stereotypical examples can still be found in the books. She stresses that publishers, however, will respond to teacher complaints and are very aware of the laws.

"One particularly fine textbook publisher has a representative in Washington who keeps up with the new trends and is constantly re-evaluating the editions to get away from sex role stereotyping. Library books are even better. The William Allen White books are sometimes great in Title IX concepts. "But even if there are stereotypical materials, I don't worry about it. They can be a valuable teaching aid. If there are blatantly stereotypical materials, pictures or stories, I let the students read it and analyze it, and make comparisons.

"Omitting books from teaching is a mistake as far as I am concerned. We can't improve learning by stamping out everything that someone thinks is negative. If we start censoring materials, then we get small interest groups who have their own biases. It's better to keep the classics, look at them, evaluate them and make comparisons. If those books are removed, what do we have to learn with? We just have a whole new set of values and lose what went before. In my opinion, the ideal way to do it is to equip children to make their own value judgments and learn to read intelligently. To implement Title IX in the classroom, one does not have to go around with a chip on the shoulder. All you have to do is be an understanding, accepting human being. The teacher is a model for the student. That is a big responsibility, but also a fact of life," Younglund said.

Diane Osborn, principal of Earhart Elementary School, said her school staff is "100 percent receptive to the concepts of Title IX." She believes the main problems come from parents who are enmeshed in roles and by conveying them to children, perpetuate stereotypical behavior. "My teachers are young, dynamic and very alive people," Osborn said. "They also are very interested in helping parents become aware of what Title IX is trying to accomplish in the schools. But there you run into people's values and viewpoints and people who are locked into their roles. A lot of that, of course, depends on the particular financial situation. And many parents feel threatened by change."

Although Osborn shares Younglund's optimism about the overall progress in Wichita schools, the Earhart principal admits that not all schools are totally involved in Title IX implementation. "It's difficult to completely change attitudes," she said. "People need retraining, and success depends on enthusiasm of the staff. However, in every Wichita public school, one staff meeting a year is required to set goals in the area of Title IX, and to identify staff problems.

"As far as textbooks go, I am convinced that materials are being carefully selected by the committee. And you must remember, publishers are out to make money. They will eventually listen and get on the bandwagon."

Coming Full Circle

Lee Goodman Starkel

Augustus 1978 began my first semester as a full-time student at Wichita State University, and I attended my first women's studies course – Carol Konek's Women in Society: Cultural Images. When I entered the room, I encountered another first: the chairs were moved into a large circle. This arrangement altered the classroom dynamics, particularly influencing the exchange of ideas and information between students and Dr. Konek. There was no hiding, no hierarchy – instead, equality personified. During the remaining two and a half years of my academic life at WSU, which extended into the graduate level, I only experienced chairs placed in a circle in women's studies classes. At first glance this seems a minor detail, but circular seating was a symbol of the faculty's thoughtfulness and commitment to something all together different, from the arrangement of chairs to the ideas considered.

In the spring of 1978, only months before my fateful first semester, the Kansas Board of Regents awarded the Center for Women's Studies its designation and approved an undergraduate major. It was a momentous achievement for Wichita State and the Fairmount College of Liberal Arts and Sciences, no less because the first women's studies courses – Women in Society and Writing by Women – were taught in the fall of 1971. Not everyone agreed the creation of the Center for Women's Studies was momentous. Women's studies faced struggles and resistance for years on campus and in the community.

During a presentation I gave March 9, 1983, in celebration of the center's first decade, I stated the following: "Women's studies has often been perceived by some faculty and administrators as unimportant and nonacademic, and described as a credit-hour thief." In spite of its detractors, women's studies was a success with students, and it quickly grew and expanded year after year. The first two classes in 1971 attracted 35 students. In spring 1974, the program had grown to 11 courses taught in seven different departments. In 1975, enrollment topped 1,000. By the time women's studies was celebrating its first decade, the program offered 29 different courses taught by 22 faculty in 13 different departments, and enrolled more than 1,500 students.

During my talk in 1983, I identified several factors for that success: "The strong administrative support necessary for any academic program to develop and thrive was always available for the department's students. Dean Paul Magelli, in particular, perceived its importance to a quality liberal education. Most importantly, the success of women's studies at WSU was founded on the exceptional caliber of the faculty associated with the program. The most talented and creative WSU faculty participate in the program. They bring quality learning experiences to the classroom and scholarly excellence to the campus. They also realize that women's lives continue outside the classroom and have successfully built connections in the community." The fruition of their community involvement led to the formation of the Women's Studies Community Council Advisory Board in 1990. The board was – and continues to be – occupied with an extraordinary breadth of community women committed to increasing the visibility of and raising funds for the department.

In September 1998, almost 20 years to the day I attended my first women's studies class, I witnessed the transfer of that circle of classroom chairs to the very heart of the WSU campus. This time, it was a circle of bricks and granite, each carved with the names of real women, to create the Plaza of Heroines. Through their efforts, women's studies faculty had uncovered women's culture and history and, by doing so, brought meaning and recognition to women's lives. The promise of women's studies for so many – and for me, personally – had come full circle.

Women's Studies and the Rise of Feminism in Wichita

Dorothy Walters, Ph.D.

For many of us, it began in the very early '70s. Something called "women's liberation" was being talked about, sometimes in whispers, always discreetly. We had heard that early-day "feminists" had chained themselves to fences, marched and gone on hunger strikes, all in the cause of women's right to vote. But this was different. Calls were coming forth for women to control their own property, to go into the workplace and claim jobs worthy of their talents, to pursue higher education, to be free agents, to be equal.

I began collecting books on the subject (only a few had appeared at that time), but writers like Betty Friedan, Kate Millett and Germaine Greer were being published. Several of us from various teaching fields noticed that women were all but invisible in the texts available for teaching. Psychology courses focused primarily on male subjects, history was mostly about men and their wars of conquests, anthropology omitted material related to women's roles in various societies.

And as for literature – well, few women writers were considered eligible for inclusion. In America there was Emily Dickinson. And of course the English could turn to Elizabeth Barrett Browning as their token female poet. Some women novelists of the 19th century could not be ignored. Otherwise, it tended to be male writers chosen by male critics, and often these were taught exclusively by male faculty. Women were conspicuously absent from both curriculum and teaching staff.

Soon Dr. Carol Konek, then an instructor in the English department, offered a class in Life Planning for Women through the extended education department. This became, in fact, the first course offered at Wichita State University focusing exclusively on women. Then I arranged to teach a class on women writers through the honors department. ("Awfully new, isn't it?" asked the then head of that program.) And then I heard that a new woman administrator had arrived on campus, and that she was seeking someone to co-teach a course in women's liberation. I immediately volunteered, though I had not met her nor did I know what her goals were. So Dr. Annette TenElshof and I taught the first class addressing women's issues. It was a smashing success. We invited speakers from the various departments of the university to discuss the status of women as subjects in their various fields. The effect was electric. Students were eager to explore this new approach to academic subject matter.

The next semester, we invited Carol Konek (known as a master teacher) to offer a second section of the class. This one also filled to overflowing. Then we asked Sally Kitch to offer yet a third section of this popular offering. This too filled to capacity. We were four women who had already thrown off the stereotypes simply by pursuing higher degrees and becoming faculty in an institution of higher learning. Our outlooks and goals matched. We loved the idea of breaking new ground, of offering students a broad view of the positions, roles and images thrust upon women by a patriarchal society.

Carol came up with the idea that we, as a society, needed an anthology of contemporary women poets who were vastly under-represented in the collections then available. She invited me to co-edit such a book, and we set out to break new ground. There was no way to know from the shelving of the poetry books in the library which were by men and which by women. We literally had to take down the books, one by one, and ferret out the ones with female authors, most of whom were little known at the time. I took a semester off to spend in Berkeley, a major center of the growing feminist movement, and there collected more women poets. Together we put together our book, *I Hear My Sisters Saying, Poems by Twentieth Century Women* (1976); it was one of the first anthologies of poetry by women writers to be published anywhere.

By now various women faculty were beginning to include sections on women in their standard courses. We felt it was time to develop a complete curriculum in a women's studies department that could offer a comprehensive view of the various disciplines from this new perspective. With the encouragement and support of Paul Magelli, dean of Liberal Arts and Sciences, we set up a committee to organize a program. I served as chair, but there were representatives from many areas of the university, including Betty Welsbacher, LaVonna Spencer and many others. We crafted a major in women's studies and soon recruited faculty (men as well as women) to offer courses in this emerging area.

We now had separated the original "women's liberation" course into two parts, one focusing on "images of women in society" and the other on "women's issues." As we progressed, we saw the connection between women's studies and other major areas now coming to the fore, including minority issues, ecology, peace and justice. In fact, virtually every department and area of the university was impacted by our presence and our activities. New courses included such titles as Women in Psychology, Women and Religion, Women and Anthropology, Women in Sociology, Human Sexuality, Minority Women, Women and Philosophy and, of course, Women Writers, as well as Images of Women in Literature.

Those who came forward to offer these classes did so in spite of pressure from some quarters to steer clear of women's studies and all it stood for. Many of the old guard saw it as some kind of threat to traditional education. And indeed, some of us who embraced these new approaches were in fact penalized, being denied promotion as a direct result of our activities in this new area.

I was chosen to be the coordinator (called director) of the new program. I had done preliminary work in the field and, in addition, I was faculty with tenure, and thus less likely to be targeted for my involvement in this controversial area. Indeed, the core faculty were all extremely strong teachers and researchers, as well as being very active in community affairs. Those faculty in the various departments who were adding courses or sections on women to their offerings were also among the most able in the university. In addition, we were supported by a highly competent corps of student assistants, many of whom had backgrounds in very responsible positions before returning to pursue more educational goals. Among others, this group included in the early years Lee Starkel, Sarah Schluss, Gail Thompson, Alexsandra Leslie, Shelley Freeman, Sylvia Thorsten, Brenda Denzler and Natasha Cook. Women's studies maintained a major presence in the various groups then forming in the city to promote women's equality, including the Women's Political Caucus, shelters for abused women and others.

Throughout this period, women's studies was under constant scrutiny and challenge from various quarters, for certain critics within the university were extremely unhappy with its successes. We were change agents, and change is not always welcome. After many such challenges over many years, women's studies demonstrated that it was highly successful by every conceivable measure, including teaching awards, academic research, community relations and student support. The final complaint of the opponents was that women's studies was "too small" and this did not look good on the charts.

Perhaps the outstanding achievement of women's studies (in addition to restoring balance to the curriculum) was to support and encourage women to complete or upgrade their education in order to step out into the world in suitable roles and occupations, to gain a better understanding of the historical and sociological forces which had shaped Western culture as a patriarchal society, and to become change agents for a more balanced society. In addition, women's studies helped and supported many young female faculty, who themselves were entering on their careers in a new era. Religion was then a flourishing department on campus, and at least three of the young faculty who taught there went on to highly distinguished careers in their later professional lives: Dr. Marjorie Suchoki later served as the head of religious studies at Claremont College (CA); Dr. Denise Carmody later was elected provost at a major California university; and Dr. Judith Plaskow co-authored a ground breaking text, *Standing Firm at Sinai*, before returning to the East Coast.

Others also won distinction in their fields. Dr. Sally Kitch authored several academic volumes, some published by major university presses and some receiving strong recognition from various national associations. Dr. Carol Konek traveled to virtually every continent in the world, speaking in support of women's issues at various international conferences (think Mexico, China, Australia, Ireland, Africa and Norway, among others). She brought this international perspective to women's studies, which became more inclusive as a result. She was named to the rank of full professor before her retirement, one of the few women on the WSU Liberal Arts faculty (and one of the few openly avowed feminists) to attain this rank.

Dr. Dorothy Billings, after many years of pioneer work in the South Pacific Islands, finally received the recognition she deserved and also was promoted to professor. For many years, she was a devoted peace advocate and worked tireless in that cause. Anita Skeen continued to write and promote poetry from a feminist perspective and encouraged students to do so as well. She published several books of poetry, and later moved to a highly ranked Midwestern university which recognized and rewarded her work in poetry as well as lesbian studies.

Indeed, another key area that was emerging at that time was what is now known as "gay liberation." This was a very hush, hush topic in the '70s, and those who were gay or lesbian carefully shielded their identities from the outside world, for the penalties were extreme.

About this time, Anita Bryant appeared in Wichita, sponsored by various conservative religious groups, to denounce gays as immoral and as threats to ordinary society. A small band of supporters of the rights of gays to be accepted as equal members of society turned out to march in peaceful protest outside the city auditorium where she was speaking. The group included many students as well as some faculty from women's studies. One woman, afraid that if she were recognized, she would lose her job (as a city employee) wore a paper bag over her head. Another, as a prank, carried a sign that read, "Gays Against Floridization." (Anita Bryant was a spokesperson for Florida Orange Juice.)

The issue of the inclusion of open lesbians was a key point of contention in the early national women's movement, and Wichita was no exception. Many feared that by including this then-controversial group, they would endanger acceptance of the overall women's rights movement by mainstream society. At one of the first organizational meetings of the Women's Political Caucus in Wichita, Nita Mark (a student and supporter of women's studies) stood up and announced that she was gay and asked that lesbian issues be included in the considerations of the caucus. Many feared that by being so bold, lesbians would be effectively barred from participation, but the opposite reaction occurred. Not only were lesbians accepted into the caucus, but many of the women there realized that they were also gay and sought a new lifestyle.

At the university, gay and lesbian students were beginning to form small discussion and support groups. When women's studies allowed these budding campus organizations to meet in one of its seminar rooms, some were fearful that the administration would be disapproving and that the program would suffer the consequences, but this was not the case. The vast majority of women's studies faculty (as well as students) were in fact heterosexual, but most strongly supported the few lesbian faculty and students in their midst.

Ours was not a confrontational program. We stressed the positive aspects of "women supporting women," rather than engaging in strident confrontation and debate. Our primary motto was "Forgiveness is easier to obtain than permission," and this principle served us well. Often by the time our critics discovered what we were up to, our success was so well established that there was little they could do to reverse it.

One interesting measure of the growth of WSU's women's studies program had to do with where it was housed. In the beginning, we were literally in a broom closet – Dean Magelli offered this space to us as all that was available at the time, and we were glad to have this humble location as our own. Later, we inherited what had been the American studies office, quarters that were larger but still not luxurious by any means. When the new liberal arts building was constructed, Dean Magelli allotted us spacious quarters, including proper administrative offices and our own seminar room and library. This office acquired a very special vibration as time went on; one could literally feel the good vibes there, especially at night when few people were about. Visitors often remarked how special the ambiance of this space was -- more homey than other such quarters, as one put it.

I, like many others, had become deeply immersed in the mythological and cultural background of this movement – the spiritual, if you will. Merlyn Stone had published her now famous book, *When God Was a Woman*. I was quite intrigued by this notion. I was privileged to visit various classes and give a one-hour lecture on this theme, complete with visual slides and references from scholars such as Joseph Campbell and Alfred Neumann. I was at the time seriously engaged in the lore of the Western goddess, as well as the role of the "feminine principle" in such areas as Taoism, creativity and other areas which stressed receptivity over coercion, openness over closed systems of thought and the central role of the mind/body connection. Then in 1981, I had an unexpected awakening of the "inner energies" (spontaneous Kundalini awakening) and from that time on, this ongoing experience became a primary focus of my life. For me, the inner energies (experienced as the ultimate mind/body union in bliss) were the essential expression of the divine feminine, the goddess within. My experience was the culmination of my personal journey into the realm of the feminine, and its impact continues to this day, finding expression in original poetry and prose as well as in helping others to navigate deep spiritual transformation in their lives.

The '70s were a crucial period for many transformative social movements, and these eventually led to a changed society. Not only were women's roles revised but other, even broader areas, were impacted. The waves of influence continue even now, as more and more discover who they truly are in their inmost nature, as physical, social and spiritual beings. I think we were indeed privileged to have been participants in this momentous transition.

Struggling for Equality as Women and Minorities

"On one hand, women's equality was clearly an issue of the time with plenty of evidence to merit it. On the other hand, issues and voices for women of color were often not addressed by the mainstream women's movement."

—Brenda J. Gray (Women, Race and Class)

From Wichita to Washington, D.C.:
How I Spent the Women's Movement
Elvira Valenzuela Crocker

As a Latina, I was never really sure which part of me was the offender when I was denied a privilege or position or was treated as though I didn't belong. But early on in my life, I knew that there were differences in the way men and women were treated, no matter their color or creed. As a child growing up in Western Kansas, I noted that my male siblings seemed to hold a more favored status in the family hierarchy. My sisters, I realized, were viewed in a supportive role to the males in our household. I remember my mother once asking me to iron a shirt for my little brother. When I balked, she warned me that when I married, after all, I would have to iron for my husband. I argued, and then I ironed.

In the first grade, I learned that I was a Mexican, as my teacher regularly reminded me and the few others like me in my class. It was the disgusted way she said it that told us this was not a good thing. I didn't suffer an identity crisis, because there were so many reminders that I was a Mexican, and sometimes even a *dirty* Mexican, from both adults and children around me. For example, my third grade teacher admonished her son --who bore the misfortune of being in her class – that on a particular test even the Mexican kid, meaning me, did better than he did.

That summer my younger brother and I enrolled for swimming lessons at the local swimming pool. As students' names were called to team up with teachers, our names were blatantly missing. It was like "the cheese stands alone." I knew the reason, but I always wanted people to verbalize their rationale on what they were doing to see if they noted anything wrong about their behavior. So, I asked why our names weren't called. We were informed it was because we were Mexican.

"So?" I responded. "Mexicans aren't allowed in the pool?" Decency and political pressure on the city fathers from a local florist who was aghast at what happened resolved that situation. We did learn to swim, and Mexicans did swim in the pool that summer.

As I grew older, I tended to notice important things – such as the fact that my teachers were pretty much all female. Administrators all seemed to be male. The librarians at school and at the city library were all female. Nurses, too. Secretaries? Of course. Did I mention that all of them were Anglo? Also notable was that our local library had few resource materials or books regarding Hispanics or Hispanic females. It was as though we didn't exist. I decided to be a writer and to help fill that void. My high school counselor advised me to major in math, so I could become a teacher. When I told him I wanted to be a writer, he said that it would be hard to make a living at it – as if teachers were paid that well then, or even in some places today. "I'm going to do it," I responded.

I graduated in journalism from Wichita State University and went on to my first full-time newspaper jobs in Dodge City and Wichita. What was quickly evident was that equal pay for equal work was not an operable concept in the business. Everyday observations of these inequities and injustices fueled my ambition to be a writer who could expose all of these things. My rationale was simple and very innocent in retrospect. I reasoned that people will correct problems or inequities if they just know about them.

My very wise parents cautioned that even when people know the problem, they don't always want to make it right. Because they frequently told us, "People fear change, and the impact it will have on their lives. People who have power generally don't give it up easily." I lived through the civil rights movement, realizing how much of what I had been taught at home was true. Racial, ethnic and gender discrimination were the epitome of that fear fueled by strong doses of ignorance and long-held practices.

By the time the women's movement came around, I was radicalized and ready to move mountains. My Wichita years were spent traveling the state with the Panel of American Women, led by well-known Wichita activist Annabelle Haupt. The panel was viewed as a tool to sensitize audiences on how women in the state had experienced discrimination – no matter their race, ethnic background or religion – just because they were women. As a reporter, I wrote about programs and people that sought to improve the lives of those who were underprivileged for whatever reason. In 1968, I spearheaded a special project to provide a Profile of the Kansas Woman to give readers of *The Wichita Eagle and Beacon* insight into who we were.

In the early '70s I spent evenings with various informal groups of women in Wichita looking for ways to sensitize and organize women politically. Local women were awakening to the larger waves going on in the rest of the country and were ready to work toward equality for women. These early gatherings eventually gave life to the Wichita Women's Political Caucus. Newspaper journalist Dorothy Wood and I, by then a former journalist, were organizing chairs.

In 1972, just as things were warming up in Wichita, I moved with my journalist husband and son to the Washington, D.C., area where I continued my feminist activities. In 1974, a growing group of bright and talented Mexican American women – primarily educators, lawyers, health professionals, employees in government and non-profit organizations, and unionists – found themselves in Washington. The women's movement was rapidly evolving and its leaders were developing the national agenda for change and equality. Chicanas realized it was critical for them to form their own organization to inject their voice into that important historic dialogue.

The Mexican American Women's National Association was created to provide that important voice. As a writer, my talents were frequently called into play to develop position papers, policy recommendations or statements delivered before Congressional committees, or in departmental hearings or meetings. I also authored many speeches delivered by our leaders and helped write many of its early publications.

MANA had many goals. In addition to being the voice of Chicanas, we sought to provide leadership training and opportunities for our sisters, to promote a public awareness of Latina issues and to work for parity within the Mexican American and larger communities. We also sought to serve as a communications link with our other *hermanas* (sisters) across the country. The male-dominated Hispanic organizations had been the lone voice for all males and females up to that point. Eventually, they learned that MANA was here to stay and could be a valuable ally and voice in their efforts too.

MANA was in the forefront of all the key women's issues of the day, including displaced homemakers, battered women and aging women. We supported reproductive rights, equal pay and the Equal Rights Amendment. We testified at hearings and participated in meetings where countless decisions and strategies were being formed on matters affecting the lives of women.

We met, we rallied, and oh, did we march. As Fran Kentling can testify, when she and other Wichita friends came to visit, they often found themselves marching with us. Each of those marches and rallies built more enthusiasm for the next battle.

One of the most valuable contributions MANA made was training our members on how to be good citizens by informing themselves on the issues, registering, voting and even running for office – local, state or national. Members also learned the importance of effectively communicating with their elected officials. We did this through annual training conferences in which I helped with program development, promotion of the events or in leading some of the workshops. Some of the earliest Latina state legislators in various parts of the country were our members. It's also fair to say that some of the first Hispanic political appointees at the national level were either MANA members or had ties with us.

From the outset, MANA was a pro-choice organization. Though there was debate in the ranks, our members viewed abortion as an important health option for women and that position prevailed. Unfortunately, sterilization abuse also was a key issue for our women. We knew of too many cases where women had unwittingly agreed to the procedure by the incomplete explanations they had been given by medical professionals. Public testimony by MANA resulted in an invitation to work with the then Department of Health, Education and Welfare to draft regulations and guidelines to ensure that doctors and clinics explain sterilization to women in their primary language.

Organizing Latinas was vital. The social indicators of the day dramatized that need. During the '70s, Mexican American women comprised the second largest female minority in the country. Eighty-five percent of us lived in Arizona, California, Colorado, New Mexico and Texas, and our labor-force participation rate was 36 percent. Yet, we were concentrated in low-paying operative and service jobs. Seventy-five percent of us earned under $4,000 a year, only one percent had incomes of $10,000. Our educational attainment was at 9.1 years; our college education rate was 1.4 percent. Our families were larger than the U.S. average. Most lived in cities rather than rural areas.

As the women's movement gained momentum, it was clear that the voices of minority women – Hispanics, Native Americans, Asians and African American women – had to be fully added to create a more inclusive national movement. So it was a time when many new national minority organizations came into existence.

Against the backdrop of demands for equal rights and responsibilities from women all over the world, 1975 was declared International Women's Year by the United Nations. In June, an IWY conference was held in Mexico City. It was both a busy and fruitful time for me. Although I was a member of the Mid-Atlantic regional staff of the U.S. Commission on Civil Rights, my agency was asked to loan me to the IWY conference staff as they prepared for the Houston meeting in 1997. In the meantime, there were state meetings being held over the country in preparation for the historic gathering. I was named to the planning committee for the Maryland conference.

My key memory from the planning experience was that we held meetings in various parts of the state to provide an opportunity for as many women as possible to participate. One meeting, held not far from Baltimore, drew a couple of busloads of anti-abortion forces. They were women, seemingly being led by men. As they entered our session, already underway, the women pulled their chairs as physically close as they could get to the members of the committee. It was a move I felt was an intimidation tactic, as did other members of our committee.

When they were allowed to speak, two of them rose. They circled the committee's table and emotionally pleaded for us to save the unborn. They declared that they would happily take one of those children into their own homes, rather than see them aborted. Though there had been plenty of conviction and certainty in their presentation, there was a definite change in their demeanor when I asked, "Would you take that child if it were a child of color?"

There was an awkward pause before they answered, unconvincingly, "Yes, of course."

In addition to my activities pertaining to the Houston conference in 1997, I served as president of MANA and led the way to renaming the organization. It became A National Latina Organization to better reflect its now growing membership that included Mexican, Puerto Rican, Cuban, and other females and a few males from Central and South America. It was not an easy transition for some who had been the mothers of the organization in its earliest years, but for purposes of being all inclusive and generating a more forceful voice for all Hispanics in the country, it seemed right.

I wrote the organization's history in *One Dream, Many Voices*. I knew it was the right thing to do when I sent the manuscript to several readers, all leaders of the organization who had played key parts in the organization's development. One of them called to tell me that she had reviewed it and it made her cry.

"Oh my God, was it that bad?" I asked.

"Oh, no," she replied. "It was that good."

Later, while attending an event at the Kennedy Center for the Arts, a MANA member sat next to me. "I just want you to know, your book is by my bed. It's falling apart, because I read and reread bits of it every night for inspiration."

I knew then that I had accomplished something important in providing Hispanic women a reflection of who they are and can be.

A Dichotomous Decade
Janice Gary Davis, As told to Elizabeth "Liz" Kennedy

Note: Before we met, I asked Jan Davis to think about her life, her career, her family and her life in the community in the 1970s. After our conversation, Jan shared a page of notes she had made prior to our meeting. I have used a dash and italicized her notes, then added any related information and direct quotations from our conversation, as applicable.

– During the 1970s, I continued to be more involved in the civil rights movement than I ever was in the feminist movement. I always related more to being black than woman.

"I have never been a woman first. My blackness is more my identity. In everything I have achieved, I think being black has helped."

In 1970, Jan Davis was 29 years old, in an abusive first marriage, raising two stepchildren and had been a teacher for seven years. She had been brought up to be a teacher or nurse, but was also told she needed to learn secretarial skills.

– Domestic Violence: Victim was blamed. Why did you stay? Filed charges, convinced to drop them. Judge reprimanded me and told me not to come back, because I dropped charges.

"The way I was raised was more in alignment with my first husband's views (in terms of a woman's traditional, domestic role and the husband as the undisputed head of the household). I always had to agree with his point of view."

Jan was expected to do everything domestic, help with the yard work and make money while being totally subservient to her husband's wishes and views. Her husband's church espoused these views, including that women should never wear slacks or speak in church. When her husband beat her, she pressed charges, but he convinced her to drop them. The judge was angry at her and very rude, offering no assistance and telling her he didn't want to see her back in court. Jan wasn't aware of community resources that could help her, but now, she said, that's changed.

– Teaching at Jefferson Elementary. Was going to teach students the Black National Anthem. Parents rebelled. Principal intervened and stopped me. Same principal accused me of stealing money from an envelope that was being passed around to raise money for something. Didn't do it. Felt accused because of my race.

– Chosen in 1973 to start Isely Magnet School for gifted and talented students. Felt chosen, because I had an excellent reputation as teacher and was black.

"I was one of six people in the district asked to open Isely as a magnet for gifted and talented children. I loved teaching at Isely, because it was a different approach. There were no letter grades. The kids evaluated themselves, and the teacher evaluated them. I taught there from 1973 to 1979."

– Always had, and still have, more white girlfriends than black. Cuz of upbringing in small town.

– Second marriage to Caucasian in 1970s.

"In my first marriage, I couldn't be myself."

Jan married Rich in 1977 and, for the first time, felt accepted for what she was – a bright and active woman with little interest in traditional domestic roles.

– Did the whole braless, short-shorts, raggedy jeans, hippie scene thing. Can't believe the way I dressed.

– Refused to stand for national anthem at Wichita State basketball games – along with white girlfriend.

– Became conscious of environment. Rode bike to school one entire year.

– Actually was somewhat resentful of white women who benefited from civil rights movement – seemed to be getting more from system than blacks.

"I can't say I was at a disadvantage as far as career growth due to a white woman, but I can remember being in conversation with other blacks about how white women were benefiting from the civil rights movement more than maybe they should."

– Hierarchy then was white men, white women, black men, black women – at least in my mind.
I can't say that feminist movement had any social effect on me or provided me with any advantages. Think if anything beside my natural gifts helped me, it was definitely my race.

"I know from watching my mom what the perception of a woman's role should be. In that respect, I am grateful to the feminist movement because that's what freed women from archaic expectations and made a lot of men feminists, like my present husband."

Women, Race and Class: A Wichita Perspective

Brenda J. Gray

During the racial turmoil of the 1960s and '70s, women's issues were the least of black women's worries. I was growing up at that time and fighting for the right to eat in restaurants, obtain a decent education and have a job. I knew that I felt strongly about women's rights and equal pay, even if I hadn't yet defined myself as a feminist. By the time I got to college, I was armed with an Afro, an attitude and a quest for justice. I was involved in black student organizations, and even then I saw the inequity of women's roles. The men always assumed leadership positions, and the women's importance was defined by which of the leaders they were sleeping with.

My earliest encounter with women's injustice was at Kansas State University when I made the women's basketball team. I was miffed the women couldn't practice in the impressive Ahern Field House. I remember my teammates and I peeping through the curtain that separated us from the nice, polished floor that was for the men's team, thinking, *Wow, this is the big time.* However, we could only get on the nice floor after the men finished practicing or when they were traveling. Our team always took a back seat to whatever schedule the men were on. Slights like this shaped my drive to become an advocate for women's equality.

Even though I didn't know how important it was at that time, I had the honor to play one semester for K-State women's basketball legend Judy Akers. It was 1971, and women's basketball was still in its infancy stage. Title IX was still being hotly debated at universities across the country. I don't think there had been any African American women on the team before then. I knew in any case it was still a new concept, that I was breaking ground. When we played our first game out of town, that purple and white uniform was very special to me. As a freshman, I was nervous and didn't know what to expect on the Division 1 level. I would soon learn what those students who sat at the lunch counters in the South must have felt.

As I got off the bench to go into the game, I heard yelling and lots of noise. In my freshman naiveté, I thought they were clapping in support of me, but after a moment I realize the noise was ape sounds from the whole gym. They are making fun of me, calling me a gorilla. I was mortified. On the ride back to Manhattan, nothing was said about the incident. It was quiet. In addition to being a second-class citizen on a women's basketball team, I had to face the humiliation of being an African American. My resolve was hardened that day.

I learned later how much Judy Akers fought for Title IX rights, even though she met much resistance from the administration. Learning about what Coach Akers had to go through was another experience that enlightened me to the inequities for women and why I was compelled to object to the injustice. It was a fire deep inside me that was ignited and grew during my adult life. Yet, I was often torn about my loyalties to the women's movement in those early days. On the one hand, women's equality was clearly an issue of the time with plenty of evidence to merit it. On the other hand, issues and voices for women of color were often not addressed by the mainstream women's movement. In the black community, there was even hostility at the thought of the "white women's movement." This contrast was particularly stark in the conservative, Republican enclave of Wichita.

I can remember so many conversations with my black sisters questioning me about my working in the movement: "Why are you there, Brenda? They are just as guilty of racism as their white men." This was like a stab in the heart for me. My experiences, my background and my family all reflected being black in America. I knew the pains, the anguish and the teachings of Malcolm and Martin. But I also knew that being a woman meant that I was not as valued, and I was less than a man when it came to my ideas, thoughts and work. This was unacceptable for me regardless of color.

Whenever I attended or participated in an event in Wichita on women's issues, I usually found myself to be the only woman of color. It was a lonely experience. I can remember several occasions – when listening to the discussion at hand – looking around the audience asking myself, "What am I doing here?" While my fellow feminists took great pains to be polite and make me feel included, we all knew that the elephant in the room was racism and discrimination against people of color, particularly women of color. There was a big void on those issues among this group of women. My presence at these events only emphasized the fact. I usually felt as though I was asked to participate in events in Wichita because of the fact that I was black.

There was guilt by the mainstream movement at not having women of color involved in their events and not addressing issues that were important to us. There was also an elitism issue attached to this problem. Many women in the movement in Wichita were middle-class women, working for their own intellectual well-being and not out of necessity. Many of these women were married to affluent men and living in suburban homes with housekeepers (usually black women). How could they know the struggles of women of color? How could they know what it means to live in poverty, not knowing where their next dollar was coming from? It was a schism that also reared its head on a national level in the women's movement.

My womanhood usually took a back seat to my being black when it came to my public displays for women's issues. Two incidents stand out for me that are proof of this. The abortion issue was front and center in Wichita by the mid-to-late '70s. A staunch pro-choice supporter, I took every opportunity to take a stand on the subject. Talk show host Phil Donohue came to Century II to hold a live telecast on the subject. The event drew thousands of women on both sides of the aisles. I was seated with a row of like-minded women, and again was one of the very few black women in attendance. It was obvious that our group was pro-choice by the times we yelled and clapped our support for what was said on stage.

After the event an older, white woman sitting behind me offered me a piece of paper and said, "I'll be praying that you find God." The paper was an advertisement for the right-to-life agenda. Mind you, there were a whole group of us, yet she chose me to hand the paper to. I took that message to mean that because I was black, I should not advocate for the death of black babies. It was an argument I had heard before. I was infuriated. I tore the paper up and yelled obscenities at her. The incident stayed with me for years and only hardened my resolve of a pro-choice stance.

The second incident took place when I agreed to co-chair the annual Women Fair/Women Art event sponsored by the Wichita Women's Equality Coalition. It was *the* event highlighting women's issues, displaying the artistic work of and distributing information about and for women. That year three women agreed to co-chair the event – myself, a Hispanic woman and a white woman minister. The Hispanic woman and I were the first women of color to head the event. When the time came to solicit vendors, we went through careful discussions about who could be a vendor. Our number one issue was they had to have respect for women's choices. That meant no anti-abortion vendors. Without knowing it, one of the co-chairs responded yes to an anti-abortion group that had applied to attend. (Afterward my Hispanic co-chair and I contemplated whether this was a set up or not). Once we found out what the group stood for, we sent a letter saying we were rescinding their invitation and returned their fee.

On the day of the event, they were there and ready to set up and participate as though they had not received our notification. I was placed in the role of sheriff to send them away. Naturally it turned ugly when they wanted to argue their point. I had no sympathy, and they were forced to leave. They called the television stations, which showed up, and before I knew what was happening, I was on the six o'clock news trying to explain our position.

It was a coup for the Women's Equality Coalition to have the face of a black woman making their case, but to this day I cannot tell you if the event was successful or not because all I can remember is the glare of the television camera in my face.

A Strong Role Model for Her Daughters

Carmen Rosales, As told to Elizabeth "Liz" Kennedy

When Concepción and Rafael Lopez opened Connie's Mexico Café in 1963, their daughter Carmen had no idea of the impact it would have on her life. By the late 1960s, Carmen was a college student at Wichita State, getting an education with the support of her parents. However, when she shared her dream of then going to Washburn and becoming a lawyer, their response was immediate and negative, "Who's going to run the restaurant?" As an adopted only child, Carmen felt the full weight of her parents' love and expectations.

By the time she married Jim Garcia in January 1970, Carmen needed only 12 credits to earn her degree. But she had lost heart when she realized law school was not in her future. "I knew I'd never go to Washburn, but I wanted to get rid of that little nagging voice that said, 'Don't be a quitter.'" Despite the birth of her daughters – Monique in 1971 and Sonia in 1973 – Carmen went back to WSU. She did it on her own, taking her daughters with her until the professors said she needed to make other arrangements, at which point she put them in a nearby day care center. She earned her degree in 1976.

Carmen had been helping in the family restaurant, but her husband was not very happy about it so she stepped back for a while. But when her parents needed her, and Carmen felt she and her husband needed the money to help their own family get started, she returned to working with her parents at Connie's Mexico Café. Carmen decided if she was going to eventually run the restaurant, it was important that she learn all she could about the business. She was anxious to learn everything from her parents, and they were anxious to teach her everything. However, Carmen's parents would get frustrated, because she couldn't give them her undivided attention because of her family, even though they were her biggest help in raising her children.

By the end of the '70s, the family had expanded to include four daughters with the addition of Delia, born in 1977, and CiCi, born in 1979. A fifth daughter, Adele, was born in 1982. According to Carmen, "We kept trying to have a boy; it was expected for a Hispanic family."

Carmen's husband decided he also wanted to be part of the family's restaurant business. It was a "big downer" to Carmen to find out that when her parents weren't there, the sales reps didn't want to talk to her, but to her husband. Despite the fact that it was her family's business, they didn't want to talk to a woman. Carmen said they felt "I wasn't significant enough to be an asset." Carmen said that when her parents were there, her mother was in the same situation. The reps would only talk to her father.

In terms of other discrimination, people also tended to make erroneous assumptions about Carmen. "In three seconds, people would see I look different from the general public, and then, when they saw all these little kids, would look at me like I'm draining the welfare system." This was a source of great distress and made her very angry.

For Carmen, the decade of the 1970s was a time of great transition and activity as she gave up her dream of becoming a lawyer, got married, worked hard to learn the restaurant business, gave birth to four of her five daughters and completed her college degree. The feminist movement was not a part of her life at that time.

However in reflecting on her life, Carmen said, "Perhaps I benefited from the women's movement. … I thought by providing a positive role model for my girls, showing them that you never give up – set your goals and achieve – that I was showing them that women can be as powerful as men. We didn't have to be overlooked, downplayed or ignored, and that little by little, each woman, each girl, could make her mark on society."

Not All Indian Women Wear Beads, Braids or Buckskin

Priscilla Zadoka, As told to Elvira Valenzuela Crocker

T he first lesson was about the difference in the treatment to which American Indian males and Anglo women were subjected. She had a Wichita Indian father and an Anglo mother. Now retired, she recalls that her father received checks at the end of the year from the leasing of lands he held in Oklahoma. The family lived in Anadarko, OK, at the time. The lease checks provided the opportunity for the family to make purchases of major necessities. One year, the family decided they needed a new refrigerator. Her dark-complexioned father went to a local store to price them. He found a model he liked. When her mother went to see if she liked it and asked the price again, "It turned out," Priscilla said, "that the price was lower."

As a high school teen, she was a top-notch student with the grades to make the National Honor Society, but it didn't happen. Students were nominated by teachers and though she bested the grades of some of those nominated, she was passed over for that honor that was very important to her.

"That really hurt," she recalls. When she was nominated for Annual Queen by two history teachers, she was viewed as a *token* and did not win. There were other cases of insensitivity. When her mother took her to purchase her first bra, the store clerk measured Priscilla and declared, "She's a B-cup. Indian girls aren't supposed to be that size."

She was the only Indian woman in her graduating class who chose to go on to a four-year college out of state. She attended the University of Kansas for a semester, and then got her "M.R.S." degree, she says. For a number of years, she was a housewife and mother and involved in parent groups at her children's schools. Eventually when living in Wichita, she and her Boeing-employed husband got involved with a group who was starting to talk about developing an Indian center. Those relationships eventually led to the creation of the Mid-America All-Indian Center.

Later she was involved in the Panel of American Women, a group initiated to share the experiences of a broad spectrum of women from a range of racial and religious backgrounds as a means of promoting understanding. In her signature comments, she always told the audiences: "Not all Indian women wear beads, braids or buckskin." It was one way in which she tried to fight against the stereotypes of American Indian women. She also became a member of the League of Women Voters, the National Organization for Women and was active in La Leche League.

While serving on the board of the Wichita YWCA she was selected to attend a IWY gathering on racial justice at New York's Hotel Americana. It was an opportunity for her to meet American Indians from over the country. Several of them decided to have a drink in the hotel bar. When they got there, they were taken aback. First of all, the name of the bar was The Wooden Indian. As they looked around, they saw so many offensive items of décor, including statues of Indians, that they asked to talk to the manager.

By the time they met with the manager, they had been joined by other Indians, Hispanics and African Americans. Explaining how offensive they found the décor, they asked him to close the bar. He was asked, "As a French Canadian, wouldn't you be offended if there were Catholic religious items used to decorate a bar?" He got their point. He didn't close the bar, but he did cover the offensive items during the conference. The bar eventually closed for about a week, and it was reopened with a more general western décor. It was an incident that made the news. It was not, however, the kind of publicity appreciated by the then more conservative Wichita WY she represented.

She has another very special memory of that event. Dorothy Height, executive director of the National YWCA and then president of the National Council of Negro Women, gave her a New York Subway token as a memento of that event.

The '70s saw her back in college at Wichita State University. She did well enough to be named the recipient of the Glen Gardner Award for Outstanding Minority Student. She was a sophomore, and it was an award that had generally gone to junior- or senior-level students. She graduated with a B.A. in general studies. In one of her earliest jobs, she worked at the police neighborhood service center at Central and Cleveland. She also worked with the Mid-American All-Indian Center in its earliest location near Central and Hydraulic. She edited the center's newsletter.

In 1985, she joined the Kansas Corporation Commission in its library, working in oil and gas drilling records. She was in a field dominated by males. She helped create an electronic base of information on oil and gas wells in all 105 Kansas counties. The repetitive hand motion she received in doing that work led to a disabling condition, so she was moved to a front desk position and assisted in the legal department. She retired after 20 years. Recently, she's been involved in Friends of the Keeper of the Plains celebrations to honor the highly visible Indian monument.

Finding a Feminist Faith

"Would the sexist language of scripture, hymns and sermons be acknowledged? Would sermons continue to batter women with their need to be subservient? What would happen to a woman 'who did not know her place'?"

—Jane Anne Richards (Grace, Faith, Feminism)

"Reverend Greta Crosby is an attorney, as well as ordained Untarian-Unversalist Minister. ... Crosby believes more and more women will be entering the clergy. 'Right now there still are problems in more traditional churches,' she said, 'but now that women know women [ministers] are okay, I think we'll see that changing.' "

—Marilynn Gump (Meet The Reverend Ms., *The Wichita Independent*, June 2, 1975)

The Path Into and Out of Radical Religion: A Personal Journey

Lana Elaine Bennett

During a weekend trip in June 1969, my husband picked up our four-year-old son and held him over the ocean at the end of a remote pier and threatened to throw him in. The boy's offense was that he had cried about something. A week later, my husband awakened me from a sound sleep, grabbed me by my throat, threw me into a corner and strangled me until I was unconscious. Thinking that he had killed me, he ran out of the apartment. This allowed me time to come around, pick up my son and get into the car. No one in those days had heard of post traumatic stress disorder, which I am sure my husband suffered from, having just returned from a two-year stint in Vietnam. But worse for me, no one acknowledged domestic violence – which he had subjected me to even before he left.

My parents had moved to California, seeking jobs, the year before I was born in 1946. Tired and bitter, because she had to work outside the home while I was growing up, Mother was controlling and increasingly religious. In order to keep track of me in her absence, she filled my life with obligation, rules and dogma. Obedience was the master. After school I was to go directly home to do chores and practice the piano, Mother's greatest love and salvation. While growing up, she found fault with anything that I was interested in. I dared not question God, who remained elusive but still held sway.

My oldest sister had moved back to Kansas several years prior and lived on a farm. I called and told her I was coming. This was the beginning of a very difficult period for my mother and me. Rejecting the notion that my son and I were not safe and not wanting me to divorce, Mother felt that I was abandoning her. I left for the Midwest with no support from home, very little money, a four-year-old and a less-than-perfect vehicle that literally died in the parking lot of a mechanic's shop on the day I arrived in Topeka.

I quickly found a job, a house and day care for my child. A young woman who lived in the garage apartment of the house I rented introduced me to a law student about to take the bar exam. He offered to help me get a divorce. There was a condition, however; I would marry him. My mother had often admonished me to make quicker decisions: "Don't be wishy-washy," she would say. A few months later, in my mother's church in California, the attorney and I married. In 1970, we moved to Wichita, his hometown, where he got his first position. I can't say the hasty marriage was a complete mistake, but the trauma of recent events had taken their toll on me and my child. I was emotionally numb.

A teacher at the day care in Topeka told me about a church in Wichita. She knew the people who ran the church's day care center. Happy with the day care, I began attending church services and making friends. My husband did not share my interest in the church, nor in much else. With little in common, we were divorced in just three years – another strike against me socially and internally. Still young, earnestly wanting to grow as a person and keep life together for my son, I became more active in the church. It was a safe place for us and rapidly became the center of our social and spiritual lives.

The minister saw social justice as central to his mission. He, along with other clergy in the area, embraced a philosophy and theological thinking that I had never encountered. They taught that churches needed to find ways to become agents of social change, not only where we lived but around the world. Religious houses, usually led by a clergyman, had been established both nationwide and outside the country. Dedicated people could live there and work within their communities. The idea was that if people were freed of the baggage of individual homes and lives, they would be better able to serve, to create a new world order. The goal was to help neighborhoods or villages organize so that they could work to improve their own situations. This was especially important in poor and/or underdeveloped areas.

In the summer of 1973, my son and I became live-in members. I soon learned I would have little time for my child and even less in which to get rest. Preparations for seminars, community outreach, church attendance and 40-hour workweeks made for an exhausting existence. Early summer brought new assignments for live-in members. Rarely did people stay in the same house longer than a year. In retrospect, one of the ways to keep people living in the religious houses was through moving them from state to state and sometimes out of the country.

It was not all bad. The summer brought special sessions that were held at the Midwestern city headquarters. These were intense, yet exhilarating, and church members from around the country were recruited to attend. In the midst of daily workshops – doing everything from strategic planning for community efforts in other parts of the world to song writing – there were huge celebrations. On the spiritual end, a two-day retreat took participants through meaningful exercises of meditation, contemplation and prayer.

My assignment in 1974 was to move to the headquarters in Chicago. Insisting that I go to school, I was allowed to attend a nearby university and live and work in the student house for the junior high and high school students. Most of these children had parents assigned either out of the country or in houses in other cities. I enrolled my son at the local elementary school in a very poor neighborhood. It was nothing to be required to hide from a gang war on the way to the subway. This was a bad situation for him, and he didn't do well in the school.

One evening my son, who was too young to be in the student house, came to see me while I was working on a rather large project of creating a crafts school for the students. He was lonely. The boy he roomed with spent the evenings with his parents, two people trying to pull enough funds together to get back to their home country. Soon after that evening, a leader of the program spoke suggesting married couples adopt the practice of abstinence. Children, he said, took too many resources and too much time. (While I was living there, several women had miscarriages. They felt it was due to exhaustion and lack of care, according to conversations in our communal bathrooms.)

Before I had moved from Wichita, I had become romantically involved with a bright and wonderful man who had stolen my heart, partly by befriending my son. He, too, had been a live-in member of the program but left before I moved into the Wichita house. It was difficult for us, but we had managed to keep in touch. I was hesitant to chance disappointment again, but in my heart I knew I was in love. By the end of 1975, I was very unhappy with my situation. When he asked, I accepted a proposal of marriage, and my son and I moved back to Wichita.

Larry and I have been active in several congregations but "church" will never be the same for me. We have found our spiritual centers and formed a relationship with the Mystery in our own ways. Through hard work and struggle, we have done what we are able to do for the world and those around us. We are active with teenagers of all stripes, while raising our own sons, and many are like family to us. I have reconciled most differences with my mother, who now lives in Wichita and has added more adoring piano students to her long list. Larry and I have not moved mountains, but then, neither did the religious group I had previously joined.

Honk for Mary

Mary McDonough Harren, As told to Dorothy K. Billings

Mary McDonough Harren had several epiphanies that led her to the women's movement. In February 1966, after she had begun to raise her daughter and six sons, she looked down at the foot of her hospital bed to see the twins, healthy new boys, and she thought: *There must be another way. The fellows who are making the decisions are sleeping all night in the Vatican.* With this she embraced the family-planning movement, and she considers herself a walking billboard for women's reproductive rights. She realizes, of course, how lucky she is to have this wonderful family. She considers herself fortunate to succeed, as she did, as the mother of seven children.

Another epiphany occurred when one day a Catholic woman confided in her that she had had an abortion and realized that she was going to hell. Mary told her, "No God I believe in would send you to hell for having an abortion!"

Mary was educated entirely in Catholic schools, including Cathedral High School in Wichita. She met her husband – Don, a Minnesota native and Marine Corps veteran of World War II -- later while he was a teacher at Cathedral High. Mary's family experienced some difficult times after her mother died and left their dad with three young children.

She recalls, "Dad was a man of courage, tenacity and love for his children – the thought of abandoning us to an orphanage was unthinkable – so he spent the last 37 years of his life dedicated to being both mom and dad to his little ones, which eventually included 22 grandchildren." When Mary's husband died and left her with her large family, she looked at her dad's example and said, "I can do it."

Another epiphany occurred later – somewhere in the '60s – when she joined an anti-abortion group consisting of attorneys, doctors, priests and businessmen. She was the only woman. She, of course, was the secretary. One day the chairman of the group called her. She listened patiently to his ranting against women who had had abortions, and remembers looking at the phone, then telling him, "Ray, there's got to be something better I can do with my life." She hung up, never to attend another meeting, and already on her way out of the anti-abortion, anti-woman movement. A new course in her life had begun.

Mary has written many outstanding letters to the editor, pointing out that the Catholic Fathers and other men are the ones who stridently oppose a woman's right to choose (and in the case of the Church, frown deeply on contraceptive family planning), though none of them can conceive, get pregnant or give birth. Further, the celibates do not participate in the raising of the children.

Mary has supported many social justice causes and considers them all interconnected. She recognizes that the steady stream of her energy comes from her Catholic upbringing. She credits the great Dorothy Day, founder of the Catholic Worker movement, for her dedication. Her main focus has been on the peace movement, of which she has been the leader in Wichita for 40 years.

She has been arrested a number of times for demonstrating at military installations, but not for some years now. She turned her own house on North Topeka into the Peace House, and there she held many meetings, arranged speakers and films, and invited Fr. Dan Berrigan to speak at Wichita State University. She also organized countless demonstrations against war, the "White Train" – which took nuclear bombs through Kansas – and the nuclear reactor at Wolf Creek.

She is quick to identify the many other groups with which she worked and whom she often joined: the Two Rivers Group, which lived in Peace House after she owned it but before she moved in; the Mennonites; and many women's groups.

She worked with many women including Annabelle Haupt, a United Methodist with strong Quaker leanings, who went to Cuba twice in the 1980s with her West Side Methodist church; Peg Vines, who re-enacted the wisdom of Eleanor Roosevelt for many groups; Fern Van Gieson, who responded to the urging of Kay Yoder of McPherson to form a branch in Wichita of the Women's International League for Peace and Freedom; and Sister Ann Catherine, who continues to make the world a better place.

Mary has always recognized that there is no peace without social justice. She has been active in the NAACP and other civil rights groups – especially those seeking justice in the gay community. She always looks especially for the implications for women in any cause she supports, but works equally with men. Her friends from the labor unions and the Catholic Church include Nick Mohr and Harold Plenart. When she left the Peace House, her colleagues turned it into the Peace Center. Pat Cameron, an early Mennonite volunteer, has continued his work raising funds for the Peace Center.

Mary now sends out her emails in the name of Molly's Brigade, in tribute to the late Molly Ivins. For the Wichita peace and justice community, Molly Ivins was a great woman, but Mary McDonough Harren is the lynch pin of our community's successful activism. When you see a demonstration for one of her causes, be sure to "Honk for Mary."

God is Coming and Is She Pissed

Kerry Johnston

In July 1978, my mother brought several T-shirts home from the Equal Rights Amendment march on the nation's Capitol. Her kids were allowed to choose which we wanted. I asked for the one declaring, "God is coming and is She pissed!" I was always one to wear T-shirts that said something thought provoking. I recall wearing this one as a way of proclaiming that God might not be a man, but I still believed in God. As the child of an atheist father and a mother who left the Catholic Church to marry him, it suited my budding rebellious nature to challenge the homestead belief systems in addition to those of the world at large.

I wore this one proudly to Brooks Junior High School one day that fall. I received the usual stares from classmates that just didn't get it, as well as the few who made I-like-your-shirt comments. No one – child or adult – seemed to be passionate one way or the other, until I saw an administrator. I do recall she seemed flustered. She told me that the shirt "might be offensive to some," and that I needed to go home and change it. I did. As my parents recall it, I was suspended until I took it off, and that may very well be how the school communicated it to them.

In my 13-year-old consciousness, however, I was more interested in letting it blow over. At that age, there's a point to which you want to rebel and then you just want it over. I wasn't an extremely outgoing young woman, despite my individuality, and I had outdone myself enough for that day. I queried some old school friends via Facebook recently; some remembered the shirt, and one or two remembered a slight controversy, but none in greater detail than I did. A few did enjoy that I brought about discussion on the existence of God, and a classmate who is now a magazine editor said, "Your views were quite progressive and against the flow of Kansas thought."

As a parent, I know I will remember my daughter's personality-shaping moments better than my own. It's just the kind of thing you do concerning your kids. Like giving them the tools to shape who they will become and letting them be who they are going to be. Then, to quote George Michael, "You gotta have faith," regardless of how it is defined.

Grace, Faith, Feminism

Jane Anne Richards

I came to Wichita in 1971, searching for a spiritual home, perhaps more a sense of place in the changing world. Yes, the promise of interesting work also added to the decision to move from teaching at the Sinte Gleska College Center in Rosebud, SD. However, as was somewhat common in that era, location and work also needed to be liberally mixed with a sense of meaning.

The Wichita public schools were in the first year of racial integration, and I believed in being part of changing the world. My husband, Bob, was hired to be part of the process while I cared for our baby and a four-year-old. Three months after moving to Wichita, we had a home and a babysitter, and I began work at Friends University. We were once again a two-career couple.

My family visited church after church. Wonderful possibilities.

Except for me. The anger that had been building in me increased. My aloneness deepened. Where could I find a place to worship? I sought a place where women could be included in ways beyond teaching children's Sunday school and preparing meals. Oh yes, one could be the consummate volunteer; but could a woman be included in the major decisions of the church? Would the sexist language of scripture, hymns and sermons be acknowledged? Would sermons continue to batter women with their need to be subservient? What would happen to a woman who "did not know her place"?

This cultural shift impacted many Wichita churches as women began to experience ways of hearing language, words of comfort and hope that valued them. Many women, though devoted to their church community, recognized the necessity of change and spoke forcefully. Resistance and time are powerful allies when held by the majority in a congregation. Unfortunately, the majority was not women who sought an inclusive spiritual home. For both men and women, this discussion created divisions and hurt. I believe the sadness and anger that many women experienced during this period of time created a chasm that has never been healed.

A gift of grace occurred for me one Sunday morning in 1972, when I visited a congregation where a peaceful woman was pastor. This was my first experience to listen to an entire group of people quietly, verbally making the change to include all who were present. My tears would not quit, and I recognized the value of language that embraces women's souls. It was this year I also discovered "Try to love the questions," a line from Rilke's *Letters To A Young Poet* which brought profound affirmation that questioning was part of my nature and most likely a lifelong trait that I could value. Not a value I had been taught in church, but one that freed my soul.

I experienced worship in Chicago with Jesse Jackson's Operation Breadbasket during the late '60s. I watched eagles circle the young Native American men during a Sun Dance in the Rosebud Reservation in South Dakota. My understanding of the world continued to increase. My search for meaning and faith expanded. Feminist writers further opened my eyes to possibilities of a world large enough to question and explore. To push back against rigid church structures no longer seemed an act of anger, but a necessity to secure space for my growth, my daughter's future and the spiritual search of my friends.

God and Feminism

Peg Vines

An eventful weekend? Yes. But was it life-changing? For me, it was – politically and spiritually. Now, 34 years after the 1977 Women's Weekend, I can look back calmly and even write about my struggle to balance my Catholicism with my fierce desire to help women. I saw the weekend and the following conference in Houston as important ways to acknowledge barriers that have been prescribed for us by custom, tradition and law. In other words, barriers to women's full participation in our nation's life.

But on that final day of the weekend, a Sunday, I had been so busy with my conference duties that I hadn't attended morning Mass in my parish. There was still time to attend the one church that offered an early evening service. So I hurried and was among its crowd.

I knew church hierarchy was not in favor of the whole idea of a women's conference, but I wasn't prepared for the tirade from the pulpit that night. The International Women's Year logo, incorporating a dove and woman's symbol, was "really a Nazi helmet upside down" ... and the hotel's air conditioning and elevator mishaps were all "done on purpose." Obviously God was not happy with feminists and the women we were influencing in our workshops.

I was thoroughly shaken from that experience.

Fortunately, my friend Gloria assured me there were other Catholics supporting women's equality and where to find them and worship together. Later I phoned the diocese headquarters and talked with an assistant to the bishop. I asked about the church's position on the ERA and, of course, it was denounced. I was told I should quit working for it. In fact, I should "quit bitching, and do what God wanted me to do."

I must add that when some friendly nuns heard my story, one of them said, "Peg, if you've been sent to hell, we'll just reach down and pull you back up!" I believe she will, because I'm still working to get an ERA passed in my lifetime.

Pursuing Health Care for Women

"When men and women took identical complaints and symptoms, both physical and mental, to the panel of physicians, the men were taken seriously, tested and evaluated over a number of visits. The women were usually prescribed Valium at the first visit and sent home."

—Joan Brussat Cole (Mental Illness: Finding My Way)

"The Kansas Coalition For The Freedom To Choose affirmed in 1978 the right of women and men to make decisions regarding their own fertility, free from church or governmental intervention, in accordance with their own individual consciences. The new organization also stated that it respected the scruples of those who reject abortion, but oppose any attempts to embody those scruples in laws, binding to all. Every American should have easy access to family planning services and until unplanned pregnancies no longer occur, that legal abortion should be available to all women desiring it, regardless of age, economic status or race."

—Equal Time, September, 1978

From Traditional Housewife to Reproductive Freedom Activist

Peggy Bowman

I arrived in Wichita in the fall of 1978 as a very traditional housewife. I was so traditional that I didn't really understand why my Sunday school class cringed in horror when my husband said: "I don't mind if my wife works if she does my laundry, takes care of the kids and has my dinner on the table at six." Then I met Margaret Simmons, my first boss when I was a Vista Volunteer at Work Options for Women. She quickly became my friend, confidant and mentor. Margaret is the force behind everything that followed. At Work Options I met many fabulous and fascinating women. I worked with them and began to understand the importance of diversity, activism and equality. I quickly began to empathize with my Sunday school class.

When my year as a Vista ended, I knew I wanted to continue to work, to learn more and explore my potential. I had gained enough confidence that when I saw an ad for lobbyist for Planned Parenthood of Kansas, I told myself that even though I knew nothing about how to lobby, I could learn. I applied for the job and was hired on the spot. Lobbying was quite different then. Moderate Republicans controlled the Kansas House and the Senate. Anti-abortion bills were rarely heard and when they were, we pretty much knew they would be defeated. We just had to present our position well, and the votes to kill the bill would be there.

Eventually I applied for the job of executive director of Planned Parenthood of Kansas. I was given the job with the stipulation that I not speak to the press. How ironic that I became Dr. George Tiller's spokeswomen for most of the '90s. During the horrible summer of 1991 when Operation Rescue invaded our city, I appeared almost nightly on the evening news.

Many others also influenced my life – too many to name. However, none were/are more profoundly important to me than my two sons. When I told them I was a lesbian they were 10 and 7.

One said, "Just as my friend Mr. Rogers says, 'I like you just the way you are.' "

The other, "Whatever turns you on." That support was overwhelmingly important to me. They have encouraged me every step of the way since then. One is a pro-choice "born again." The other is more like me – a liberal through and through. Both are feminists, and I take full credit for that.

Mental Illness: Finding My Way

Joan Brussat Cole

When I was 10 years old, my mother became seriously depressed following the birth of her third child and began a lifelong struggle to remain functional in spite of it. At that time, little was known about depression or how to treat it. At first, my father did not seek professional help for my mother; instead he tried, in a loving manner, to help her himself with the aid of a few close friends. He told us that it was "a female problem" and seemed unable to accept her condition as serious – though it greatly resembled the situation of her mother who also experienced deep depression. Because the family would not allow my grandmother to be declared "legally insane" and placed in the state mental hospital, she never received treatment. Instead she remained in the family home, sitting in her rocking chair and muttering threateningly to all who passed her for a decade until her death. At that time the stigma against mentally ill persons and their families was overwhelming and further isolated them from others.

My mother's depression deepened until she could not get out of bed. In despair, my father took her to a physician who, eventually, arranged admission in the mental ward of the university hospital 200 miles away. For the next 25 years, my mother was admitted to that hospital at least every other year. There she received shock treatments and was prescribed a variety of drugs in an attempt to find one that would enable her to remain at home and able to participate in the family's activities. She was one of the first patients to be treated with lithium that provided the best, although temporary, relief. To my knowledge, she did not receive talk therapy to any great degree, which today is used extensively with many patients.

Little education on my mother's illness was given to my father by the doctors and nurses who treated her. In turn, he offered scant comfort and explanation to his three daughters, who were 10, five and six months old when her depression first manifested itself. We were a close and loving family; and this frightening experience drew us closer; we did not share our mother's condition with others for years. When my mother returned from the hospital, shockingly thin and weak, we waited fearfully for the "dark cloud," as she described it, to return and necessitate another trip to the state hospital. My mother's illness marked us as different and strange to many people in our community of 50,000. Thus, carrying on was not always easy.

As we grew older, we worried that the same symptoms might manifest themselves in us as they had appeared in one of my mother's siblings and in a cousin who committed suicide in her early 30s. I did not experience depression until 1978 when my first husband left me for another relationship. As a single parent with two young children, no job and no financial resources, I became despondent and could not decide how to proceed. I thought of my mother often during that period. I sought help from my family doctor and a psychiatrist who was also a friend. Both wanted to prescribe antidepressants. When I told my psychiatrist friend that I did not want to simply take drugs, but instead wanted assistance in looking at my life and finding solutions to my situation, he recommended a woman social worker in his practice. Then and over the remainder of my life, she has provided the professional expertise I needed. With her help, I looked at my life in general and developed a path on which I began to move.

My first positive step was to find a job as a planner for a national health-planning network created by Congress. I was assigned the development of a mental health and substance abuse plan for the 23 Kansas counties that we served. This necessitated researching the prevalence of health problems, past and current treatment of these diagnoses, providers of services to persons suffering from mental illness and substance abuse, and developing recommendations for prevention and treatment of these problems. When I sought examples of existing plans that might provide ideas for my work, I found that none existed.

Also, there was little research available. One of the few studies that I found demonstrated major bias against women. When men and women took identical complaints and symptoms, both physical and mental, to the same panel of physicians, the men were taken seriously and tested and evaluated over a number of visits. The women were usually prescribed Valium at the first visit and sent home. Other research that I conducted with local providers confirmed this disparity. I spent almost nine months on my plan. When I completed it and submitted it to the national headquarters of the Health Systems Agencies, it was well received and distributed to the other HSAs across the country as a model.

Subsequently a friend invited me to join the local board of the Mental Health Association. He was a member and believed that my personal experiences and the history of my family would bring a needed, and missing, perspective to the board. At first, I declined. Eventually I concluded that several things in my life were presenting opportunity for me to finally deal with the issue of mental illness that I had assiduously avoided all of my life. I joined the MHA, and my education continued.

Next I was invited to join the Kansas Mental Health Association Board of Directors and did so. While I was attending a board meeting in Topeka, I met a man who had formed a support group in Topeka for persons who had received in-patient mental health treatment. He had suffered from bouts of terrible depression and had been hospitalized several times. He learned of a support group, traveled there for training and began the Breakthrough chapter in Topeka. He invited me to attend one of their meetings; then he began a full-court press to convince me to initiate a similar organization in Wichita.

In 1978, I approached the local Mental Health Association and asked permission to create such a group. I was turned down twice. The third time I asked to hold two open houses in December to see if there was interest in a Breakthrough chapter in Wichita. The board agreed and told me that if 25 people attended and showed interest, they would consider sponsoring a support group.

This was a bold move, because MHA's focus was advocacy for the mentally ill. It had not provided "direct services" to persons who had experienced mental illness, and the board was not sure that it wished to do so. *The Wichita Eagle* responded positively to my request for help and wrote a substantial article on our plans. We held two open houses. More than 150 people attended; most were women who spoke of their depression and sadness, but there were a significant number of young men who told us they had been diagnosed as schizophrenic.

I returned to the Mental Health Association board and was given the go-ahead to form a Breakthrough chapter and create a committee of MHA and Breakthrough members to plan meetings. All of the members who offered to serve on the committee were women. We decided to hold monthly meetings in my home with the help of the MHA assistant director. And so, in 1979-80, Breakthrough became a program of the Mental Health Association. At first, we intended to include family members. However, early on, it became apparent there was need to provide a safe place where family dynamics were not an issue. I struggled over that decision, because I remembered how great my family's need for support and education was. Fortunately, in time, a support group for families was developed with the help of the MHA.

My husband and four teen-aged children participated in Breakthrough meetings in our home and interacted with them, which was a wonderful learning experience for them as well. We taught life skills that so many of our members lacked in the hope that they would learn ways to solve problems early on rather than avoiding them until they grew to crises. We taught them how to shop for and prepare healthy meals, how to use public transportation, pay bills and other things that the members requested. It was exciting to watch them grow in confidence, to volunteer at agencies and even find part-time jobs with our assistance.

After the membership grew to almost 70, our home could not accommodate the projects and training we wished to provide. I sought another venue and went to several organizations for help with funding and volunteers. For a while, we met in a church and Episcopal Social Services granted funds. Later we held our meetings at Venture House, but it became increasingly clear that there was a great need for more individual help and professionally trained staff to work with the members. The needs of this population were and continue to be overwhelming. They became overwhelming to me personally, as well. Breakthrough members came to my home at all hours, day and night, for counseling and help. I was a wife, mother of four and working two jobs outside the home. Clearly it was time to develop a program that could offer more and better assistance to the Breakthrough members.

The Mental Health Association took their project to several organizations and asked them to take it on. Today there is such a program. Breakthrough House offers a full-time comforting and stable environment with trained personnel and a variety of programs. I am pleased to have been one of the catalysts along the way. As is so often true when volunteers initiate a program, the greatest benefit, I believe, came to me. I learned about mental illness, especially in women, and the prevention and treatment of it. I learned how to encourage women and men to seek treatment in a non-threatening way and, in some cases, accompanied them on visits to competent mental health professionals. Also, I finally looked at my family's "secret" in the light of day, talked at length with my sisters and other relatives about the genetic risk in our family and the need to remain vigilant for signs of it.

We have come a long way since I was 10 years old – but much remains to be done. Women must speak more openly about mental illness and teach others that, just as we seek professional help for broken bones, we must go to quality mental health professionals when our psyches are broken and troubled. As courageous women (and men) demand and receive quality, appropriate mental health care and treatment, they shall find their way out from under the paralyzing "dark cloud" of depression and sadness.

I know this to be true.

Living In Fear of Pregnancy
Andrea Ramsay

I was born in 1943. My husband and I attended the same junior high and high school, though we did not begin dating until our senior prom in 1960. We were married later the same year. My mother was from a large family and had been a licensed practical nurse. Although I considered her fairly progressive about telling me the facts of life, and I had read some "health" pamphlets in junior high explaining the mechanics of how one became pregnant, I knew little about birth control. I had never seen an obstetrician or had a vaginal exam before getting married. By the time of my first visit to an obstetrician, I was five months pregnant with our first child, who was born in 1961. Within 15 months after his birth, when I was 19 and my husband was 20, we had our second child. Neither pregnancy was planned, and I didn't want a second child so quickly after the first.

I do not recall any of the several obstetricians I had seen explaining available birth control methods. Certainly none of them offered any prescription. Within five months after the birth of our second child, I was pregnant for the third time, also unplanned. There were some difficulties in the early weeks. I began hemorrhaging, but as luck would have it, I was in the doctor's office for a pregnancy test at the time and was given some pills that stopped the threatened abortion. The doctor never explained that the threatened spontaneous abortion might be an indication of birth defects. I carried the baby to term, but some of his internal organs had developed outside his body (omphalocele). He could not survive the rigors of labor and was stillborn in 1963.

Enough was enough. My husband and I just wanted to take care of the children we had. We knew we did not want another unplanned pregnancy. In 1964, I asked my doctor for birth control. He discussed IUDs and birth control pills. He would not prescribe an IUD, because he believed they caused abortions rather than preventing pregnancy. I didn't care. Birth control pills were available by that time and were acceptable to me, although I worried about their effectiveness and would panic when I forgot to take one as scheduled. I had also heard it might not be healthy to take birth control pills for years on end.

In 1969, my husband and I knew we did not want to have more children. I saw a doctor and requested to have my tubes tied. The doctor refused. He said I was "only 26 and only had two children." I was frustrated and disappointed to tears, but it did not occur to me to seek a second opinion. I was still naive enough to think the doctor was the ultimate authority. I thought he spoke for the whole profession.

We moved to Kansas in 1970, and my husband was taking college classes. Our children were both in school. I was working as a legal secretary, the sole support of our family. Four years later, the thing I had feared for 10 years on birth control happened.

I was pregnant. Whether I had forgotten that critical pill one day, or it just failed, I did not know. By 1974 abortions were legal, though not easy to get. After talking with my husband, who said the final decision was mine, I decided to seek an abortion early in the first trimester. A Wichita hospital had been offering the procedure, but was being picketed by protesters and was not taking any new patients. I could find no one else locally who would agree to perform an abortion for me. I learned of, and made an appointment, at a women's clinic in Lawrence, and my husband and I traveled there for the procedure. I suffered from nausea on the way home, but I knew we had made the right choice for our family.

I was determined never again to experience constant fear of an unwanted pregnancy or abortion. In Wichita I went to a doctor again to request a tubal ligation. Because of all that had brought me to that point, I was not going to take no for an answer. When the young resident began his spiel to determine whether I really had thought through the decision and really wanted the procedure, my face drew taut. I leaned forward and raised my voice: "I do not want another child!" The young resident stopped the mechanical spiel, explained the procedure and scheduled me for surgery.

Finally, at age 31, I experienced the triumph of determining for myself what would happen to me and my body.

Women Alive and Well

Marni Vliet, As told to Lee Goodman Starkel

Like so many others, my path to launching the Women Alive and Well health fairs can be traced back to Carol Wolfe Konek. In 1974, I encountered Carol while standing in line in Henry Levitt Arena to register for classes at Wichita State University.

"Enroll me in something," I said to her. "This is the first day of the rest of my life." The memory of that cliché somewhat pains me today, but I was a mother with two toddlers and ready to re-incorporate the life of the mind into my everyday routine and complete a master's degree. Carol enrolled me in my first women's studies class, Women in Society, that she taught at the downtown Wichita library. Her goal was to inspire students to pursue their intellectual curiosities through various class projects. I arrived with a ready-made inspiration that grew out of my own experience with childbirth.

Hospital policies at that time, and for decades previously, banned fathers from delivery rooms. The recent births of my two daughters, Sasha and Whitney, brought home the irrelevancy and absurdness of these policies, and I was driven to find ways to change the hospital environment. The women's studies class was the perfect vehicle for studying this issue. As I launched into my research, my thinking about this issue expanded. Physicians were primarily male, and they held the keys to the knowledge about women's health. I came to believe that it was vital for women to know more about childbirth and their health in general, and to rely less on the medical profession to control their experiences with their own bodies.

Building on the spirit of inspiration gained from the Women in Society class, I persuaded WSU to develop a combination degree incorporating courses in women's studies, the College of Health Related Professions, the College of Education and the newly founded KU School of Medicine-Wichita. I had found my calling – the advancement and betterment of health for women and for the community at large. It was heady times. Coming on the heels of the civil rights struggle, American women were finding their voices for the first time and discovering that the personal is political. Locally, the City of Wichita established the Commission on the Status of Women to champion equality.

The rising women's health movement and holistic health movement galvanized many women like me. It was natural that women championed prevention and wellness, because it was typically women who facilitated and guided the family's health. However, men primarily managed the health system at that time. Providing information to women in our community seemed an obvious solution to me. I submitted a proposal to CSW at the start of 1976, describing the need to host a Women Alive and Well Health Fair. Soon after, the city commission, as it was then called, granted permission for the fair and provided partial funding and a half-time staff person to assist. Then the real work began. The Commission on the Status of Women formed a health committee, and a series of meetings were scheduled in offices and homes throughout the city to brainstorm what the health fair would include. I contacted everyone I could think of to join the endeavor.

Soon an agenda was formed. Speakers and workshops would focus on women as health consumers, human sexuality, birth control, pregnancy and childbirth, body awareness, menopause, women and drugs, nutrition, holistic medicine, psychology of women, self-defense, acupressure and massage, and Hatha Yoga. Speakers agreed to participate for free or for travel expenses only. The idea of art as another form of health also seemed appropriate. Dance and music activities were incorporated into the programming, and an art exhibit was planned. Women Health/Women Art was taking shape.

Additional funds were raised from the KU School of Medicine-Wichita, thanks to Dean Cramer Reed. The Wichita Child Care Association agreed to provide child care free of charge. Brochures and posters were printed and distributed throughout the city. Local television and radio stations aired several promotions, and *The Wichita Eagle* ran numerous feature articles, written primarily by Carolyn Kortge.

The first Women Alive and Well Health Fair was held Oct. 9, 1976, at city hall. The brochure read, "Women's health issues are unique, precious and too often misunderstood. It's time for a happy end to the 'don't worry your pretty head' theory of women's medicine. We must know our bodies, appreciate them and be aware of changes. The medical world is evolving toward prevention rather than cure, and it's time women hopped on the bandwagon."

And did they ever hop on the bandwagon. Hundreds of local women turned out for the first Wichita women's health fair. They filled city hall. They listened to dozens of speakers and workshop panelists, tried yoga and t'ai chi, learned basic self-defense techniques and watched informational filmstrips on topics related to pregnancy and childbirth. It was a powerful and profound experience for everyone in attendance, and for me. The feedback was overwhelmingly positive, and the Commission on the Status of Women decided a second health fair would be held. We learned a great deal from the first event, including the need for more space. An even more ambitious schedule was planned for the second Women Alive and Well fair. The interpretation of health would be stretched, and the concept of women owning their bodies would be embraced.

The second health fair was held April 8, 1978, at Coleman Junior High School. Two national speakers – John Travis, M.D. and Lonnie Garfield Barbarch, Ph.D. – were invited to present. Dr. Travis discussed wellness education and individual responsibility for health. Dr. Barbarch talked about healthy approaches to sexuality. The list of workshop topics expanded to include women and mental health and widowhood. The body awareness workshop added topics unknown to most Wichitans, including biofeedback and aerobic dance. Discussion groups ran throughout the day and provided a safe environment for women to talk about divorce, displaced homemakers, menopause/aging, parenting, self-defense, spirituality and health, understanding our sisters, and work options. An art exhibit was again part of the health experience. Once again, attendance was overwhelming.

After 1978, the health fair became part of WomenFair/WomenArt. Issues related to health became part of a larger dialogue about women's lives and experiences occurring across the nation, and Wichita women had successfully joined the discussion. I had grown from this two-year adventure. I learned so much listening to women talk about their bodies and their health, most for the first time in their lives. This new awareness formed the basis of my master's thesis where I interviewed hundreds of women following childbirth at Wesley Hospital.

The relationships built during this time eventually led to my position as CEO of the Kansas Health Foundation. Service in a philanthropic organization is an enormous privilege and a serious responsibility. Remembering my early experiences with the women health fairs, the Foundation developed grassroots leadership opportunities, increased the quality of information available to make good health decisions and highlighted the importance of the earliest years – children from birth to five, the best time to begin promoting a healthy life.

As I reflect on Women Alive and Well, I believe most of what I needed as an administrator was learned during those early days. From the women participating, we heard how they felt like they were listened to for the first time. They felt they were equal and important members of society, as Carol Konek had taught us. They helped make change possible, which defines the work of philanthropy. These passionate voices of the 1970s are still being heard.

Planned Parenthood of Kansas

Kris Wilshusen

"No woman can call herself free who does not own and control her body. No woman can call herself free until she can choose consciously whether she will or will not be a mother."
—Margaret Sanger, founder of Planned Parenthood Federation of America

Margaret Sanger was wise and courageous enough to say this aloud in the early 1900s. But women knew this reality long before that – even if they could not put it into words of their own. Still, nearly a century after Sanger battled for reproductive justice, women face the same realities in controlling their fertility.

Recognizing the need for reproductive health care and contraceptive services, Sanger opened her first contraceptive education clinic in 1916. This ignited grassroots organizations across America that fought for better methods of birth control and an end to birth control laws. In 1939, these grassroots organizations joined together to form the Birth Control Federation of America, which eventually was named the Planned Parenthood Federation of America. It would take years before Planned Parenthood affiliates would be established across the nation.

Early in the 1970s, Junior League of Wichita convened a panel to discuss issues facing the community. Ann Fugate, a member of Junior League, wanted someone from PP to sit on the panel to lead the discussion regarding teen pregnancy. When Ann went looking for a representative, she discovered no one, because Wichita had no PP clinic. In fact, there were none in Kansas west of Kansas City.

Like Margaret Sanger, Ann was unable to abide such a lack of services for women. She asked to have her Junior League project be that of establishing a Planned Parenthood clinic. But Junior League of Wichita was unwilling to support her on a project connected to such controversial subject as birth control. Unstoppable, Ann found a person in Missouri who was able and willing to help her begin the process of establishing a Planned Parenthood affiliate in Wichita.

Ann put together a group of dedicated individuals that created Planned Parenthood of South Central Kansas. A once-a-week clinic was held in the Kansas Children's Service League building in west Wichita. With the help of a part-time director and many volunteers, the clinic offered birth control services and counseling. It became apparent from the overflow of patients at each clinic session that much more was needed to meet the demand for birth-control services. She began strengthening the board by calling together a group of professionals in Wichita who dealt with issues of teen sexuality and pregnancy. The group included doctors, nurses, ministers, social workers, staff from SRS and school counselors, among others.

From this group also came some of the members of the first board of directors for, what was now Planned Parenthood of Kansas. This board included Rev. Bob Eades; Ruth Luzzatti; Merv Silverman from the Sedgwick County Health Department; Melba Madden, RN; Dr. Dan Roberts with Wesley Hospital; and, of course, Ann Fugate. Over time, the board secured a site of its own, added clinic hours and staff, and intensified education programs. This board struggled with raising funds for the newly formed Planned Parenthood of Kansas. The Rev. George Gardner, who joined the board in the mid-'70s, remembered Ann going before the Wichita City Council to ask for funds.

"With all her beauty and grace, and cane in hand, Ann walked to the front of the room to make her pitch." Rev. Gardner credited her success in getting funds from the city council to what he labeled as "cane politics." This accomplishment was not long lived. The city, just as Junior League, did not want to be involved in a service they considered controversial.

Despite many funding and political controversies throughout the '70s – just as the decades that followed – PPK endures today as Planned Parenthood of Kansas and Mid-Missouri. Providing comprehensive reproductive health care services to the women of Wichita continues to be a challenge. Many of the struggles have moved from the streets to the legislature and courtrooms, thus becoming less visible but no less a threat to women deciding " … whether she will or will not be a mother."

"It is not enough," Margaret Sanger also said, "to look backward with pride, justified as that pride might be. We must look forward with hope and confidence too. The real lesson of the past is that it shows us what can be done for the future."

Organizing for Political Clout

"In five of the state meetings Right-To-Life and Anti-ERA representatives won a majority of the state delegations. "Operation Wichita" was their statewide plan to make Kansas the sixth state. They introduced at least ten resolutions against gay rights, abortion and federal funding for day care centers."
> —Margalee Pilkington Wright (Kansas Women's Weekend)

"An invitation to join The Wichita Women's Political Caucus in order to:
*Get women represented in elective and appointive political offices
*Gain policy-making positions in both political parties
*Work for legislation that promotes women's priorities at all levels of government
*Raise women's issues in every election
*Recruit and rally behind candidates of either sex who support women's priorities
and humanist goals
*Work to correct injustices that diminish the dignity of every human being"
> —Wichita Women's Political Caucus flyer, 1974

Breaking Stereotypes: Going From Mrs. to Ms.

Correne Green

My '70s experiences brought a true child of the '50s to a new view of the world. I was the dutiful daughter, responsible, a good student and careful to be seen and not heard. Coincidentally, those are the hallmarks of a child in a family where one parent is alcoholic. I was not encouraged to think outside the box. My behavior was deeply ingrained, and it took something strong, almost explosive, to shake it. I left my parents' home, married and had two daughters. I stayed home until both of them were in school. Soon PTA called, and I began with room mother duties and meetings about school board concerns.

Then I found the League of Women Voters. These women were no lightweights. Their studies included the constitutional amendment of one-man-one-vote, Red China (yes, we heard all the jokes), water conservation and more. Suddenly, I was knee-deep in facts, figures and newfound imperatives. And I had a revelation: I had the brains to understand the issues, and I could think!

Growing awareness of the feminist movement led me to new women's organizations. I attended a meeting at the home of Glendora Johnson, a Kansas Women's Political Caucus member. It was great fun with interesting women and good conversation. I was chatting with someone about how a mechanic had fixed my sometimes-unreliable car, with just a "flick of the wrist" under the hood. "I could never do that," I said.

A woman standing nearby turned and said, "Of course you can." I was stunned; of course I can? She continued, "You just have to learn how." Her name was Carol, and I later learned she was Carol Konek, a name I recognized as a mover and shaker.

So this is consciousness raising, I thought. I joined the caucus.

Their goals were so close to mine. I was active in the Republican party, but no political party had women's issues as a top priority. Unfortunately, I voiced a thought I shouldn't have at one of the Republican meetings: "I didn't join the party to bake cookies." Some people objected, so the caucus was a natural home for me. Members sought to recruit and elect women candidates, and they would teach us how. Additionally they were prepared to make changes on many fronts. No cookie baking needed. Later, I was the caucus Republican liaison.

We were not a one-issue organization; there were big issues, small issues and injustices everywhere. We tackled them all. Looking at some of them now, I am aghast how often we couldn't control even the tiniest personal things of our lives, but we could succeed in caucus goals. Here are some can-you-believe-this? examples:

Alma Carter brought to our attention that Southwestern Bell, when it listed only one of a household in the phone book, usually listed the husband's name. We had a letter-writing campaign to change the "usually-the-husband" policy.

Martha Hodges was active at the rape center and on the caucus rape task force. We all had heard horror stories of women who wouldn't press charges against a rapist because of the treatment they received in the justice system. She wrote a letter to District Attorney Vern Miller requesting him to assign women prosecutors to rape cases. (Do you remember how long it took to convince the police to use rape kits at the hospitals?)

Glendora Johnson reported she had registered a complaint with the Advertising Counsel, because they had no women on their program. They asked her if she wanted to participate. She did.

Peg Vines wrote a letter in response to an anti-ERA editorial by George Doyle at KFH radio. She urged us to get our message out using radio.

We had to be ever vigilant. Our legislative committee and our lobbyist kept us updated and ready to act. We prioritized our interests and developed strategies to push legislation. Legislative topics we targeted included displaced homemakers; credit discrimination; child care; adult care homes; state family planning centers; female inmates and the penal system; sexual offenses; child abuse and neglect; public assistance; pregnancy disability; flexible hours act; abortion; and estate and gift taxes. These battles took months or years to decide. Indeed, some of these are still in flux. Our attention to these matters and many more put the debates in front of the public and provided information that may not have been available otherwise.

The caucus members were busy at every level -- local, state and national. The third NWPC convention took place Sept. 9-11, 1977, in San Jose, CA. Martha Hodges and I were Wichita delegates. I was so excited I don't even remember the trip or the hotel. Entering the convention center, a mass of energy immediately engulfed us. I know my jaw dropped. There were women everywhere – earnestly conversing, making campaign buttons, selling books and tapes. There were workshops of every kind. During the convention, I met a little keg of dynamite named Barb Mikulski, a congresswoman from Maryland and now in the Senate. She was everywhere, and she was generously sharing information and inviting us to call her anytime.

At lunch one day, I sat beside Garry Trudeau – cartoonist, male feminist and television journalist Jane Pauley's husband. I was in awe of the California fundraiser who talked nonchalantly about events she held on a yacht featuring celebrities. Oh, my. There were speeches from our founding mothers as well as from newcomers. I remember Jill Ruckelshaus' speech most vividly, not the words but the spirit I felt as she spoke. It was a real stem-winder and gave me goose bumps! It was the kind of speech you want to hear from your leaders. Talk about getting the juices flowing. I returned home filled with new enthusiasm, new energy and ready to tackle anything.

Opportunities in the caucus abounded in Wichita. Whatever your particular interest, there was a committee, a task force, seminar or clinic to attend. I served as program chair, Republican liaison, rape task force chair, key committee member for Wichita and, in 1978, I became chairwoman of the WWPC. I remember energy, debate, actions and meetings, meetings, meetings. Our Political Action Committee swung into action that year by adopting the by-laws. We were soon choosing candidates to support with funds, labor, advice and almost anything else they needed.

The next step was asking women to enter the bruising battle of election politics. Numerous women transitioned from the volunteer world to the professional. Nancy Landon Kassebaum, who began as a Maize school board member, won her campaign for U.S. Senate. She represented the state well and became a woman who was asked frequently for her opinions on issues of the day. A woman we saw frequently at every level was Kathleen Sebelius, an advocate for women in the criminal justice system. She became a legislator; insurance commissioner; second woman Kansas governor; and currently serves in the Obama Administration as Health and Human Services secretary.

Notable for long-running state legislative careers are Jo Ann Pottorff, who went from the Wichita School Board to the state legislature, and Belva Ott who also was a long-time state legislator. Ruth Luzzati was instrumental in much of the state legislation that helped us achieve our early goals in the '70s. She provided the expertise needed to establish the Women's Crisis Center, an important haven for battered women and children. These are just a few of the women who made incredible impact on our lives.

The '70s contributed a record number of advancements for women in every arena of life. The laws changed, job interviews changed, our language changed, our insurance changed and how we thought about ourselves changed. We met each challenge, chore and test, and we swept them away to make room for the next needed change. Every time there was a woman or women who stepped up, we stood in support of each effort. Along the way, we met our neighbors, our friends, new people who became friends and even a few famous people. And we found ourselves.

Women Elected to Office in the 1970s
Correne Green

In the 1970s, the Wichita and Sedgwick County women who were elected to offices in Wichita, Sedgwick County, Topeka and Washington D.C. are:

Marie Warden	Sedgwick County Clerk
Dorothy Van Arsdale	Clerk of District Court
Jean Wilkerson	Clerk of Common Pleas Court
Edwana Collins	School District 259
Jo Brown	School District 259
Evelyn Whitcomb	School District 259
Ruth Luzzati	84th State Representative District
Connie Peters	Wichita City Commission
Ruby Tate	School District 259
Sharon Hess	87th State Representative District
Ardena Matlack	93rd State Representative District
Geneva J. Anderson	101st State Representative District
Bette I. McCart	Sedgwick County Register of Deeds
Dorothy K. White	Sedgwick County Clerk
Belva Ott	92nd State Representative District
Elizabeth Donnell	School District 259
Patricia King	School District 259
Jo Ann Pottorff	School District 259
Nancy Landon Kassebaum	U.S. Senator
Joyce Focht	School District 259

Source: Sedgwick County Election Office

The Blonde in the Bikini
Melissa Gregory

And there it was. The billboard loomed over the I-135 interchange at First Street just east of downtown Wichita. You could not miss the gorgeous young woman. She had long, blonde hair, wore a little yellow bikini and big smile, and lounged across the 30-foot expanse. The billboard read: Coleman – Coolers and Jugs.

No, you could not miss it, and the Wichita chapter of the National Organization for Women would not let it go unchallenged. NOW had been loosely organized in Wichita for some time. I was not the first president, but I was the president on this summer day in the late '70s. I drove over to see it after work the day Kathy Klusman had called to tell me about it. There was no mistaking the image, the message, the size of the damn thing. And the blonde in the bikini? Well, the jugs on the billboard were not just something to keep your iced tea cold.

The Coleman Company was an icon. It stood for something in Wichita, and it was pretty much all good -- a local company with a good reputation. Coleman was a nationally recognized brand, and we thought the blonde was probably on display along highways across North America. Momentum for the women's movement at the time was being fueled by conversations among women questioning and challenging the traditional roles they had been assigned.

The general mood in the United States was raucous. We had been in recession through much of the first half of the 1970s. Richard Nixon resigned as president in 1974, and after the war in Vietnam ended in 1975, every topic was open for discussion and challenge. Economic reality put a harsh focus on women in the workplace. Two fronts were clearly defined: first, the rights of women in domestic matters and second, workplace equality. At the time women in the workforce made 59¢ for every dollar earned by a man. The use of a pretty blonde in the little yellow bikini was not unusual or intended to be subliminal. She was just another example of how women were portrayed then. She exemplified an image of women that appeared in advertisements, movies and television of the day.

There were very real barriers to equal employment opportunities, equal pay and advancement. Objectification of women was the norm. Women were challenging assumptions that they were taken care of by men and that they didn't need to support themselves financially. There was no consideration that women could find personal satisfaction and pride in accomplishment in the workplace, let alone contribute to or fully support their families.

Wichita NOW had an annual budget of around $450 at the time. Membership was based on common ground, no dues. We were a spirited group who marched in parades and occasionally picketed. My recall is that the most we had in common was gender and the recognition that this was a time for change. Decisions were based on consensus. We were offended by the billboard and thought other people would be too. This was not complicated. We wanted Coleman to take it down. We thought a good place to start would be for me to write a letter to the company president to let him know that the billboard offended the members of Wichita NOW. We decided to start from our position on the moral high ground. We would decide what our next step would be after we got a response or non-response from the company.

I wrote the letter, citing recent statistics from a book titled *Gender Advertisements* that showed the affect advertising images had on how we view ourselves and others in society, and on our treatment of other people. I respectfully requested that the Coleman Co. remove the offensive billboard. I received a very polite response from the president. He told me he appreciated our point of view, but this billboard was part of their summer marketing campaign, and as a practical matter, they would not take it down. He also told me he had shared the letter with his wife, and she had told him I was right. I responded to him with another letter and told him that, with all due respect, the fact that the billboards were fait accompli was not a good enough reason to leave them in place. I asked him again to please take the billboards down. The billboard was soon replaced by one with another image.

Later that summer I attended the NOW regional conference in Denver with another Wichita NOW member, Donna Meis. In conversation with one of the national board members, I was surprised to hear that the billboards had been brought to their attention as well. The blonde in the bikini had been part of a national advertising campaign. But NOW had many other issues that required its attention and no action was taken. It was noted that the billboards had been taken down, but they didn't know the Wichita chapter had been in contact with the company until I included the letters in my quarterly action report. It was very unusual at the time for a local organization, like Wichita NOW, to correspond with a national corporation. We were simply not that experienced, and our projects tended to be local, personal and hands-on. I can only attribute the decision to start by sending a letter to our unbridled enthusiasm and optimism. I cannot say that the billboard in Wichita or anywhere else was taken down because of the concern we raised.

In recalling this incident, I firmly believe it unlikely this scenario would happen in 2010, as it was resolved with civility, restraint and reason with no threats of lawsuits or boycotts necessary. I think this can be attributed to the fact it was a local conversation. The company headquarters were in Wichita, and the letter had come from the Wichita chapter. The incident also reminded me of many of the good women I knew from those times. I am embarrassed that I cannot recall everyone who was involved by name. Cindy Bell was part of the original group, and she brought in her sister Donna Meis, who brought in Jo Kyle Stevens. Donna and Jo went on to fill leadership roles and expanded the organization. They are both deceased, as is another former president, Joyce Purcell.

Wichita NOW was one of a number of women's organizations that were active in Wichita during the 1970s. Some of the organizations were better organized than NOW and had more specific agendas. Each one attracted and appealed to a different demographic. The members were predominantly white women. NOW was considered to be the most radical and confrontational of the groups, and we were proud of it.

We all came together after Wichita Women's Weekend. When the Wichita Women's Equality Coalition was formed after that weekend, it became the voice for consensus issues and was active for a number of years. There is no question that my experience in Wichita in the 1970s, and the opportunities I had as a member of NOW, challenged me and set me on a path that led to a career I have enjoyed greatly and lifelong friendships that I treasure.

I Think We Have Won

Maxine Duncan Hansen

At the ripe age of 86, my view of the rise of women in society has length, breadth and depth. I think we have won. During the 1950s and '60s women were becoming more visible in public sector roles, both political and economic. And by the 1970s, there were definite signs of new choices for women in our changing world.

Those of us who remained homemakers after our children were grown discovered ways of furthering the role of women in society by offering continued visibility in policy roles and public service. I had served eight years in a local elected office in a Chicago suburb, had been stimulated and challenged by the experience, and was reluctant to give up this newly expanded lifestyle when we moved to Wichita in 1975. At the time we moved, I stood on the threshold of becoming the next state president for the League of Women Voters of Illinois. I had looked forward to fulfilling this challenge.

As it turned out, that was to happen in its own way. I was elected president of the League of Women Voters of Kansas in 1976. This visibility provided a two-year exposure to Kansas state government and a quick immersion in the Kansas political scene. It resulted in an appointment by the governor of Kansas to a four-year term on the Kansas Governmental Ethics Commission. I also received an appointment to serve on the Wichita Urban Renewal Board, a highly controversial issue in conservative Wichita. I was appointed in 1977 and became chair in 1978.

This very visible role in contentious policy questions was followed by an appointment to the Wichita/Sedgwick County Planning Commission in 1981. My very good friend, Margalee Wright, had just been elected mayor of Wichita. She did me no favor. That board consisted of nine other members, all of whom were involved in business and real estate careers. I found myself the lone voice speaking for neighborhood people and issues. In 1983, Mayor Wright appointed me to the executive board of the Private Industry Council where I remained until 1985. My last role in public policy was an unsuccessful bid for the Wichita City Commission.

My public policy roles were visible. Not as visible was my commitment to the quality of life for all women. During my 10 years in Kansas, I served on the YWCA board, and for two years, I volunteered evenings at the Women's Crisis Center for abused women. I served as vice president for the Planned Parenthood board in 1984 and '85 and co-chaired Operation Holiday, the Interfaith Ministries program which provided for the needy at Christmas. Supporting one of my own joys, I served on the Wichita Symphony Society executive board for two years.

This was my journey, providing growth rewards for me personally, but it was much more. It was an opportunity to push for expanded roles for women in all facets of community life. Today's women are not as available for this kind of time commitment. And that is the good news. Today women can define their skills early and pursue their dreams in almost every phase of our society. Sometimes, watching the newsmakers across all fields in our present society, it seems there are more women in prominent roles by the week. Yes, I think we have won.

New Voters in Kansas

Marilyn Harp

Early in the '70s, a transformational event took place in the right-to-vote movement. On July 7, 1971, the 26th Amendment was ratified, changing the voting age from 21 to 18. The unfairness of forcing young men to serve in the military before they were old enough to vote became a focus of youth activism during the Vietnam War.

In 1970 Congress passed an extension of the Voting Rights Act to set the voting age at 18. When that was ruled unconstitutional, because it affected local and state elections, Congress passed and sent to the states the 26th Constitutional Amendment for ratification. The amendment was passed by the required three fourths of the states in just 107 days. This is the fastest ratification process of any amendment. Kansas adopted it as the 14th state, two weeks after it was sent out by Congress. This haste was motivated by the Kansas Legislature's fears of the confusion that could ensue if youth were allowed to vote for president and congressional candidates, but not state and local candidates, in the upcoming 1972 election. Rapid passage was also facilitated by Congress sending the amendment to the states during the spring legislative season, allowing ratification without special sessions.

With the constitutional amendment ratified, the stage was set to convert these newly enfranchised youth into registered voters. I was directly involved in this effort through the Youth Action Council, ostensibly a bipartisan effort, but sponsored by the Sedgwick County Republican Party. Efforts targeted recent high school graduates because we could obtain mailing lists for that group. The time frame for registration was short, since many of this group would be leaving their parent's home for college within a month. I spent many hours during that summer hand addressing invitations to 5,000 youth. Technology, like computerized mailing labels, was not available.

The biggest obstacle was that voters could be registered only by staff of the election commissioner, and that could occur only at the official county office. Because of the interest in efficiently registering this group, the first ever off-site registration event was scheduled for a mid-August Saturday evening in Linwood Park, Wichita. To bring out the young people, a pizza party with live music was planned. A prize of an airline ticket was offered in a drawing for all who registered to vote on that day. The effort was a modest success, getting some young people ready to vote in the November national and local elections.

Nationwide, voter turnout for this group was at its historically highest rate. However, any expectation that voting by this group would change the outcome of an election in Kansas was short-lived. That year, George McGovern was defeated in his bid for president by Richard Nixon, who received 68 percent of the Kansas vote.

I suspect my involvement in registering voters in Wichita led to my lifelong interest in women suffrage issues, and particularly the Kansas aspects of that struggle to pass the 26th Amendment. The motivation of enfranchising draft-eligible men was certainly a reason it passed. The fact that women could not be drafted did not prevent their inclusion in this amendment. That fight was waged by our grandmothers and our great-grandmothers, from 1848-1919, and led to the automatic inclusion of women voters when the age was lowered.

Key Kansas Laws Pertaining to Women's Rights Passed During the 1970s

Victoria Mork

Congress passed the Equal Rights Amendment in March 1972 and, as required by law, sent it to the states for ratification. That same year, the Kansas Legislature ratified the ERA. According to Jim Lawing, who served in the Kansas House of Representatives for District 86 from 1975-77, there was only seven minutes of debate. The ERA would have, if it been ratified, amended the Constitution by declaring that "Equality of rights under the law shall not be denied or abridged ... on account of sex."

In 1868 Kansas criminalized abortions, with an exception to save the life of the woman. The Kansas legislature revised the abortion laws in 1970 to allow for abortions to preserve a woman's life, her physical or mental health, in cases of rape or incest, or when the child would be born with disabilities. Finally in 1973, the year the Supreme Court legalized abortion, state legislatures enacted a large number of fertility-related laws. Abortion continued to be a major focus of the new laws, but not the primary focus as more than a third of new legislation pertained to family planning and maternal and infant health issues.

Women in Kansas were awarded the right to sue for loss of consortium in 1975. This change in the law made it possible for women to have the same privileges as men, allowing recovery of damages for the loss or impairment of "such person" instead of "woman," as the law had previously stated.

Sedgwick County Representative Ruth Luzzati, District 84, served in the Kansas House of Representatives from 1973 through 1986. She blazed trails for Kansas women. Her legislation to provide employment and other services to help homemakers displaced by dissolution of marriage or other loss of family income was passed in 1976. The displaced homemakers law required the secretary of human resources to establish one urban and one rural pilot multipurpose center to provide counseling, training, services and education for displaced homemakers to assist them in becoming gainfully employed. Staff positions were to be filled wherever possible by displaced homemakers. Wichita was the site for the urban center.

One final bit of 1970s legislation occurred in 1976, when a law was passed to ban pay toilets. This practice of pay toilets was especially discriminatory to women, as men had other choices!

Sources: Kansas Session Laws, 1972, page 1431; Kansas Session Laws, 1975, page 686; Kansas Session Laws, 1976, page 664 ; Lawing, Jim; Lawyer, U. of Kansas, J.D., 1965; Kansas House 1975-77

Running on My Husband's Name

Jo Ann Pottorff

After 12 years of serving on the Wichita School Board, my husband, Gary Pottorff, decided not to seek re-election. I was surprised when he told me he wasn't going to run again. I hadn't had any political ambitions, but I decided to go to the school board meeting. As I sat in the meeting on Monday night, the evening before the filing deadline, I made the decision that I would run for the school board. At 10 o'clock the next morning, I filed for the position in the election commissioner's office and prepared a press release. *The Wichita Eagle* story stated that school board president Dr. Gary Pottorff chose not to run for re-election, but his wife, Jo Ann Pottorff, filed just two hours before the noon deadline.

There were 21 candidates running in the 1977 primary. The newspaper had a practice of interviewing candidates running for election, but they didn't interview me for the primary. When I read the endorsements in the newspaper and knew that I hadn't been interviewed, I called the editor and asked why. I was told they thought I would vote on the school board just like my husband. As it turned out, the endorsement wasn't important. The article in the newspaper after the primary election stated that Jo Ann Pottorff, wife of retiring board president Gary Pottorff, took top spot in the primary with 12,852 votes. I received more votes than the two incumbents running for re-election.

One of the radio stations called to asked why I was running on my husband's name. I told them it had been my name for 20 years. A newspaper article at the same time said two school board hopefuls, Jo Ann Pottorff and Elizabeth Donnell (wife of city commissioner Dr. James Donnell), insisted they were running on their own names. When I introduced myself to voters, I always introduced myself as Jo Ann Pottorff, not Mrs. Gary Pottorff, nor did I mention in my campaign literature that I was a former school board member's wife.

I was qualified in my own right to run for the office. I had firsthand experience with the classroom as an elementary teacher near Manhattan, KS, and as a substitute teacher in the Wichita public school system. I also worked with the Cooperative Urban Teacher Education program as their elementary specialist and earned a master's degree in Urban Education from St. Louis University. A letter from a voter said I was talented, attractive and had an "independence of thought." I told voters I was interested in the end product of the school system, particularly in career and special education, parental involvement, and increased state funding.

For the general election, the newspaper still failed to interview me and still didn't endorse me. It endorsed Jerry Lessard, Elizabeth Donnell, Ken Kimbell and Pat King. However, I came in first among the eight candidates and received 20,405 votes, which was 25 percent. The headline in *The Wichita Eagle* on April 6, 1977, the day after the general election, read: "BOE: It's Pottorff, (Don) Miller, King, Kimbell."

Many people contributed my victory to name recognition. However, two years later, an article in *The Wichita Eagle* said, "Jo Ann Pottorff has made a name for herself." People also started asking my husband Gary, "Are you JoAnn's husband?"

The Long March to Equality

Carolyn S. Russell

July 9, 1978, I had little trouble finding the National Mall. I just followed the women dressed in white, many wearing gold or purple sashes. The Mall was packed with thousands of people. It took me 30 minutes to find those from Kansas, but they were there, a small group of about 25. We had gathered to march to the Capitol and let the country know that extending the deadline for ratification of the equal rights amendment was serious business to many American women. We were represented by every state, marching on the anniversary of Alice Paul's death, the woman who authored the ERA more than 56 years ago. A large banner said, "We're here for you, Alice Paul."

The march started at 12:30 p.m. and had been in progress for more than an hour before our Kansas group began to move. Walking in lines of 24 down Constitution Ave., the last in that long mass didn't arrive at the Capitol until 3. It was so hot! The humidity was nearly as high as the temperature. I was starting to feel the symptoms of heat exhaustion, and I had only been there an hour. Still, I wouldn't have wanted to be anywhere else. The pavement was sizzling. Once in a while someone would run to the side and walk barefoot in the grass to cool down or scoop water from a fountain, recovering enough to continue. There were no quitters here, though. The spirit among us was so high and buoyed further with chants: "What do you want? ERA. When do you want it? NOW!"

When we reached the Capitol, people split up to sit, rest and enjoy the speakers. Some went wading in the fountain. They listened to Bella Abzug, Marlo Thomas, Midge Constanza, Jean Stapleton and Ellen Bernstein, among others. I managed to make my way through the crowds and over a couple of stonewalls to stand within 10 feet of Gloria Steinem when she was introduced to the roaring thousands before her. I shot a final roll of film while she was speaking, then turned around and looked at the blanket of more than 90,000 people surrounding me. It was getting late, and I had to leave for the trip home, but it was so difficult to walk away from the crowd of unified women and men who had joined together and demonstrated how strong they could be when they worked together.

Fragments, 1970s

Fern Merrifield Van Gieson

Becoming Aware

I didn't keep what I should have kept. Most I sent on or simply let a name, a paper or a memory slip away. So many names and faces in my thoughts, but with whom I worked on what project I can't always securely say. What I'll share are fragments, possibly already put down more accurately somewhere, but maybe not.

As I recall the essential tools of the volunteer women's movement in the '70s were the telephone, the U.S. Post Office, the bulletin board and 6x4- or 4x3-inch file cards (Please don't misplace, lose or drop). And of course the typewriter and some place to do copying. Coming together, considering different strategies, doing that calling on issues and for candidates, getting those mailings out, feeling frustration, making the legislative contacts, rallying, walking the districts, celebrating in the exhilarating atmosphere of sisterhood.

Much earlier, from experiences and friendships that came to me, I had become aware – though imperfectly from my position of privilege – of the systemic inequality with its associated discrimination, hardship and harm, under which African Americans were suffering in the United States. By 1953, I was joining with others in various efforts toward change.

It seems strange now, but within the comfort of a sheltering, supportive, though patriarchal family, and then with work, family loss and a failing first marriage, I was slow to recognize the systemic inequality of women. I viewed as personal occurrences the negatives that I had observed or experienced. As I opened my eyes to the reality of women's status, the women's rights movement became more and more a learning tool and a cause.

It also helped me to broaden my perspective in other directions. Until Elvira Valenzuela, now Crocker, told me one time about being at age eight the audacious catalyst for a successful effort to open the Garden City municipal swimming pool to Mexican Americans, I was unaware of the extent to which Hispanic people in Kansas suffered the ills of inequality and discrimination. I don't remember the occasion, but I do remember the conversation. And it was through the friendship of lesbian and gay people that I became aware, as I had not been, of the scope of their denied civil rights.

Kansas ratified the Equal Rights Amendment in 1972. I can't say now why I wasn't among those actively working toward that goal. I supported it, but I didn't work for it. Worse, I can't even say who the leaders of that effort were, nor have I been able to locate that information. A terrible thing about ignorance is that you don't know that you are. Sometimes what I may have rejoiced in as a new awareness has turned out to be only a minimal lifting of the ignorance veil. Nothing is simple. Everything is interconnected.

From Growing Awareness to Activism

It was in the election cycle of 1972 that I fully grasped how central to change committed political action is, and how important it is to reconstitute our government to include those who have been systematically kept outside the decision-making framework. Later, as I learned more about congressional and state house governance and the power of the majority, I relinquished my '70s feminist bipartisanship. I then firmly identified my continuing imperative to elect progressive Democratic candidates closest to my political and social philosophy, at every governmental level with my first priority, election of women. Parity is still a distant goal.

As I know what moved me from growing awareness to activism on civil rights issues, I know what moved me from growing awareness to active feminism. It was a speech made by U.S. Rep. Bella Abzug at Wichita State University. She heralded the necessity for women to act politically, to reject governance without input from women, to elect progressive women at every level of government and to pass the Equal Rights Amendment. She noted that she was among the founders of a new bipartisan women's organization, the National Women's Political Caucus and urged that local and state chapters be formed immediately. Rep. Abzug was a dynamic and persuasive speaker, and she had an audience that was fired up to act.

Both the Wichita and Kansas Women's Political Caucuses were founded in 1972. The rush was on to elect women and to speak out on political issues. I was unable to attend the first meeting called by Dorothy Wood, later Belden, to form the Wichita Women's Political Caucus, but was at the next one in the downtown library garden room. Elections were held. Dorothy Wood was elected our first chair, and we began our work. Through the efforts of Dr. Kay Camin of WSU, who was a member of the NWPC National Council as Kansas' representative, the caucus' 1974 National Conference was held in Wichita. I think every Wichita caucus member worked on some phase of that effort.

A continuing focus was electing women to public office, and there were both local and state level bipartisan 1970s successes. Women were appearing in the state legislature and on boards and commissions. Connie Peters, later Kennard, became Wichita's first woman city commissioner. Rep. Ruth Luzzati's extensive background in the League of Women Voters, encyclopedic knowledge and legislative smarts, made her a positive force in the Kansas House for many terms.

In 1976, I became chair of the Kansas Women's Political Caucus with strong support from an active and able board, including Alma Sanford Carter, now Sanford, Annabelle Haupt, Mary Feeley and Martha Hodges from Wichita. KWPC worked to locate and train potential feminist women candidates for state office, as well as campaign managers, and to increase the number of women on appointed state boards, councils and commissions. The state caucus also initiated a bipartisan feminist political action committee, the KWPC PAC, with separate leadership and accounting to research, endorse and provide funds to feminist candidates.

Another emphasis on my part was expansion, both in numbers and size of local caucuses. Our women's rights lobbying project, providing a lobbyist for the broad range of feminist issues in Topeka during the legislative session, was already active under the leadership of Kathleen Sebelius, a KWPC vice-chair for legislative affairs. Periodically throughout the legislative sessions, a legislative bulletin updating and seeking action was sent by mail to all members. Telephone alerts were added in emergencies.

With slowing state ratifications of ERA, an increasingly vocal opposition moved into an active effort aimed at getting state legislatures to rescind ratifications already accomplished. In a speech in June of 1976, Rep. Ruth Wilkin of Topeka said, "I am constantly amazed to discover I am pleading today with the Kansas Legislature not to rescind Kansas' ratification of the Equal Rights Amendment in almost the same words used by this outstanding women over 100 years ago." She then quoted the eloquent feminist, Clarinda Nichols, who had sought to have equal rights for women written into the Kansas Constitution at the time it was written. Feminists worked to strengthen defense of ERA in Kansas. The Wichita Caucus with KWPC and Kansans for the ERA produced a brochure – Why Kansas Should Stay With the ERA – that was distributed across the state. Kansas did not rescind.

In June 1977, less than a month before our Kansas Women's Weekend, part of the U.S. observance of International Women's Year (IWY) mandated by the U.S. Congress, KWPC received an alarming letter from the chair of the Ohio Political Caucus. She warned that the Ohio state conference and a number of other states had been dominated by well organized anti-ERA participants and the result was that votes on both delegates to the National Women's Conference and core resolutions were swept by women's rights opponents.

At KWPC's initiative, an emergency meeting was held of Kansas organizations supporting ERA. Twelve organizations were represented. All agreed to contact their members immediately to re-enforce our previous outreach by stressing again the urgency of getting as many pro-ERA women as possible to the women's weekend of July 15, 16, 17. The result was that delegate slots to the National Women's Conference were split, however all but two of the core resolutions presented by the Kansas IWY Coordinating Committee passed. All votes were very close, foreshadowing the struggles ahead.

Also in 1977, some of us got together at the Wichita YWCA, an incubator for feminist activity and organizations, and considered how our goals could be furthered in Wichita by organizations working together. Out of that meeting the Women's Equality Coalition was launched. Made up of individuals and organizations, WEC worked on a variety of projects.

The same year – still needing three more states – efforts to ratify ERA were stalled with an impending deadline of March 22, 1979. With impetus from the National Organization for Women, Rep. Elizabeth Holtzman introduced an October bill to extend the ERA deadline. In 1978, unsure whether congressional extension votes would come in the current session or in the next, Kansas feminists were trying to cover both possibilities.

KWPC brought U.S. Senate candidates Nancy Landon Kassebaum and Bill Roy together to speak at our state convention in Wichita. The standing-room-only event garnered wide media coverage. The hottest among a number of issues discussed was the ERA extension. Kassebaum stated her support for ERA, but opposition to extension. Roy stated his support of both ERA and extension. She defeated Dr. Roy in the November election, but did not have to vote on extension as it was passed before she was seated in January 1979.

Since my term as KWPC chair was ending, I had agreed as a NOW member to coordinate the National NOW Emergency Extension Project in Kansas. The Wichita chapter of NOW had been formed earlier in the 1960s. I have Polly Miville and Anneke Allen in mind as among the founders. It was reinvigorated in 1974, staying on track for women's rights since then. We acted through local NOW coordinators and KWPC members and other contacts where there was no NOW chapter. Volunteers called those on shared pro-ERA lists providing information and asking that contact be made with Senators Dole and Pearson, urging them to vote for ERA extension.

In a letter to Kansas NOW president Melissa Nachbor (now Gregory), I wrote at the end of the project, "To my knowledge letters and public-opinion telegrams that would not have been sent otherwise did go to the senators as a result of the extension project from Emporia, Hays, Manhattan, around the Oakley area of northwest Kansas, Topeka and Wichita. Certainly the laurels go to Julie Craft who made the Wichita project a successful one."

I am not absolutely sure how our senators finally voted, and I have been unable to find a record of individual votes. However, ERA extension with a new deadline of June 30, 1982, was passed in early October 1978. We had a second chance to get the requisite number of state legislatures to agree to pass the ERA so the U.S. Constitution would specifically guarantee equal rights for women. Still remaining alert to possible rescission attempts in the Kansas Legislature, ERA activities after the extension passed were directed elsewhere. As part of an NWPC project, some teams of WWPC members went to Oklahoma, because that legislature had voted against the first attempt to pass ERA. We were asked to help by pro-ERA state legislative candidates.

One weekend Jan Calderon Yocum and I drove down. Our work there was not memorable, but I do still recall what she told me over that weekend of her childhood as a Mexican migrant farm laborer, its hardships, hard work and discrimination. Another weekend a carload of NOW members drove down to help at the NOW booth at the Oklahoma State Fair. We circulated through the crowds handing out pro-ERA ratification fliers and talking with some fair goers who wanted to talk with us. Sadly, once again the Equal Rights Amendment failed to be ratified.

Kansas NOW Is Continuing

KWPC, WWPC, Women's Equality Coalition and their contributions are now history. But Kansas NOW and Wichita NOW have persevered and are still continuing the pursuit and protection of women's rights. And Kansas NOW is continuing the tradition and necessity of having a feminist lobbyist in Topeka during state legislative sessions on behalf of needed legislative decisions over the broad spectrum of women's issues with email alerts when action is needed. If you haven't already, add your voice.

Weekend Was Eye-Opening;
Needs Retelling in 2002
Peg Vines

For thousands of women, the Kansas Women's Weekend – held in downtown Wichita 25 years ago this week – was the eye-opening political experience of their lifetimes. Can it be that our daughters and granddaughters haven't even heard of it? Each state and territory had been ordered to hold "a public meeting of women of all ages, incomes, races and religions to take a serious look at the status of women and press for changes in policies that obstruct women's equality." It was mandated by Public Law 94-167, an outgrowth of the observance of International Women's Year.

I served on the Kansas committee. Our task was to ensure that participants voted on the resolutions listed on a core agenda ballot, select delegates to the national conference in Houston that November, and create a Kansas plan of action. When we met early in 1977 to plan our statewide meeting, we couldn't have imagined what lay ahead. We hoped for 2,000 registrants, with 1,000 a more realistic total. As it turned out, 4,350 persons attended some aspect of the gatherings held in the Holiday Inn Plaza, Century II and the public library.

Kansas was one of the final three states to meet. We should have realized that some issues on the core agenda had become so controversial that the anti-groups would attend in large numbers and spark confrontations. By July, we had become one of a handful of states targeted by the Mormon Church as part of a highly organized coalition to disrupt sessions by asking continually for points of clarification, points of order, etc. Their plan of action was spelled out in a guide for Operation Wichita.

The opening press briefing on Friday was delayed, because crowds were so dense in the halls that reporters couldn't get through. More registration desks were finally set up as lines grew longer and longer. In addition to planned events, the 36 hours that followed included a lawsuit (resolved by allowing extra observers during the elections), an elevator accident in which nine persons were slightly injured, several people fainting due to air conditioning problems and a call to the calling of local police to disperse a crowd that refused to leave an adjourned session on Alternative Lifestyles.

The Wichita Eagle devoted many columns and photos to the Women's Weekend, naturally headlining "tempers flare" on issues of reproductive rights and the Equal Rights Amendment. But it also ran in-depth reports of the informative workshops on women in crisis, job equality, displaced homemakers, older women and media representation of women.

Friends and foes of the women's movement struggled for the right to speak for the women of Kansas in the general session dealing with resolutions and selection of delegates to the national conference. Eventually, 17 resolutions supporting women's rights were passed, including the ERA; the child care and reproductive-freedom resolutions were closely defeated. A newspaper editorial called it ironic that the ERA resolution was passed while 17 of the 20 delegates selected represented the anti-position, which was likely the result of bloc voting. A headline read: "Both Sides Claim Victory." Some might review the events of that weekend and see only the negative side. Historically, however, it has usually been easier to organize against an issue than in favor of one.

But I ask those of you who were there, and committed to the movement, to elaborate on my tale with a little local-history lesson for your daughters and their friends. Tell them your own war story. But also tell them how that historic, hectic weekend became the impetus to form women's coalitions in Wichita and Topeka, coalitions to keep the spirit of the International Women's Year alive and to advance our rights.

Found Souvenir
Peg Vines

Among my Women's Weekend "souvenirs" was this letter from the brand new Women's Equality Coalition, dated August 27, 1977:

Dear Sister,

On behalf of the members of the Women's Equality Coalition, we want to thank you for your time and effort in making Kansas Women's Weekend happen. It was an enriching experience for us. We were excited to discover many sisters from all over the state and shocked to learn how many people were ready to deny us our rights.

It was because of this experience that the Women's Equality Coalition was formed. As a result of the weekend, we realized the need to coordinate our efforts and the need to be organized. The impetus created at the weekend will not be lost. Individual women and existing organizations will work together through the coalition to disseminate information, share leadership and provide opportunities for women to make considered choices in their lives. In addition, the coalition will work toward strengthening women's positions in society by affecting decisions at local, state and national levels.

We are grateful to you for making Kansas Women's Weekend possible. The sisterhood we discovered and the lessons we learned will be the basis for future action. We owe that to you.

Thank you.

The letter was signed by Judy Jones, Alice Schulte, Dorothy Walters, Melissa A. Nachbar, Joyce L. Hardy, Vicki Catlett-Newby, Sharon F. Poindexter and Correne Green.

Some 1970s Federal Actions Impacting Women's Rights

Diane Wahto

Congress

1970   House holds hearings on sex discrimination in education.
1972   Senate votes to submit Equal Rights Amendment for state ratification.
1974   Equal Opportunity Act stops sex or marital status discrimination.
1976   Hyde Amendment passes Congress.
1977   Congress bars federal funding of elective abortions.
1978   Nancy Landon Kassebaum (R-Ks) becomes a senator.
1978   Congress votes to extend ERA ratification deadline.
1979   Law passes prohibiting discrimination against pregnant or disabled employees.

Supreme Court

1971   Court rules 1964 Civil Rights Act pertains not just to overt discrimination, but also to practices that are fair in form but are also discriminatory in operation.
1972   Court rules unconstitutional to prohibit sale or dispense contraceptives to single persons in Massachusetts.
1973   Court rules an abortion decision is between a woman and her physician (*Roe v. Wade*).
1973   Court rules employment ads cannot state gender.
1975   Court rules Louisiana cannot deny women the right to serve on juries.
1976   Court rules unconstitutional Missouri law that required a husband's consent for a first trimester abortion.
1977   Court rules Medicaid money to fund elective abortions unconstitutional.
1979   Court rules a law requiring a physician to attempt to save the life of a fetus is unconstitutional.
1979   Court rules unconstitutional Massachusetts law that required single underage girls to get permission from parents or a judge before they can have abortions.

President

Nixon administration:

1970   Col. Elizabeth P. Hoisington and Col. Anna Mae Hays are commissioned the first female generals in American history.

1970   President appoints Harry Blackmun to the Supreme Court.

1972   President signs Title IX of the Higher Education Act.

1972   Equal Opportunity Commission (EOC) gains enforcement powers.

Carter Administration:

1976   Patricia Harris, first black woman to serve in the cabinet, appointed Secretary of Housing and Urban Development.

1976   Eleanor Holmes Norton appointed first woman to head U.S. Equal Opportunity Commission.

1977   First woman Secretary of Commerce, Juanita Kreps, sworn in.

1978   Susan B. Anthony silver dollars minted.

1979   Shirley Hufstedler named first Secretary of Education.

Sources: American Chronicle: Seven Decades in American Life, 1920 -1980; Lois Gordon and Alan Gordon. Published by Crown Publisher, Inc., New York,1987.

The Women's Chronology: A Year-By-Year Record, from Prehistory to the Present by James Trager. Published by Henry Holt and Co., New York, 1994.

The Timetables of History: A Horizontal Linkage of People and Events Based on Werner Stein's Kulturfahrplan. Published by Simon and Shuster, New York, 1975.

Kansas Women's Weekend

Margalee Pilkington Wright

"We the people of the United States, in order to form a more perfect Union ... " Those first words of the Preamble to the Constitution capture the purpose of Kansas Women's Weekend. The United Nations International Decade of Women was 1975-1985. Congress requested meetings as an outgrowth of the 1975 International Women's Year Congress in Mexico City. Fifty-six public meetings were funded to allow all American women an opportunity to inform Congress of their concerns. Kansas' share of the national allocation was $26,915, which paid for materials, printing and facilities. The meeting was held in Wichita.

Dr. Kay Camin, dean of the College of Business Administration at Wichita State University, was selected coordinating committee chair by the 45-member Kansas International Women's Year coordinating committee, a group charged with developing a meeting to interest a wide segment of Kansas women. Diane Lewis was vice-chair. Camin said in a June 19, 1977, article in *The Wichita Eagle*, "We are mandated by Congress to talk about what progress we've made, where we want to go, barriers that still exist and recommendations to lesson those barriers." The state meetings were to prepare for a national women's conference Nov. 18-21 in Houston. Delegates to that meeting were to be elected, along with a core agenda of women's issues, in order to find areas of general agreement among American women to include in the report to the president and to Congress.

Kansas was allocated 20 delegates to the Houston conference. The state coordinating committee prepared a slate of 20 candidates to be nominated at Kansas Women's Weekend. According to regulations, it was to be balanced according to age, race or ethnic group, income level and religious affiliation. Anti-Equal Rights Amendment forces also submitted a slate of delegates. Individuals could be nominated from the floor, as well. The eventual election of 13 pro-family delegates from Kansas had little impact in Houston, because they would be outnumbered there at least three to one.

The core agenda included 15 issues: arts and humanities, child care, credit, education, employment, Equal Rights Amendment, female offenders, health, legal status of homemakers, international interdependence, mass media, older women, rape, reproductive freedom and women in elective office. Workshop sessions were organized around the core agenda topics resulting in position statements to be considered during the general session.

Wichita was selected by the coordinating committee as the site for Kansas Women's Weekend because of its size and large number of media outlets. Century II, Holiday Inn Plaza, Broadview Hotel and the Wichita Public Library housed the event July 15-17, 1977. Essential business was to be conducted on Saturday. Registration began Friday, and workshops were held both Friday and Saturday. Sue Horn Estes was registration chair. The coordinating committee felt that a meeting in which women could vote on delegates, recommendations, the core agenda and participate in workshops was in the spirit of the mandate. Twenty regional meetings had been held in April to encourage participation. Registration fee was $2, and proof of Kansas residency was required.

In her final report, Diane Lewis noted that the coordinating committee cautiously hoped for 2,000 registrants. An estimated 4,170 persons attended some aspect of the meeting, which began at noon Friday and ended shortly after midnight Saturday. Kansas, it was learned about 10 days before Kansas Women's Weekend, was one of a handful of states targeted by the Mormon Church. Disruptive tactics were planned by Stop ERA forces, antiabortion foes, the Mormon and Catholic churches, and others. Lewis also noted that during the 36 hours, in addition to the events of the meeting, there was a lawsuit, an elevator accident in which nine persons were slightly injured, several persons fainted, and supplies and materials were depleted within hours after registration opened.

Because of the large crowds, it was impossible to accommodate everyone who wanted to be in a workshop or on the floor with the registered delegates at any one time. The fire marshal worked with organizers to manage the crowds, and doorkeepers created a system that would be fair to all. It was a difficult task. The anti-forces complained that they were slighted at every turn with emotions running high on both sides. Police were called to disperse a crowd that would not leave an adjourned session on Alternative Lifestyles. Pat Storey (Ranson) was presiding officer at the general session, a very difficult task with plenty of parliamentary maneuvers.

It is important to note that Kansas, on March 28, 1972, ratified the Equal Rights Amendment and became one of the 35 states to do so. At the time of Kansas Women's Weekend, three more states were needed for a total of 38 for the amendment to become an official part of the U.S. Constitution. It had been passed by the 92nd Congress on March 22, 1972, and submitted to the states for ratification with a deadline of seven years.

The clock was ticking, and the pro/anti activists were working to gain momentum for their side. The three-section amendment read simply:

> Section 1. Equality of rights under the law shall not be denied or abridged by the United States or by any state on account of sex; Section 2. The Congress shall have the power to enforce, by appropriate legislation, the provisions of this Article; Section 3. This Amendment shall take effect two years after the date of ratification.

The League of Women Voters of Wichita was asked by the coordinating committee to manage the election for delegates and the core agenda ballot. As president of the league, I was responsible for the election process. Gwynne Johnson, past league president, was election judge, and Maxine Longstaff was invaluable to the process.

A voter card received at registration was required to vote, and ballots, voting booths and ballot boxes were on the balcony of Century II above the large meeting space where Saturday's general session was held. Opponents of the ERA were upset that the league was managing the election because the League of Women Voters USA had a position in favor of the ERA. The league had agreed to allow observers, but the number and their placement had not been settled. A lawsuit filed against the Kansas coordinating committee and the league by four anti-ERA women was settled during negotiations before a Sedgwick County District Court judge. The league agreed to all requests for observers, permitting representatives of the anti-ERA groups to observe all aspects of voting and tallying during the election of delegates and the core agenda items. In an effort to accommodate the larger numbers attending the meeting, polls remained open until 10 p.m. on Saturday. No one who wanted to vote was denied the privilege of voting. Counting the ballots was done by league members and lasted all night and into Sunday midmorning.

Phyllis Schlafly was the leader of an organization called Eagle Forum. Its sole purpose was to stop the women's movement and the ERA. Sylvia Turnis led the local effort. These women, along with other anti activists, worked to disrupt the meeting at every turn. Mormon and Catholic men stood at the end of the rows to tell the women how to vote on issues. One of the great fears of the anti-forces was that women and men would be required to share public restrooms. It was quite a sight to see one of these women coming out of the men's room, because waiting lines were so long for the women's restrooms. There were many moments of irony and plenty of bonding between those with similar values. Before the weekend, a number of women's organizations had joined forces to plan for positive action on the ERA and core-ballot issues. This effort proved quite useful in the final analysis.

Gloria Steinem was the invited speaker, another source of contention between the pro- and anti- ERA forces. She was an outspoken leader in the women's movement, and was a member of the National Commission on International Women's Year, which established ratification of ERA as the top priority of American women. She participated in Kansas Women's Weekend all day Saturday and spoke to the general assemble at 7 p.m. Other invited speakers for workshops included Lynn Caine, author of *Widow*, Laurie Shields, national coordinator for the Alliance of Displaced Homemakers, and Josephine Hulett, national field officer for the National Committee of Household Employment.

In a July 10, 1977, an article in *The Wichita Eagle* titled "ERA Time Bomb Ticks Toward Women's Weekend," reporter Carolyn Kortge noted that Kansas was one of the final states to meet prior to the national conference in Houston. In five of the state meetings, Right to Life and anti-ERA representatives won a majority of the seats of the state delegations. Operation Wichita was their statewide plan to make Kansas the sixth state. They introduced at least 10 resolutions against gay rights, abortion and federal funding for day care centers.

Election results were announced at noon Sunday on the patio in front of the Holiday Inn Plaza where more than 1,000 women had been waiting for several hours. Delegates to the Houston conference from Kansas included 13 anti-ERA members from their slate of candidates, a highly organized strategy. The remaining seven delegate spots went to women nominated by the coordinating committee. Several Wichita women paid their own way to Houston as observers, including Peg Vines, Gloria Bonwell, Anneka Allen and Pat Lehman. The ERA resolution had passed the general assembly just after midnight on Saturday with 1,149 in favor and 942 opposed. It was the end of a tense general session on resolutions that lasted more than eight hours.

More than 2,000 Kansas Women's Weekend participants passed 18 resolutions dealing with women's rights that became the Kansas Plan of Action to be distributed to state legislators and the governor. The 20 newly elected delegates would carry them on to Houston. Both sides had won something, and each left with an ever-deeper resolve. The debate on values continues to this day.

In a letter to the editor, *The Wichita Eagle*, July 26, 1977, league member Ruth Richards claimed it was worth it because of the educational value to women. An editorial noted on July 22 that it had been successful and "… the most positive thing of all is that it didn't all end when the last vote was counted and the last participant had gone home. Issues raised, discussions heard, acquaintances made and strategies hatched will be with us for a long time to come."

For me personally, it was the first time ever that my husband had been responsible for our daughters, ages seven and eight, without my assistance. It was an experience of empowerment that moved me deeper into the feminist movement and our quest for equality. The lasting impact, and one that changed my life, was summarized by the quote that adorned the poster side of the program:

"I believe we will have better government in our countries when men and women discuss public issues together and make their decisions on the basis of their differing areas of experience and their common concern for the welfare of their families and their world … Too often the great decisions are originated and given form in bodies made up wholly of men, or so completely dominated by them that whatever of special value women have to offer is shunted aside without expression …." – Eleanor Roosevelt, U.N. General Assembly, December 1952.

Candidate for City Commission – 1979
Margalee Pilkington Wright

"We already have one woman!"
"You have never run a business."
"What about your family responsibilities?"
"What does your husband think?"

Those are the kinds of comments I heard during my run for the Wichita City Commission in the winter of 1979. Having just completed my term during a turbulent time in city politics as president of the League of Women Voters, my women friends suggested that I run for city commission.

The first woman to suggest it was Mary Umansky. I will never forget the feeling I had when she said it, and a few weeks later I began the process. It required an extensive campaign committee, because the race was citywide with the top three candidates being elected. There were 81 candidates in the primary. Family and friends were supportive, and a remarkable campaign organization unfolded with my mother, Dora Pilkington, as volunteer coordinator. I felt an explosion of passion. I wanted to make a difference, to prove that women did have a place in the community's decision-making process. To me it was a matter of simple justice to have equal representation. Walking door-to-door through the deep snow and hearing citizen concerns about our city remains one of my best memories.

I came in fourth on election night. Three businessmen were elected. My feminist perspective became stronger and more deeply etched in my soul because of that race. I resolved to run again. I did, and I won. I also resolved to support women of substance for any public office. And, I have.

Embracing Our Artistic Gifts

"'Creative Kansas Women' was the theme for the performing and producing artists participated in Kansas Women's Weekend Art Show and Sale, July 16-17.

Over 60 artists came from throughout the state to display their creations in oil painting, printmaking, sculpture, watercolor and acrylic painting, pottery, batik, weaving, macrame, drawing, metal sculpture and enamels.

Groups of amateur and professional women participated in poetry reading, ballet and tap, gymnastics, magic shows and musical performances."

—*Equal Time*, August, 1977

"We realized we couldn't keep going to college forever simply because we didn't have a place to show our work when we left the university. We heard there was an artist co-op in Kansas City, MO. There were none in Kansas. We decided an art co-op seemed a good opportunity for women to band together and provide a place to display and sell their work."

—Betty Richards (Gallery XII)

Gallery XII
Betty Richards

Some blame it on the Age of Aquarius. I guess that works as well as anything to explain what happened to the mass consciousness during the '60s and '70s. Equally, a mystery to me is why this hit some of us and completely missed others. By the time I was 40, the life I had been living for the past 18 years had become unbearable to me. I was married to a man of a generation who had been taught to believe that a husband was free to do as he pleased once he made the money and paid all the bills. If the children got in trouble or the house didn't function well, it was entirely the woman's fault. This seemed a belief accepted by most of the women I knew. It didn't appear to bother them that they were second-class citizens. In fact, they didn't even know they were.

I'd never thought of myself as a rebel, always too anxious to please, but for some reason the unfairness of my unappreciated role as a wife, mother and woman became unacceptable to me, and I rebelled. In 1970, I dropped out of bridge club, and quit teaching Sunday school and playing golf, as well as all the other things that had become meaningless to me. I enrolled in art classes at Wichita State. My friends thought I'd lost my mind. My husband emphatically agreed. After all, didn't I know my place was at home?

When I arrived on the WSU campus, it was a hot bed of movements: the antiwar movement, civil rights, gay rights, human potential. The seeds had been sown for the women's liberation movement too, which was to come full blown later in the '70s. It was also a time when some were beginning to question religion in favor of spirituality and exploring Eastern thought. Once on the campus, I met women of a completely different consciousness, women who were no longer willing to play along with the roles society was imposing on them.

A number of the art-major women I associated with were concerned about equal rights for women in the art world. Until this time, the works of women and minorities were rarely displayed in most museums and galleries. A movement had started in the '60s to fight this unfair system, but it wasn't until the '70s that artist co-ops began to appear around the country as an answer. By 1977, Shirley Glickman, Sara Pat Ehrke and I had been taking art classes at WSU for more than seven years. We realized we couldn't keep going to college forever simply because we didn't have a place to show our work when we left the university. We heard there was an artist co-op in Kansas City, MO. There were none in Kansas. We decided an art co-op seemed a good opportunity for women to band together and provide a place to display and sell their work.

The three of us found an old house on East Douglas. It took a little imagination; the house had been many different things, the last being a used record store that had all its walls painted black for some reason. Before inviting other women artists to join, we set up the by-laws and figured the financing so new members would know exactly what they could expect. When considering who to invite, it was equally important that their work be of a high quality and that they be women of like mind who could get along well together. Twelve women soon formed Gallery XII: Barbara Mallonee, Joan Danneberg, Lucinda Foster, Marty Healy, Mickey Leiter, Joyce Schyler, Beth Sifford, Jean Shellito, Joan Ray and the three of us.

We worked together to strip floors and spread white paint over the black walls. Officers were elected, and each woman was given a space to hang her work on a revolving plan so that everyone would have the benefit of the most prominent place during a month of the year. Members were to do all the work, from hanging the walls to sitting the gallery. Working together helped form strong bonds between us. By the grand opening, we all were friends as well as partners.

In spite of our husbands' skepticism about the gallery lasting, "because that many women couldn't possibly get along," 30 years later Gallery XII still thrives. There are now more than 20 members. The women have proved their point, and now admit male members. However, the women are the ones who have kept it alive all these years. The founding 12 women artists knew we were as capable as any man of producing meaningful works of art and that we had the right to have our work seen.

Confessions of a Born-Again Actress
Connie Bohannon Roberts

The creative urge is fragile enough in most of us so that it requires great support. And that is what this article is about. Over the years, I have taken increasing joy in the work with my students. I'm a drama coach. Like for many coaches, the activity itself became so absorbing, so creative, that I no longer did acting myself. I tried, and often succeeded, in creating group support systems for my students within our classrooms. Only recently did I admit I wanted such a support system for myself. However, creating such a system creative endeavor in the arts for the adult woman is hard to come by.

A way to achieve that goal is to begin by asking for the help we need. That's not the whole of it, but it's a big part. As adults who want to see our selves as self-sufficient, it's difficult to say, "I need your encouragement to do this," whether it is paint, dance, act, sing. And sometimes as adults, we are afraid of appearing silly. My first step began in Carol Konek's WSU Office one day last December. It was raining, Christmas was coming and I definitely was not in the Christmas spirit. In fact, I felt immobilized

"You're just suffering from temporary paralysis of the spirit," Carol said. "In fact," she went on, "I'll tell you what happens with me when I feel that way. Usually, I'm repressing some creative energy and when I do that, it turns crazy in me."

"Carol, I think I want to act again. And I think I want to write again. You know, it's been twelve years since I've acted. Six years since I've written."

Carol listened and then she said, "When I'm feeling low, there's something I tell myself to try to liven myself up. I say, 'Carol, I love you.' And 'Carol, you are a wonderful person, and 'Carol, I will never, never leave you.' "

I walked into the December dusk. I was trying to say, "Connie, I love you," but it was weighing heavy on my tongue.

The next week, my friend Dr. Myrliss Hershey talked with me about doing a workshop at a state conference on "Gifted Education." The workshop was to focus on special challenges in tapping creativity in women. As Myrliss and I talked, it became clear that I would begin the workshop by presenting in dramatic form some of the challenges facing women. Then we would divide up into small groups for discussion. Here was the chance for me to act for the first time in a dozen years. I felt almost dizzy with the kind of risk that made me want to hide. But there was Myrliss telling me I would be good.

And later, Mary Jane Teall enthusiastically agreed to coach me, pronouncing, "You will be better than ever. You'll see. You'll be better, because you've experienced more, lived more. Work, wait and see."

Slowly, women began to present themselves to me. The characters included a child, a bride, a housewife, a single mother, a prostitute, a woman in childbirth and an 85-year-old woman. About eight weeks before the conference, I began working with the real-life women who would lead the small group discussions: Wichita high school teachers, Connie Bradley, Cynthia Rutherford and Mary Lashley; WSU faculty, Dr. Carol Konek, Women Studies graduate assistant, Donna Larson, and Sedgwick County Cooperative developer of programs for the gifted, Marian Davis. The women gave me much support as I prepared for the conference.

Finally, the day of the conference arrived, and there I was, opening Off-Off-Broadway in Hutchinson, Kansas at the Holidome. My homemade stage was adorned with Granny's homemade quilt, one of those sewn-by-hand-every-stitch friendship quilts made by her 1938 quilting Bee in Putman County, Missouri. Like Linus and with his blanket, I felt more secure performing on that quilt. It seemed to have a symbolic importance, because the women I was portraying formed a kind of emotional patchwork. "A celebration of creativity," Myrliss called it, "featuring prose and poetry, which portray the pathos significance of women's roles."

A number of men at our workshop surprised me with their feeling and understanding. I realize that statement sounds like inverse chauvinism. I had thought my presentation would be understood primarily by women.

Chuck Thompson, coordinator of social studies for Wichita Public Schools said, "I think that global discrimination against women is more subtle and pervasive than any discrimination leveled against a minority group. I don't know how intelligent women deal with this. They must sublimate a hell of a lot. Rationalize. ... I think the greatest enemy of women is simply other women who carry a limited view of their own humanity. Those women will try to repress those in their own group, much as some slaves suppressed those among their number who decided they wanted to be a human being."

The workshop was done with the idea of learning to tap creativity in our female students. Maybe we women have to start with ourselves. I don't ever want to hide under Granny's quilt again "in a temporary paralysis of the spirit." Rather, I want to use Granny's quilt as a trampoline – to leap high, to stretch, to reach out. To rejoice!

"Women's Art;" Whatever That Is[1]

Novelene G. Ross

In 1974, the Wichita Art Museum organized *Mr. Godey's Ladies Revisited*,[2] June 25-July 21, one of the earliest museum exhibitions devoted exclusively to contemporary women artists. Museum staff conceived the project in response to the momentous news that Wichita was to host a three-day meeting – June 28-30 – of the National Women's Political Caucus. Moreover the local conference organizers had arranged for the museum to host an evening reception for the delegates.

The roster of special guests encompassed many of the individuals who were to become the popular culture icons of the feminist movement such as Gloria Steinem, who had founded the National Women's Political Caucus in New York just two years earlier; New York Democratic Congresswoman Bella Abzug; and Frances (Sissy) Farenthold, national chair of the National Women's Political Caucus. Also among the celebrities was liberal cartoonist celebrity Garry Trudeau, creator of the syndicated comic strip "Doonsbury" that had introduced a feminist character call Joanie Caucus. Additional national and local political luminaries were Olga Mader, representing the Coalition of Labor Union Women; Mary Louise Smith, co-chairperson of the Republican National Committee; Kansas Gov. Robert Docking; and Wichita Mayor Garry Porter.[3]

I was three or four months into my new, full-time position as curator of education at the museum, when *The Wichita Eagle* reporter, Dorothy Wood Belden, called me to ask if the museum was going to do anything special for the upcoming caucus reception. First it flustered me to receive a call from a woman that I considered to be a celebrity on the order of Brenda Starr, a popular comic strip character styled as both a top reporter and a femme fatale,[4] and I knew nothing at all about the NWPC. All I knew was that I wanted to please Belden. After conferring with George Vollmer,[5] then acting museum director, we decided it would be appropriate to the honor of hosting the event, and to the museum's mission, to organize an exhibition of women artists from Kansas. Since the museum did not have a curator of collections/exhibitions at the time, I eagerly volunteered to undertake this project.

It was our policy to design special exhibitions, whenever possible, to reflect upon the WAM permanent collections. Recently we had been mounting shows from the lesser-known collections in our permanent holdings. As part of this effort, we had just presented an exhibition of Americana that included fashion plates from the 19th century American women's magazine *Godey's Lady's Book*. Research for that collections' exhibit prompted the choice of the title for the assemblage of current works by women artists. The title of *Mr. Godey's Ladies Revisited* emphasized contemporary artists' rejection of the roles as ornamental subject, consumer and cheap labor allotted to women in the past, as exemplified by the bustled and corseted fashions of the 19th century. It also asserted that the current feminist demand to the hard-won achievements of the arts professions' suffragettes.

In particular, the exhibition title meant to reference the hundreds of women that journal publishers, such as Louis A. Godey, employed in the days before color lithography and photography, to work in an assembly line, hand water coloring every fashion plate illustration in the total run of each issue. More importantly, however, the title referenced the pioneering vision of feminist and distinguished journalist Sarah Josepha Hale.[6] Hale edited *Godey's* from 1837 to 1877, raising the subscription rate from 10,000 to 40,000 in two years, and to an impressive peak of 150,000 by 1860, publishing original manuscripts by American authors and devoting several issues exclusively to women writers.

Having been active in the Kansas arts community as a studio arts and art history major at Wichita State University, as a lecturer and now as a WAM staffer, one of whose duties was to organize monthly art sale exhibitions for the museum's sales and rental gallery,[7] I had many contemporary artist contacts. I immediately began calling everyone I knew to in order to gather names and conduct studio visits. Most of the exhibitors were Wichita artists, but we were able to include outstanding women artists from other Kansas college towns, including El Dorado, Hays, Lawrence, Manhattan, Topeka and Winfield.

We assembled 62 objects of diverse media – paintings, graphics, sculpture, fiber and ceramics – from 23 artists, most of whom were graduates of university art schools or current art department faculty at Kansas colleges and universities. Looking at the range of styles and the competence of individual works in retrospect, I would say that the schools had done their job. The work on display reflected a professional level of craft and a sophisticated knowledge of the imagery and techniques practiced in the art centers on the coasts.

What distinguished *Mr. Godey's Ladies Revisited* from the look of a show one would have gotten had the exhibitors all been male was the emergence of aggressively feminine objects, artworks that asserted identification with the stereotypes of "women's work," "romantic sentimentalism" or "earth motherhood" by means of the traditionally feminine associations of their materials, hand skills and imagery. A particularly baroque example of the latter was Ranel Harrell's stuffed pink satin *Heart*. This sculptural wall piece fairly swooned with wet emotion under the influence of stiffened lace rising and falling in agitated rivulets around the heart's puffy bosom, itself weighted down by a withered bouquet crying in slender drips of yellow ribbon, and winking back sequined tears. Harrell's *Heart* is a classic of its kind. In her subsequent art, she elaborated upon her delight in obsessively detailed, anxiously precious collages of small found objects that emitted intimate and visceral associations with women's lives.

Judith Burns is another artist represented in the exhibition whose personal vision resonated with various themes of the feminist movement. Burns' perception of the dominant sexual power inherent in the female body might have been the most subversive assertion in this exhibition. In the first look at her image, *Nude on a Tapa I*, the viewer might see her pastel rendering of a female model, reclining on a cloth draped over the studio floor, to be a decorative interpretation of the traditional academic nude, the latter convention denounced by feminist art historians as the "male view" or the fantasy conceived by male painters designed to appeal to male delectation of a sexual object. A viewer might indeed need to see more than one of Burns' many depictions of the female nude, executed during this period and over the subsequent course of her career, to perceive the subtle insinuations of what the early 20th century moderns called *élan vital*, or the secret inner essence of being.

In this work Burns' bird's-eye rendering of a muscular body, lush with rosy color and sudden swells of fat, slowly curves and angles its way across the space of the canvas in a serpentine embrace of the blankets and floor beneath her – a background that in Burns' rose, green and brown tones and expressionistic marking, conjures up the suggestion of a garden floor. Yes, it is the male conception of that old devil-woman Eve, but here woman willingly adopts the long-despised persona of Eve, luxuriantly exercising her effortless power of being.

At the time, I remarked to reporter Belden that I didn't think any of the artworks in *Mr. Godey's Ladies Revisited* were avant-garde. However, upon reflection, I would say that the exhibit's gender-oriented pieces were cutting-edge statements, mature realizations of the ideas and yearnings of an era as experienced within a particular moment. The idea of flaunting taboo or denigrated subjects and sentiments in face of the worldly "art czars" was as modernist as Manet, but the gender content was definitely new. It expressed the edginess of the early 1970s in the U.S. at the moment when the revolution was just spreading from an awakened few to young women on campuses everywhere who were meeting to explore the symbols and symptoms of oppression in consciousness-raising sessions. Looking back, I can see that the gender-themed pieces shown at the Wichita Art Museum in 1974 were every bit as advanced as artworks of similar intent then emerging on campuses and in galleries around the nation.

Donald Mrozek, art writer for the *Manhattan Mercury*, voiced the objection raised by all the critics of the period – most all of them male, but also by some women artists – that the claim of women to offer a gender-specific contribution to art production undermined their demand for equal recognition of their creative potential. He argued that if women persisted in employing such stereotypically feminine media as sewing, or domestic imagery such as aprons, fans, etc., they ran the risk of ghettoizing their art.[8] The critic's dire predictions did not come to pass. From the 1970s on, women entered the studio professions in ever greater numbers, some pursuing themes shared by men and women, others exploring women's particular experiences in the world -- all of them successfully embroidering the richness of our understanding of the human story.

1 Partial title of a preview of the WAM exhibition by Donald Mrozek, art critic for the Manhattan Mercury, i.e., "'Women's Art,' Whatever That Is, debuts in Wichita display," Manhattan Mercury, June 16, 1974. (In the WAM archives)

2 References for this exhibition include the WAM's exhibition archives that contain a full catalogue inventory of the artists participating, objects displayed, partial documentary photographs, printed brochure and press clippings, among the latter a review of the exhibition in The Wichita Eagle and Beacon Sunday magazine, "Women's Art Displayed," Modern Living section , June 30, 1974.

3 Most of the information about the 1974 meeting of the National Women's Political Caucus in Wichita derives from an unsigned news item in *The Wichita Eagle*, "Women's Political Caucus Opens Today," Friday, June 28, 1974, was one of the press clippings held in the WAM's exhibition archive file. For additional firsthand information I interviewed Wichita civil rights/feminist activist Fern Van Gieson. She graciously volunteered to contact the NY office of the National Women's Political Caucus and to obtain a contact for the NWPC archives (that I have not yet followed up). I also spoke with Nan Porter, Colleen Kelly-Johnston and Peg Vines. The latter had the honor of meeting Bella Abzug at the Wichita Airport and driving her to the conference. Vines said Mrs. Abzug proved to be a firm commander, brushing aside the instructions the Wichita coordinator had given Vines and demanding to be taken first to her hotel, before being driven to the conference.

4 Dorothy Belden would have whooped with laughter, or else scolded me, if she had known of my misguided romantic ideal of her and her struggles in the journalism profession. Well, Belden did have red hair like Brenda Starr, and I was right to admire her leadership. Dorothy's character and talents inspired many. Following a difficult first marriage and divorce in the 1940s, she shouldered the responsibilities of three daughters and entered the male world of the newspaper business. Her subsequent 45-year career in journalism encompassed the positions of TV/movie critic, art writer, copy editor and Sunday magazine editor for The Wichita Eagle. In the 1970s she emerged as a fiery civil rights advocate – unsuccessfully attempting to organize a newsroom union, successfully promoting women's rights by suing the newspaper for equal pay, joining the National Women's Political Caucus and being elected chair of the Wichita delegation, Upon retirement from the paper in 1980, she took up teaching and the cause of aging. She earned a master's degree in gerontology at WSU, and then assumed the editorship of the local paper Active Aging which she elevated to a professional publication and through which she recruited and honed numerous young journalism students into professionals. After her death from cancer at age 76 in 1999, her protégés and admirers dedicated a brick engraved with her name to the Plaza of Heroines at WSU. The following references about Dorothy Belden were graciously provided to me by Rhonda Holman, Wichita Eagle editorial staff writer: Shannon Littlejohn, "One of the Real Heroines Among Us," Opinion section, Sept. 24, 1999; Travis D. Lenkner, "Activist, Newspaper Editor Dies at 76," obituary, July 25, 1999; Margaret Allen, "Belden Lets Go of Career But Not of Beliefs," feature article, Nov. 26, 1989; Jennifer Comes, "Teaching, Learning Always Part of Dorothy Belden's Life," editorial section, June 20, 1988.

5 George Vollmer's favorite memory of the event occurred during the museum's evening reception when he found himself seated on a gold-upholstered sofa in the director's office (a souvenir of the more baroque tastes of a previous occupant). The space served as the "green room" for the evening's special guests. He joined royalty, squeezed as he was between the statuesque figure of Steinem and the fleshy Abzug, wearing one of her magnificent signature picture hats.

6 See Ruth E. Finley, *The Lady of Godey's: Sarah Josepha Hale* (J. B. Lippincott Co., 1931) for the story of Sarah Hale's amazing history as a fighter for progressive social policy and for recognition of the artistic validity of American talent as opposed to the slavish adulation of European writers and artists. Louis A. Godey can be credited with the courage and wit to abandon the then common practice of American publishers to simply pirate the writings of English and European journals for reproduction in their own publications, and to instead hire American writers to produce original manuscripts and to pay them a good fee to do it. Godey, a marketing genius who recognized talent when he saw it, succeeded in hiring Ms. Hale away from the journal she had inaugurated on her own called the *Ladies' Magazine*, in which she had already begun to solicit American writers to produce subjects specifically of interest to American readers.

7 It was common in the 1960s and '70s for museums to operate a sales gallery as a revenue source, and as a service to local artists because private art galleries were almost nonexistent in Midwestern cities.

8 Mrozek, op.cit.

Kansas Contralto

Myrna Paris, As told to Marilynn Gump

Contralto Myrna Paris credits Kansas roots for her brilliant career in a difficult, competitive field. "I'm proud to have grown up in Kansas. I got a great education ... and I don't think Kansas is as conservative as people think. There's a lot of blue in that red state," Myrna said in an interview from her home in Pittsburgh, PA, where she has lived since 1976. "There are plenty of good, open people out there." She admits that being in the artistic community may have skewed her perception. "Theater is just different. They've always accepted all types ... blacks, gays, women, Asians ... it's about who you are, not what you are."

She has sung leading roles in opera and musical theater all over the country, including twelve stints at New York City Opera. Among her most acclaimed vehicles are *Sweeney Todd, The Ballad of Baby Doe,* and numerous Gilbert and Sullivan, including *The Mikado* and *The Pirates of Penzance.*

She grew up in the vanguard of the baby boomer generation, born right after World War II. As we entered early adulthood, the traditional values and assumptions we had grown up with were violently shaken. Out went pantyhose and bras; out went our primary identification as future wives and mothers. In came war protests, civil rights movements and the promise/expectation of lives in the work force.

"My first, real sense of empowerment came through my sorority. I was a Tri-Delta; we were known as the smart girls, the overachievers. The sorority was trying to teach us how to be empowered. I guess it worked better than they intended, because in my junior year I dropped out when I realized they were racist."

Myrna had entered Wichita State University planning to major in journalism. She says the department at that time was just terrible. There were two male professors, who couldn't stand each other. One of them started a rumor that Myrna was having an affair with the other one.

"I got called into the dean's office," she says. "I wore this beautiful, yellow sweater set, a skirt, heels, my Tri-Delta pin. I convinced him the whole thing was ridiculous -- which it was! I guess that was my feminist awakening; it was like, okay, men can throw anything they want at you." The experience led to her transfer to the School of Music, with a double major in voice and music education. She became smitten with the theater department and wanted to take classes there, as well.

"The music people were like, 'We don't require you to take theater classes,' and 'you've fulfilled your requirements.' They just didn't get it that I wanted to take those classes. We were so lucky at WSU to have Dick Welsbacher, Audrey Needles and Joyce Cavarozzi. They were all into non-traditional casting, and they were so supportive and encouraging to their students."

Part of Myrna's success in opera has been due to her acting abilities, skills that many singers just don't have. They may have great voices, but they can't create characters. Myrna's expertise in both has increased her reputation and her value to casting directors. During her career at WSU, Myrna caught the attention of Jim Miller, then director of Music Theatre of Wichita. He used her in four productions, including a much-lauded portrayal of Dulcinea in *Man of la Mancha*. Outside the theater world, gender equality wasn't quite as prevalent. In 1970, when Myrna graduated college, the newspaper still listed jobs in the classified ads as: "Help wanted – male" and "Help wanted – female." She auditioned for a job as soloist at First Methodist Church. She knew the man who was bass soloist there, and he told her he made $100 per month. Myrna was offered the job of mezzo for $60 per month. "I said that I knew the bass made $100. They said, 'Oh, we never pay our women what we pay our men.' I couldn't believe they just said that right to my face. Couldn't they at least lied and said, 'Oh, you know, budget constraints'?"

She declined the position, much to her mother's (a devoted Methodist) outrage and dismay. She took, instead, a production job at a start-up alternative publication, *The New Newspaper*, edited by Barry Paris. "He paid everybody exactly the same – $75 a week. Reporters, production people, men, women, everybody got the same amount. Of course, that was for working about 14 hours a day."

At the time, Myrna was in a dying marriage to another musician. As that relationship burned out, she started one with Barry, whom she married in 1975. Within a year, they had a baby girl, delivered by the only female ob-gyn in Kansas, Dr. Ruth Petterson.

"She was wonderful," Myrna recalls. "She talked me into taking Lamaze, and she was so encouraging. 'Oh, you've got big hips; you'll be fine,' she told me. She delivered babies barefoot, just in the surgical booties. She said, 'I've ruined so many shoes.' "

The family moved to Pittsburgh, where Barry had a job on the local newspaper. It was there that Myrna found the first of what she considers two big breaks in her career: meeting Robert Page, who at the time was head of music at Carnegie-Mellon University.

"His wife and I both got solos in the Bach Choir, and we just hit it off. She asked her husband if he'd take me on as a student. He told her wasn't taking any more students, but she said, 'You'll want to take her'. So he deigned to allow me to come over one night and sing for him. We've been together for 32 years. They call me their third daughter, and I call my whole career the 'Robert Page ripple effect.' He's recommended me for so many things. He got me the audition in Kansas City for my first *Sweeney Todd*, which was a big deal, because I wasn't what they call 'managed'." *Sweeney Todd* went on to be a pay-the-bills role for Myrna, as she repeated the role many times around the country.

The second break for Myrna was being cast as Mama McCourt in *The Ballad of Baby Doe*, in the 1994 season at Central City, CO. *Baby Doe* hadn't been produced in many years. "The money wasn't very good," Myrna said, "but the carrot on the stick was that they were going to do a cast recording." Back in Pittsburgh, Myrna had an out-of-the-blue call from New York City Opera asking her if she'd audition for the Mama McCourt role.

"When I answered the phone, I thought it was a telemarketer," she laughed. "They asked if I could come in the next day. I'm, like, uh, could we do it maybe middle of next week? But it had to be the next day, so I drove through a pounding rainstorm to New York. They were kind of rude, kind of dismissive, and I thought about what a fool I had been to go to such an effort for nothing." But get the role she did, and she continued to work in New York almost every season, until the management changed and her contacts were ousted.

Myrna has also sung in Wichita productions several times. She was in Music Theater's *Phantom of the Opera* in the 2005 season. She praises the director, Wayne Bryan for his fairness and directness with the performers he casts. "I have so much respect for him." She also has done two roles with Wichita Grand Opera, both in 2008: *Pirates of Penzance*, and *Faust*, with her old pal from WSU, Sam Ramey. "The last time we had performed together was in 1968," Myrna said. "It was our fortieth anniversary."

Today, Myrna teaches private students and occasionally takes a temporary teaching position in university music departments. She says the young women take for granted things like equal pay that was so dearly paid for back in the day. "They have no idea," she says. "They take it totally for granted that they'll be treated fairly."

Facing Crimes of Violence Against Women

"On August 18, 1976 … the Wichita Women's Center opened. Carolyn Conley was CSW president at the time. The center operated a 24-hour hotline for counseling and referrals, and also provided living space for five residents. Within months, added bed space allowed residency for up to 12 women and children. It took us about a year to realize that the overwhelming need was to serve abused women solely."

    —Peg Vines, (We Were Midwives at the Birth of the Women's (Crisis) Center)

"The time of night, the victim's previous history of 'giving away' what had been taken by force, the clothing – all of these are held against the victim. Society's posture on rape and the manifestation of that posture in courts help account for the fact that so few rapes are reported."

    —Wichita Area Rape Center Newsletter, circa 1978

We Helped Battered Women

Carolyn Patton Conley

In 1974, the Wichita City Commission voted to establish the Commission on the Status of Women. I knew after what I had been through that I needed to be a part of that commission so I could begin to help other women gain some rights and equality. It was an amazing experience for me. Up until that time, the majority of the women I knew, especially socially, were either secretaries or the wives of male friends and associates. These women were nice, but didn't have any real interests other than children (which I didn't have), movies and gossip magazines. I was amazed, thrilled and overjoyed to finally be in a room full of women who were interesting, interested in what was going on and who wanted to do something about it. Many of these women remain friends today.

While on the commission, I took a stack of magazines on vacation to catch up on some reading. One of the articles I read was about a woman who had run away from home and hidden in a neighbor's garage to avoid being beaten by her husband. I was shocked. I must have grown up in a sheltered environment, because I had no idea such things happened. I almost wrote the article off as a piece of sensationalism, until I remembered it was in a highly respected magazine -- not an exposé one. It made me realize that if a well-known magazine wrote about a women being beaten (it was in the "My Problem, and How I Solved It" section), there must be others living in the same dire situation. I knew something had to be done to help these women.

I could hardly wait to get home and call my friend, Myrne Roe, who was currently president of the commission. When I got back to work, there was a message from Myrne asking me to attend a meeting, which I had missed due to my vacation. I called Myrne, excited to share my idea, but she was excited too. I let her go first, and she told me the commission had an opportunity to apply for a grant to help victims of domestic violence. Then she asked what my news was. I'm sure she was surprised when I told her that I had just learned about domestic violence and thought we should do something about it. As a result of that grant, the YWCA Women's Crisis Center was formed. At first, the YWCA board was not so sure that Wichita needed a shelter for displaced women and children, but in the middle of our discussions, the newspaper reported that two women from Oregon and their children had been found in Wichita living under a bridge near downtown. By the time the first shelter was ready to open, I was president of the CSW.

On the day the furniture was to be delivered, the shelter manager and I sat on the curb waiting for the trucks. Up walked a very bedraggled woman carrying a pillowcase with all her possessions. She had been locked out of her apartment after moving from Pennsylvania with her boyfriend. A social service agency had told her about the new shelter and had given her a dollar voucher for food. We explained to her that there was no furniture, and we would not actually open until the next day.

"I'll sleep on the floor and share my voucher with anyone else who comes tonight if you will let me stay," she pleaded. And so we were in business.

Life Without Parole

Jolene M. Grabill

The Attack

Monday, Dec. 19, 1977, I arrived home about 6:30 p.m. after doing a little Christmas shopping downtown with my mother. The only couch I had was a small love seat, so I grabbed a blanket and cuddled up on the living room floor to watch my 10-inch black and white television. Sleep ensued. Around 7:15 p.m., I was awakened by a tall, black stranger hovering over me with the quilt from my bed.

Today, 34 years later, I am still working through emotional scars from what happened next. He had crawled through my bedroom window to do me harm. His violent attack lasted less than 30 minutes, but in truth, it's lasted more than 30 years. In 2008 the Kansas Department of Corrections notified me that my attacker died in prison of natural causes. His struggle was over, but I continue to serve a life sentence, without parole.

I am convinced of two things: The first is that if it had been my sister on that floor instead of me, she would not have survived. I fought nuclear weapons; she married an Air Force guy that refueled them. We are night and day. I'd bet my savings she has never uttered the phrase "consciousness-raising," let alone attend such a gathering. Secondly, I am convinced my then short history in the women's movement saved my life that night. As the attack unfolded, all the lessons I learned from consciousness-raising groups, feminist workshops and personal safety conversations with friends came into sharp focus.

The intruder bound and gagged me with items he had scavenged from my bedroom and clothes hamper. My favorite peasant blouse became a gag stuffed down my throat, and curtain ties bound the quilt around my feet. My struggles against such restraints proved futile. His cruelty continued as he brutally raped and sodomized me. Over and over. Time and my thought process slowed as I lost access to oxygen. Even in my dizzy state, I realized one thing was clear: To survive, I needed a plan. That's when the women's movement came to my rescue.

Systematically I tried each specific strategy for dealing with an attacker I could recall, and systematically my attacker tightened the ties binding my mouth, throat and hands in response. His swift firm tightening tugs made it progressively harder for me to breathe. The gag muffled my attempts to scream before sound could leave my throat. My kick to his groin grazed only his lower leg. He clearly had the physical upper hand, and I was running out of oxygen. Even so, the sound of his words lived in my head for years, "You wanna die? I'm gonna make you die." Clearly, he was unaware how close to death I already was. Soon, only the final survival strategy remained: "If all else fails, play dead." Upon that realization, I made a conscious decision to slow my labored breathing (gasping, really, by that time) and play dead. His abuse continued as I quieted my breaths.

Even now I am horrified to read the police notes of my own account of his actions. He was brutal and relentless. Worse yet, he was skilled. In the early minutes of the attack he held my head to the floor and gruffly whispered in my ear, "You're gonna be a tough one, aren't you?" I was not his first victim. I knew the attacker believed I was dead as I felt him covering my body head to toe with the afghan off the love seat, an odd act of humanity given the circumstance. I heard him rummage through the desk drawers near my feet, followed by the sound of the back door closing. A welcome silence followed. Still, I lay frozen in fear of his return.

The Vision

What happened next will be difficult for some to believe; yet I can remember it like it was yesterday. I was floating in the air above my own body looking down. Instead of accepting the sight of my bruised and still partially bound body, my mind substituted a memory of a horrifying image I'd seen in a *Ms. Magazine* story about abortion. It was a black and white picture of a woman laying face down, naked and bloody, dead of a botched abortion. I struggled to reconcile what had just happened to me with the finality of this magazine image, which my subconscious mind obviously thought would be less painful than the sight of my immediate terror. I specifically remember telling myself, "No, that's not you. That doesn't have to be you!" It was the second time that night I made a conscious decision to live.

By that time, it seemed clear the attacker would not return. I struggled to stand up and go for help. This took a couple tries, given my light-headedness, but soon I was sitting on my neighbor's couch as she called the police and the rape crisis center.

Recovery and Criminal Justice Intertwine

Police discovered the attacker had stolen $10 and my car. My missing car key chain also had keys to my parents' house. I couldn't avoid alerting them to call the police should my stolen car show up in their driveway. I assured them I was okay and that I would be over in the morning. Unfortunately, they learned of the attack through a 6 a.m. phone call from a friend who had heard my name broadcast as a rape victim on a morning radio show reporting the overnight police blotter.

I returned to the apartment only once to move out. By New Year's Eve, I was able to stop wearing sunglasses to cover the broken blood vessels in my eyes and face. I resumed functioning and took a job at Legal Aid, even though my car was still missing – leaving me feeling particularly exposed and continually violated. One day, during this time, I found myself seeking the security of the only place in Wichita designed to be totally safe. I sat on a couch at the Women's Crisis Center for 45 minutes between work meetings. That was the first clue that my emotional recovery would prove more difficult than I anticipated.

Over the next months, I met with police detectives on a regular basis, participated in two police lineups and allowed myself to be hypnotized, all without success. The hypnotism was particularly disappointing. It almost worked, but just as my mind started to allow details of my attacker's face to come into focus, his head rolled away like a TV test pattern with a lost signal. I was now seeing a therapist on a regular basis.

The man who attacked me eventually bragged about killing two women to a co-worker who happened to be a police informant. The first murder victim he described was 65-year-old Marion O'Leary. The other one was me. This confession ultimately led to his capture and trial for O'Leary's murder and for the rape and/or sodomy of me and six other women. Even though I knew I wasn't his first victim among this group, chronologically I was the first victim. With the exception of O'Leary, of course, we all did our part during the trial. Our attacker, Harold Kidd, went to prison. He eventually pled "no contest" to 23 counts and received 10 prison sentences, two of them for life. My car was eventually found abandoned only two blocks from O'Leary's apartment.

Among the other victims was a second older woman, Margaret Hutchinson, who lived alone just north of downtown. Margaret and I sat next to each other while waiting to testify at the preliminary hearing. I can recall her round, yet withdrawn, wrinkled 80-year-old face telling me how sad she was that her attacker stole her wedding ring. Only later did I learn she had also been raped, but was unable to acknowledge it.

That kind soul died between the preliminary hearing and the trial, a common occurrence I learned, in older rape victims. In my mind, Margaret was actually Kidd's second murder victim.

Every Woman Has a Story

To my knowledge, after the trial I was the only one of Kidd's victims to speak publicly about sexual assault or the specifics of our case. Speaking out was one way I could pay back the women's movement for saving my life. It was also a good way for me to reclaim my life and my own personal power. My first public act was to write an article for Wichita's short-lived feminist newspaper *Equal Time.* "It Happened to Someone You Know" appeared in the February 1978 edition. Opposite my article was a companion piece written by my friend, Linda Gebert.

Gebert opened with this line: "Rape is the ultimate violation of the self, short of homicide, and is an act of violence and humiliation in which not only is the victim's very existence threatened and her inner and most private space invaded, but her autonomy and self-control are totally demolished," thus spake Dr. Elaine Hilberman. I had no idea when I first read those words how true they were, and how many years I would work to rebuild what my attacker took from me.

I did know that every time I spoke to a group about sexual assault I felt stronger. I would face each new audience knowing I was looking into the eyes of several future victims, and hoping that my remarks would better prepare at least one of them to survive the ordeal. There were also calls and unexpected knocks on my door from still traumatized rape victims sent by a friend of a friend who knew I could handle hearing that victim's story when they could not. I was a safe place for victims to land and tell their stories.

I learned an ugly secret in those days. Almost every woman has a story of violation. If not a personal story, she has one about someone close – a daughter, a sister or a friend. Though whispered between women in safe corners and discussed at feminist gatherings, many of these stories go unreported. Each time life calls out my identity as a rape survivor, I hear these stories still. They color our souls.

Kansas Parole Board

By far the most crucial telling of my story happened in front of the Kansas Parole Board. Three times I appeared before members of the board to speak against Harold Kidd's parole. Fearful of having to face members of his family if I appeared in Wichita, I testified each time in Topeka.

At the first appearance, I was flanked by four friends who sat at my side and held my hands while I testified through my tears. We were so afraid of possible retribution by the offender's friends or family, one of my friends talked with the media so my name would not appear in stories about the hearing. That was 1993, when Kansas law allowed the board to deny parole for a maximum of three years. I couldn't imagine going through the process every three years for the rest of my life, let alone asking my friends to endure it so frequently. Thankfully by the time I was back in front of the board in 1996, a new law allowed a 10-year pass that was enacted partly in recognition that asking victims to relive their experience every three years was too much. I made one of their first appearances under the new law.

In 2006 I told the board that, although the actual attack lasted only minutes, it continued to shape every day of my life: "What is certain is that Harold W. Kidd gave me a life sentence on Dec. 19, 1977. I've been tough. I've been a survivor. But to this day, I still stay up far too late at night, convinced if I'm awake it will be harder for someone to surprise and hurt me ... "

About 16 years after the attack I was diagnosed with Post Traumatic Stress Disorder. To learn more about that diagnosis, I borrowed a social worker friend's diagnostic manual and finally discovered the full impact that night had on my life. The words I read lit a fire of recognition inside me. They went something like this: "Even though the precipitating event may have only lasted a few minutes ... it may cause the victim to experience recurring trauma for the remainder of his/her lifetime and to delay major life decisions and commitments such as marriage and children."

"It is true the attack when I was 23 years old threw my life off track," I testified. "I stand before you at the age of 52, never having married or had children. Did I delay those life decisions because of what Kidd did to me? I ask myself that question often, but only God knows for certain. However, my life has been rich and full, even without a family. But understand, I got the life sentence. Every person I get close to eventually must be told the story of Dec. 19, 1977, and how it affected my heart and my soul. Everyone."

That testimony and the board's deliberations resulted in a November 2006, letter notifying me Kidd was denied parole for another 10 years. Pleased and relieved, I hoped to put this all out of mind for the next decade. Sixteen months later, in March of 2008, I received a second letter from the Kansas Department of Corrections. This time I was told that Harold Kidd had died in prison of natural causes. I wanted to feel relief, but as I stood in the foyer of my home and read the letter, a second and then a third time, all I could feel was anger. He was free of his sentence, but I was still serving mine.

My three parole board appearances had not felt like major traumatic events, because I had advance warning, was able to prepare for the inevitable flood of emotion and had control over whether or not I wanted to participate. However, notification of

Kidd's death was a surprise. Neither my friends nor I quite knew how to process this news. A social worker friend struggled for several days with what to say or do before calling just to admit her concern and confusion. She also told me about trying to find a card for the occasion. Of course, this made us both laugh and me to wonder what such a card might say. My anti-death penalty brain quickly produced a rhyme that shocked us both: "Sorry to hear your attacker died. If it'd been up to me, he would've fried!"

Thirty-Three Years and Seven Therapists

The past 34 years I have learned that emotions are like onions. Just when I get one layer peeled off, another unexpected occurrence causes the edges of a new layer to peel. Seven therapists have helped me work through this process. The work of a particular therapist was critical. He used a Gestalt therapy technique known to be productive with child incest victims, but not tried with rape victims. It allowed me to reclaim my power during the assault. It was as if he inserted several new slides at the front of my mental slide tray of images from the attack. When retelling my story, those new slides allowed me to get the wisdom out of the experience without reliving it. This was a transformative process for me.

Once in Santa Fe on a photo shoot, I experienced a round of victim trauma during a photography workshop. On the second day of shooting nude models, I was working with a female model curled up in a fetal position on top of a large smooth rock and covered in gauze-like fabric. As I watched my instructor's hand reach down to poke some sheer fabric deeper in her mouth, something fundamental shifted inside me. I even asked the model if she could breathe in there. That night I edited images until after midnight; then I took my still unsettled feelings to bed. It wasn't until the next morning in the shower that I realized my victim feelings had again been triggered. This experience took me back to my therapist at the time.

To aid our process for this round of work, she asked me to remember one single image from Santa Fe that might represent what triggered the trauma. I went home, chose the image and made an 8x10 print. As I studied it lying on an otherwise blank desktop, the *Ms. Magazine* image once again came to mind. I had unknowingly taken a fine-art version of the *Ms.* photo. That *Ms.* photo that emerged from the archives of my soul during the attack turns out to be quite famous in the pro-choice movement. Taken by a Connecticut police department officer, it is a photo of 26-year-old mother of two, Geraldine "Gerri" Santoro, as she laid nude, face down, alone and dead from a botched abortion. A quick Google search of her name will lead you to her amazing story.

My Hope

Women have made much progress in the 34 years since a man unknown to me nearly took my life as a way to prove his own personal power. Yet rape remains a daily threat to women in cities across our nation. I survived the attack, because other women helped me prepare to defend myself -- not only physically, but also mentally. It is my hope, that in some small measure, the telling of my story will do the same for other women.

Thank You, Anita Hill
Trix Niernberger

I cleaned out an old desk and found a business card I had been given more than 20 years ago. I never forgot that encounter. My job was to secure medical care for those without health insurance. The man represented doctors who could provide that care. At a forum where we were introduced, he said we should meet and handed me his card. I dropped it in my purse and walked to my car energized that we might be able to craft a local solution. When I retrieved the card to call him the next day, I saw he had written a note on it: "Please call me, re: you're cute." His solution was not what I had in mind. I never called him.

Years earlier, I worked in Topeka at the Division of Budget for the State of Kansas. I was told I was the first female budget analyst hired by the director of budget. A few congratulated me for breaking the gender barrier. The director was an icon in the State House, surviving Republican and Democratic governors for almost 30 years. Gruff, with a pipe in his mouth, would call me by his secretary's name, Betty.

As budget analysts, we worked long hours around the Christmas holidays to prepare the Governor's budget, which was presented in early January to the Kansas Legislature. In 1979, each budget analyst presented recommendations to the governor personally. When it was my turn, I took my seat at the conference table in the Kansas State House, with the director, his deputy, the governor and two male aides.

The budget director told an opening joke. I remember the punch line: "They both smell like fish." One of the objects he was referencing was a woman's vagina. There was laughter. I was nervous and naïve and felt insulted. With that introduction, I presented my budget recommendations. When I said Kansas needed to expand the maternal and child health program, because some women were falling through the cracks, I heard more laughter. A male friend had to explain to me later that the men's minds had wandered again to vaginas.

Little gifts awaited my arrival each morning at the budget office – quotes by Phyllis Schlafly, Bible passages or editorials against the Equal Rights Amendment. All supporting evidence, gathered by my co-workers, proving women were inferior to men. Sometimes, I would pretend the messages were not there. Sometimes, I brought in pro-ERA articles and told the guys to circulate them.

Once I walked out of my cubicle and exploded at all of them as they gathered to watch my reaction to that morning's dropping. One of the men responded by saying I was cute when I got mad, and they all laughed. I let it all get to me. I developed chronic back pain and felt exhausted. Some nights I never moved from the couch after I got home. My fiancé decided we weren't right for one another.

The term *sexual harassment* didn't exist then. It would be more than 10 years before Anita Hill told the story of "Long Dong Silver" to white male Senators who responded by attacking her character and her mental state. Although she was blamed for not filing a complaint against Clarence Thomas, I knew why she had not. We had been the same age, 25. Had she filed a complaint, it would have been her word against that of her male supervisor. Just out of law school, she could have lost everything she had worked for.

With her stature as a law professor in 1991, she felt obliged to speak about the character of a man nominated to our highest court. After Thomas was confirmed, we learned the Senate committee never called three others who were subpoenaed to provide supporting evidence. Women were angry that Anita Hill was not taken seriously. The following year, a record number of women ran for public office and won. Five won U.S. Senate seats and 24 were elected to the U.S. House. Thank you, Anita Hill. For taking risks despite the consequences. For providing women with the courage to speak about sexual harassment. For making the workplace less burdensome for women. For encouraging women to run for office.

I trust the Kansas State House is not what it used to be. Because of Anita. Because two women have served as governors since then. And because the first female governor, Joan Finney, appointed a woman, Gloria Timmer, to serve as budget director.

Wichita Area Sexual Assault Center: Early History

Robyn B. Puntch

The Wichita Area Sexual Assault Center was established as the Wichita Area Rape Center in late 1974 by a dedicated group of volunteers who created a crisis line, organized a speakers' bureau, and sought to persuade law enforcement and hospital emergency room personnel to allow them to provide training in dealing with victims of sexual assault. Among those early volunteers were Martha Hodges, Marilyn Harp, Nancy Caldwell, Linda Gebert, Kathy Warren, Sue Dondlinger, Jolene Grabill, Jackie Sivley and Susan Crockett-Spoon, to name but a few.

In 1977, a Law Enforcement Assistance Administration grant enabled the organization to hire Linda Teener as its first executive director, and for her to hire Jane B. Brummett as an administrative assistant. I would become Linda's replacement two years later with the mandate to expand programs and to obtain replacement funding for the three-year grant.

In 1980, United Way agreed to provide a percentage of the agency's annual budget. By that time, professional training for police and hospital workers was provided on a regular basis, and the membership of the center's board had changed somewhat to include influential representatives of those entities.

Hundreds of talented volunteers and many staff members have served the center since its inception. Building off the work of the charter members, staff and volunteers over time have been able to change attitudes and affect significant increases in rates of reporting, as well as provide a high standard of support and care for those affected by sexual assault.

Revisiting Domestic Violence:
One Woman's Story
Rachel, Reported by Susan Melvin, D.O.

Rachel* grew up on a farm in Kansas. After graduating from Kansas State with a bachelor's degree in journalism, she became a reporter for a regional newspaper. She met Jack at work where he was one of the editors. There was an immediate and strong attraction. He was intellectually oriented, and Rachel found this refreshing. The first year, they were happy; Jack made an occasional insulting remark in social settings, which Rachel found disturbing, but attributed it to the "alcohol talking."

As a father, Rachel remembers Jack as patient and caring, and said that he was always a very good father to their son, Jeff. However, the difficulty started when Rachel opted to stay at home to do freelance work and care for their son. Cruel and demeaning comments and verbal batter began to occur in both private and public places. Rachel remembers being publicly humiliated, especially in social settings that included friends from the local university faculty.

During this period, Rachel sought psychological help for decreased self-esteem. Her first visit was to a psychiatrist who wrote her a prescription for anxiolytics and told her to go home and care for her husband and child. She threw away the prescription and sought out a female psychologist through family services in her Kansas town.

Their son, Jeff, was about three years old when the first episode of physical batter occurred. Rachel was known, and still is, for having a very quick wit. While at a party, someone made a joke, and Rachel responded with a quick remark. Jack became enraged and immediately slapped her across the face in front of their friends. Rachel accepted this and, for years, thought she had caused the situation because of her mouth. Over the following year, there seemed to be more demeaning remarks and an attempt to destroy Rachel's self-worth, but she was a survivor. Recognizing that the marriage would not survive, and being encouraged by friends to leave, she planned for self-sufficiency and went back to school to obtain her teaching certificate.

She remembers that, during this time, a church friend came to her home requesting a donation pledge for the church's annual canvass. Rachel explained that she could not donate, because she was not working. Upon hearing this, Jack became enraged about her lack of financial contribution to the household and her ongoing, "unnecessary" education, and verbally assaulted her in front of her church friend. When her friend left the house, Rachel confronted Jack and explained how embarrassed she had felt. Hitting ensued. Rachel suffered many bruises but did not seek medical care, because she was embarrassed. Ongoing verbal and physical battles became customary, and Rachel frequently wore concealing clothes to cover the bruises and made up stories about walking into walls and tripping on stairs. Her secret was well protected

– after all she socialized in professional circles and was active in the community. She managed to maintain her own identify and social life against Jack's protests.

Eventually things became intolerable, and they separated. However, within days, Jack became attentive and doting, and agreed to join Rachel in counseling. Rachel wanted to provide a family for their son. After a three-month separation in which the bad behavior stopped, she agreed to give it another try. Yet she also continued her separate bank account that she had opened at the onset of the separation. Once back under the same roof, the verbal abuse resumed. Rachel believed that if she would just watch her mouth, she could prevent the abuse from happening. She survived by becoming more involved in outside activities and less intimately involved in the relationship.

Then one night, Jack, under the influence of alcohol, wanted to take Rachel and Jeff for a ride. Rachel refused, so Jack went for a drive alone and got in a serious car accident. Rachel was called to the emergency room and remembers wishing Jack would die. At that time, Jack's family physician did gently probe about their marriage and habits, but the probing stayed very peripheral, and he never asked direct questions. Rachel says that she probably would not have told Jack's doctor, but that she would have told her personal family physician if she had ever asked her. Rachel states that she would not have lied to her own physician.

The guilt Rachel felt over wishing Jack dead haunts her even now, 30 years later. Rachel agreed to take Jack home from the hospital, where she continued to care for him for another three months while he was in a body cast. During this time, Jack got sober. She put on hold the plans for divorce she had been considering because of the guilt she felt for wishing him dead.

Once healed, Jack's old patterns resumed almost immediately. Finally, after about a year of ongoing abuse, she noticed that her son, then nine years old, was starting to become emotionally involved in the disputes. Rachel filed for divorce. Besides her psychologist, her attorney was the only other professional to whom she disclosed the abuse. She also had a few friends who were aware and supportive of her plans. Jack accompanied Rachel to the attorney's office to "talk her out of the nonsense of divorce." When the attorney quoted the necessary fees, Jack said that he could not afford a divorce. Rachel declared, "I can," and wrote the check from her own account.

During the interim, Jack tried the same old tactics of smothering her with kindness, but this time, she refused and sought support from two close friends. But Jack did not stop. Although he was a man who never attended church, he sought help from Rachel's minister to try to "bring Rachel to her senses." Sensing the situation was no longer within his control, Jack started stalking her, initially by phone and, then, by driving back and forth in front of her house, all the while cursing her and calling her names. Then, suddenly, he became silent, deathly silent. He did not show up in court for the divorce trial. But after the divorce, he started making death threats.

Rachel, trying to continue her community activities, planned a swimming party for the church choir. Hearing of this, Jack called to inform her that if she went through with the party, he would come over and kill her in front of all her friends, and that if he did not kill her then, he would kill her the next day at her son's football game. She went ahead with the party, and he did not show up; however, he did show up the next day at the game.

Rachel's brother, informed of the situation, accompanied her. When Jack arrived at the game, her brother immediately approached him and kept him occupied, aborting a scene. After that the threats continued. Jack even broke into her home and stole an heirloom rifle, then called her, threatening to use it as the murder weapon. Rachel called the police and obtained a restraining order, but his behavior did not change. The police told her there was nothing they could do until an actual crime was committed.

Over the next two years, the stalking and threats became a way of life. Occasionally Rachel would stay at friends' homes for safety. She found herself backing out of community and professional functions, especially if the media was involved, because every time her name was in an article about one of her activities, Jack would become enraged and the stalking would resume. Rachel remembers a time when her son was 13, and he and a junior high school friend were at home when Jack showed up. Her son's friend answered the door and later presented Rachel with a handful of bullets, exclaiming, "See you don't have to be afraid anymore!" He apparently had talked Jack into emptying the gun and giving him the bullets.

Through all of this, Rachel had continued her education and completed her master's degree. She had also taken a position on the board of the teacher's union. But, finally, after 16 years of ongoing abuse, she realized that Jack would continue to control her life if she stayed in the community, so she took a job in another state. Intuitively, Rachel was a survivor; she sought her own therapy early, continued her education, established financial independence, and maintained her own identify and circle of friends. It took her many years but she, ultimately, found her way out alive.

*The author's real name has been changed to protect her identity.

Source: "Revisiting Domestic Violence: One Woman's Story by Rachel" Excerpted from an article by Susan Melvin, D.O., published in the *California Family Physician*, November/December 1994

We Were Midwives at the Birth of the Women's (Crisis) Center
Peg Vines

In August 1975, when Myrne Roe was president of our city's first Commission on the Status of Women, she received a call from Mardy Binter (now Murphy), a city employee, saying that federal money for a women's crisis center was available, but the commission would have to apply for it and be accepted.

As CSW vice president, I attended an emergency meeting early the next morning when the commission agreed to pursue the idea. We were so excited that we ignored the fact that the commission was still in its own infancy, had few members with experience in grant writing (I had none at the time) and most daunting, the grant proposal's deadline was three days away. The clock was ticking. We quickly tapped about a dozen experienced women, and some men, from the community-at-large to guide us through a marathon grant-writing session, much of it at Mardy's home. I think I contributed all of two sentences while my friend Jan Yocum applied her considerable grant-writing savvy, learned in the child-care field. Some of us took turns holding Mardy's infant child so she could assist other writers who arrived, contributed their special know-how, and then left. All that day and into the night we persisted so we could make deadline. The grant was awarded to CSW.

However, as a city advisory board, CSW did not meet the criteria for overseeing the crisis center. We needed to find a respected organization that would assume leadership of the project. And that presented a challenge considering some attitudes about women's roles that were prevalent at the time. We heard the question: "By providing an escape place for women, wouldn't we be helping to break up the family?" And, yes, some even played the shame game: "Well, she made her bed, now she must lie in it."

What's more, we were told to *document* how many women would need such a sanctuary. "After all, weren't there already overnight places like the Salvation Army? Or churches or charitable organizations like the American Red Cross one could call in emergencies?" Yes and no. The safe haven that *we* envisioned for destitute and abused women should be more than a stopgap – more than a roof over them until they went back to the same abusive environment. It should provide knowledgeable and supportive resources to restore hope to the women as they worked to turn around their lives.

CSW members Shirley Haines and Rayetta Furnas joined Myrne in negotiations with the local YWCA board, hoping that group would accept responsibility for the new project. Two key women, whose leadership was especially instrumental in these efforts, were Executive Director Susan Crockett-Spoon and Board President Ethel Smith.

On Aug. 18, 1976, with the YWCA as sponsor, the Wichita Women's Center opened. Carolyn Conley was CSW president at the time. The center operated a 24-hour hotline for counseling and referrals, and also provided living space for five residents. Within months, added bed space allowed residency for up to 12 women and children. It took us about a year to realize that the overwhelming need was to serve abused women solely. So this became the center's priority. Other agency placements were available for women not requiring the protection or special support the center could provide.

Later, the program became known as the YWCA Crisis Center/Safe House. Two more moves to confidential locations had increased the facility size to accommodate up to 32 women and children. Also, during those years, through educating the public, there developed a growing sensitivity to the issue of domestic violence. Referrals began coming in to the center from a wide variety of sources, including emergency room physicians and nurses, private physicians, mental health centers, Social and Rehabilitation Services, churches, Legal Aid, the American Red Cross, local universities and businesses. Sometimes residents would hear a public service announcement or see a poster or billboard that help was available. Then they would follow through on that information at a crucial time – perhaps to save their lives.

One particular television movie about a victim of domestic violence – *The Burning Bed* – in the mid-'80s prompted at least 100 immediate calls on the state crisis hotline, plus others on the local line. For a week, the phones kept ringing. Many of the calls were from women who were virtually prisoners in their own homes – not allowed to go out, had no transportation and had small children. They hadn't realized that his hitting them and beating them were acts of domestic violence. When they watched the movie's star, Farrah Fawcett, they began to realize "that's my story, and that's me on the screen. I didn't realize there was any way I could ever get out."

In the law enforcement and court systems, there were also changes. A city ordinance went into effect requiring mandatory arrest and charging of the primary aggressor of domestic violence if evidence indicated a crime, regardless of whether a victim wanted to prosecute. Also, the center placed a victim advocate in the city prosecutor's office at City Hall and later provided victim advocacy at the district attorney's office for felony-level domestic violence cases.

Now wouldn't it be gratifying to learn that all our efforts have stopped the violence, and there's no more need for a center to house domestic violence victims? Obviously that hasn't happened. But today the center is still providing a safe place for women and children to escape from violence. In addition, it has a special focus in its outreach programs teaching about the cycle of violence, and then teaching preventive methods.

r Choice

Speaking Up and Speaking Out

"The momentum was unstoppable as we women found our voices and realized we could become effective agents of change. Equal Time newspaper, our local monthly feminist paper, ran a calendar on the back page of each issue. There were often so many meetings and events in a given day or week, that our staff of five writers could not cover them all, so volunteers were recruited to attend and take notes."

—Linda Bell Gebert (*Equal Time*)

The '70s Pantsuit Controversy

Elma Broadfoot

To wear pants or not to wear pants at work was the big question and controversy at the start of the 1970s. I was one of seven workingwomen photo-featured on the cover of the October, 1970, The Wichita Eagle section called "Of Interest to Women."

Oh yes, pantsuits were the talk of the town, especially in the corporate offices of the local banks, utility companies, hospitals, doctor and dental offices, public school classrooms and the local newspaper. According to the "Pants at Work" *Eagle* feature story, it was talk that led to one bank sponsoring a pantsuit style show in their main lobby for women employees "to show styles that are acceptable in business." But style shows were not enough; women were polled to determine their interest in wearing pantsuits at work, and ultimately there were corporate policies about pantsuits.

One bank's policy stated: "In general, employees should be neat, wear clothing suitable for business and avoid extremes of dress. If women employees of our bank should, on occasion, wear pantsuits, they should be those with jackets or tunic tops in matching colors and must be at least hip length. The fabric and style of pantsuits must be businesslike and not of the leisure or sportswear type."

Another bank's policy further clarified "that women employees have permission to wear pantsuits appropriate for office wear. These will include only jackets and tunics with slacks, no blouses or sweaters with slacks, no extremes or hostess-type outfits. Tellers and other public-contact employees wear uniforms. The article further stated that the 30-member Intensive Care Unit at a local hospital had adopted lime green slacks and white tunic tops as mandatory uniforms for 'modesty's sake and to give freedom of movement.' An administrative assistant in a dental office noted, 'Working with children, you do a lot of bending and lifting and you can ruin a pair of hose a day. A pantsuit makes both the patients and staff happy.'"

Speaking of pantyhose, one local utility company junior executive who wanted to wear pantsuits to her office said that she kept tearing her pantyhose on a chair that needed repair. She sent a memo to superiors with an ultimatum: Repair her chair, or she would put all pantyhose she bought on her expense account, or she would start wearing pantsuits. Her chair was picked up the next day.

I don't remember there being a policy about women wearing the miniskirt or what complementary style pieces to make an outfit. A miniskirt hit somewhere between hip and knee and had its own challenges in terms of bending, lifting and getting in and out of vehicles. How in the world did the miniskirt ever fit into any description for proper business attire? They came just before the pantsuit and, in many instances, forsook any bend toward modesty's sake.

Perhaps the entire furor over pantsuits can be summed up with the quote from the president and chairman of the board of one bank: "We men hate to see the passing of the mini!"

Equal Time With *Equal Time*
Linda Bell Gebert

Themomentum was unstoppable as we women found our voices and realized we could become effective agents of change. *Equal Time*, our local monthly feminist newspaper, ran a calendar on the back page of each issue. There were often so many meetings and events in a given day or week, that our staff of five writers – Mardy Binter (now Murphy), Sherry Eslick (now Buettgenbach), Ruth Ann Messner, Carol Dannar and I – could not cover them all, so volunteers were recruited to attend and take notes. Glendora Johnson was our business manager. Volunteers also got their hands dirty with printer's ink, helping us label and bundle the papers for bulk mail delivery each month to subscribers.

It is revealing to take a look to see how many events took place in one random week in May, 1978: National Organization for Women meeting, Wichita Area Rape Center Board meeting, Family Day Care Association meeting, Big Sisters Orientation, *Equal Time* meeting, Women's Equality Coalition meeting, Displaced Homemakers meeting, Wichita Women's Political Caucus Meeting, the City Employees Women's Association and a report on the ERA extension from a NOW national board member. Earlier in the decade most of these organizations would not have existed. Women made it happen.

It was thought important to give credit to several organizations and people who did not have separate pieces written in this anthology about them for one reason or another, but definitely are deserving of mention. Fortunately, they were covered in *Equal Time*, so our archive of issues was invaluable in helping us remember the women involved as well.

In the June 1978 issue, board member Sherry Eslick wrote a lengthy investigative piece on the state of children whose mothers work and do not have adequate means of child care available to them. These women work out of necessity, some at night shifts, some needing care after school until they get off work. Child care options had not kept pace with women entering the work force in great numbers, and not just for "mad money" but to survive.

The article illustrates the problem: "Three Wichita children spend five nights a week sleeping in the back seat of the locked car, in the hospital parking lot … their mother works as a nurse's aide and there are no child care facilities at that time … A 10-year-old boy goes to school only on Monday, Wednesday and Friday; his 11-year old sister goes on Tuesday and Thursday. Playing hooky? No, they must stay home and be responsible for their infant brother … [the mother] cannot find a child care center or home that takes infants." The state Department of Social and Rehabilitation Services estimated that there were 23,316 mothers working full time in Sedgwick County in 1977. Of their children, 4,427 were in licensed child care homes or centers and 53,863 were not.

After exploring the options, the piece concluded with:

> "There are many steps toward improvement of child care which must be made together. But one of the major steps, which is the starting point for all the others, is a mass reorientation of thinking toward child care. It's not just a mother's problem. It affects every segment of society because it affects the development of our children into adults. It affects employment, the economy, taxes, consumers, providers… These groups and individuals must accept some responsibility, but it appears that women must lead the way."

In February 1977 Ruth Ann Messner covered the incorporation of Big Sisters with Big Brothers. She wrote:

> "[The] associate director of Big Brothers-Big Sisters, Inc., and the former director of Big Sisters (founded locally in 1974), said that by using the best parts of both programs, the new organization hopes to create more recruitment programs, better community exposure and service. …Big Brothers of America and Big Sisters International merged in June, 1977, and provided the groundwork. Since then, that pattern has been followed all over the country, but our merger is the first of such magnitude."

In July 1978 Mardy Binter (now Murphy) organized the "Other Kansans Seminar on Poverty" and was successful in recruiting the indomitable Flo Kennedy as keynote speaker. Ms. Kennedy offered to do a benefit for a worthwhile organization while she was in town, and *Equal Time* became that benefit. Flo Kennedy was an attorney, an outspoken black woman, publisher of many books and fighter for many causes – as far ranging as decriminalization of prostitution, women's reproductive freedom and the efforts of the Penobscot Indians to legally regain their land. She filed class action suits against two major industries, claiming their huge advertising budget increases contribute heavily to inflation.

Mardy's article said of Kennedy: "In her jodhpurs and leather hat, she rides into the ring on the bronco of inequality, injustice, discrimination, murder and violence. She stays on for the full count singing 'Our Mother Who Art in Heaven.'"

Equal Time ceased publishing in January 1979.

Free To Be, a Feminist Bookstore and Gallery

Linda Bell Gebert

In the summer of 1977, with the Women's Weekend approaching, I rented a small space on East Douglas, two rooms upstairs over the original location of the women's art cooperative, Gallery XII. This was to be a painting studio for me – a "room of one's own" – and a small, informal gallery of my work and that of other women.

Through association with other feminists and their enthusiasm for the idea, my new space morphed into that of a shop as well, with feminist bumper stickers, mugs, T-shirts, cards and other such ephemera. We had a newfound delight in advertising our mindset to the world. A postal carrier was much perplexed by delivering frequent boxes with the return address of "Women's Terrorist Society and Sewing Circle." That sentiment was on our best selling T-shirt. He eventually asked, "You're not real terrorists are you?" I explained what we were, but wondered if he actually thought "real" terrorists would give a return address?

I handed out flyers at the Women's Weekend advertising this new space, Je Suis Femme. I stayed with that name for a time, but realized that too many people were confused by it and wondered just what sort of establishment it was. I received more than one phone call asking "Is this Jesus Femmie, and what is it?"

The bookstore also became the editorial room for planning *Equal Time*. The space could best be described as "fun and funky." As such, it had a certain counterculture cachet that seemed fitting. One display area for ceramics was built like an Incan pyramid from scrounged wooden shipping crates that had housed tombstones. Cards and records (remember LPs?) were displayed on discarded drug store displays.

Mardy Murphy and Linda Kohl approached me about also including books, an idea I embraced wholeheartedly, so it morphed once again. At this juncture, it seemed a good time to change the name, so we became Free To Be Bookstore and Gallery. We carried the latest in feminist literature and nonfiction in this burgeoning field, as well as classics by such women as Virginia Woolf, Willa Cather and Doris Lessing. Mardy's particular love of poetry meant that we also included many books of poetry and poetry chapbooks.

We subscribed to other feminist newspapers and magazines, so the faculty of Wichita State University's women's studies program was a great support. Faculty frequently recommended us as a source for materials unavailable elsewhere for student's reading and research. We also had gay and lesbian literature and nonfiction not available in the mainstream bookstores at the time. We carried Olivia Records, from a California women's music company, and their all-time best-selling record, Chris Williamson's *The Changer and the Changed*. This did not go unnoticed. Members of The Way, a religious organization, arrived unannounced one day to pray for us, the "daughters of darkness." We said thanks, but no thanks.

Yet another development came with the arrival of a holistic health program at Newman College, the National College of Naturopathic Medicine. Midwifery was part of their curriculum, although Kansas law dictated they could only "catch" babies, not "deliver" them. When the program departed from Newman for Portland, OR, the midwives trained in the program wanted an outlet for their literature, so they joined with us as well.

It was a heady two-and-a-half years, and we definitely felt like we served a real need in the community. But life and other demands intervened. Mardy moved to California, and I needed to work full time again, so Free To Be closed. Not soon after, the "big box" bookstores began carrying feminist and gay/lesbian literature and independent bookstores such as ours all struggled. Many closed. It's a positive that this body of work is part of the mainstream now, but there was a certain satisfaction to being a counterculture endeavor and filling a need while it lasted.

Feminist Leader Locally and Around the World

Carol Konek, As told to Nita Mark

Carol Konek was born in Meade. Her father was a Socialist, an atheist and a vegetarian – in Kansas! He taught her to question everything. Therefore, her questioning of the rights of women and their roles was natural to her, and she assisted many women in that process. She moved to Wichita in 1954 and began to make history.

As cofounder and faculty member in the Center for Women's Studies and associate dean of Fairmount College of Liberal Arts and Sciences at Wichita State University, Carol was in a position to act on her interests in global women's issues, women's recovery from chemical dependencies, and academic resistance to the inclusion of women and minorities in the curriculum. She was a proponent of increasing the visibility of the university in community affairs and organizations, creating a program of excellence and opening doors and pathways for women. She became a role model for many. Carol frequently spoke to service organizations and religious, political and educational groups. She was very interested in helping women achieve recognition for their accomplishments. She was a sponsor for gay and lesbian organizations on campus.

Carol emphasizes how much fun it was to be a part of all of the exciting changes taking place for women in society. She participated locally in the National Organization for Women, Women's Political Caucus and the Women's Equality Coalition. She also attended many national conferences, including the National Women's Studies Association and the Higher Education Council of Colleges and Universities.

In 1946, the United Nations established the Commission on the Status of Women and the Branch for the Advancement of Women. In 1967, the U.N. approved the Declaration on the Elimination of All Forms of Discrimination against Women. Following this, it declared 1975 International Women's Year and set the first World Conference of the International Women's Year in Mexico City. After this meeting, 1976-85 was declared the United Nations Decade for Women. The Mexico City meeting was a precursor of things to come. Every state had a meeting to elect delegates to Mexico City and to vote on an agenda to improve women's status. Carol was elected at Kansas Women's Weekend to be a delegate from Kansas.

There were many men there to tell "their women" how to vote -- to try to usurp the agenda and to co-opt and intimidate women. It became obvious that there were many differences between male-identified women (mostly through their political and religious philosophies) and feminists. Carol said that frustration was experienced by many as support from some women was difficult to obtain, and it was unfathomable to many of us that any woman could vote against issues that were clearly in the best interest of women.

Carol said the gathering in Mexico City was exciting and thrilling. She met many interesting and accomplished women from all over the world. Many of these women were far advanced in their thinking and acting for the benefit of women, especially in the areas of teen pregnancy, birth control and sexual slavery. At the conference, they worked on issues on which they were united and held workshops to discuss such issues as equal rights for women, workplace concerns, hunger, birth control, control over their own bodies, sexual slavery, agricultural, politics, getting women involved and elected to office, education, strategic planning and building coalitions for social change.

For Carol, the discussion related to sexual slavery was especially enlightening. Previously she hadn't thought much about the transporting of women across borders for sexual purposes. She realized that city officials, feeling the need to offer "gentlemen's entertainment" were using Wichita women to attract conventions. This was not something that most middle-class white women had thought about or acknowledged before.

Carol next attended the UN World Conference to Review and Appraise the Achievements of the UN Decade for Women in Nairobi in 1985. She was most animated about this meeting, saying that the women of Nairobi were so happy to be hosting the meeting. They met the conference participants with joyful singing and dancing and wonderful hospitality rituals. The issues and workshops were much the same at each conference. Sometimes they felt as though they were not making progress but the attendees and speakers were different. Therefore, the opinions were different and, in places, advancements were reported. The awareness of problems worldwide also increased and could, therefore, begin to be addressed. At the Nairobi meeting, Women's International League for Peace and Freedom, of which Carol is a member, hosted a peace tent where women taught each other strategies for creating social change and implementing strategies for local and global peaceful change.

In 1995, WILPF sponsored a peace train from Helsinki to Beijing. Carol said that being aboard that train was a frightening experience. The train was frequently boarded by police – uniformed, armed teenagers who went through their compartments and generally intimidated everyone. The riders were constantly under surveillance. When asked why they were intimidated, Carol said, "They were young, not very intelligent, not well-trained, had an exaggerated sense of their own importance, and they had guns. I've never liked people with guns."

Carol also was a participant in the UN's Fourth World Conference on Women, which was held in Beijing in 1995. When asked why she thought the Chinese government was supportive of hosting this meeting, she said she thought it was the expectation that they would draw rich women to China to help their economy. Along with economic benefits to the country, they wanted to support birth control to limit populations, especially of poor people. This was true in China and the rest of the world, including the U.S.

Again, at this meeting, they looked for signs of increased awareness and advancements. As before, they sometimes felt that they were stuck rehashing differences, but they were also learning how to help without being obstructive. She said there was always growth in individual awareness and learning. She thoroughly enjoyed the opportunity to attend these international conferences. As a result of these experiences, she developed and taught courses on Global Women's Issues and Women and Peace.

Carol is a woman who has provided a lot of knowledge and support to innumerable women. I cannot think of a better role model than Carol.

What She Said

Diane C. Lewis, Compiled by Fran Kentling

The following are notes from speeches made by Diane C. Lewis (1937-2009) during the '70s.

July, 1970: Women's Rights Conference, Wichita

I have been asked to talk with you this morning about the need for a women's movement. To some people the notion of women's liberation is foolish in such difficult times – the rise of black power, student power, gay power, consumer power, but women power?

After all, consider the woman today, especially the American woman:

- More leisure time at her disposal than any of her forbearers.
- A higher standard of living than any of her ancestors.
- Suddenly freer because of the pill.

Prospects are good for the passage of the Equal Rights Amendment – which will make it illegal, according to the U.S. Constitution, to discriminate against people on the basis of sex.

And only last year in Kansas, a bill calling for equal pay for equal work was passed by the Kansas legislature.

As ads for that woman's cigarette say: "You've come a long way, Baby." But to what, and from what?

The ERA was first introduced 47 years ago. Four decades ago. Before most of us in the room were even born. It was 1923. Women had just gotten the vote, there were no television sets, few two-car families and no 40-hour workweeks or spaceships or walks on the moon or vacations with pay.

And now, almost a half-a-century later, the bill may be passed. When the bill for Kansas' equal pay law was first introduced in the state house, a Sedgwick County legislator told his colleagues that passage of such a bill would be the end to (separate) men's and women's restrooms. While laughable, the comment probably cost a few votes for equal pay.

Earlier this year, a Wichita city commissioner indicated publicly that women who receive welfare – actually aid to dependent children – were no better than prostitutes and many of them had babies just to receive higher welfare allotments.

A young woman applying for a job as a computer programmer at a local hospital is quizzed about her birth control practices. Is she on the pill? What are her plans for a family? No man was ever subjected to such indignities. Another woman is asked to make a five-year commitment for a semi-professional job.

In nearly every part of American industry, women are systematically given lesser jobs. Listen to this: Of 31,000,000 women workers, a third are secretaries or clerical workers and more than a fifth are service workers – domestics, waitresses and the like. Only a small number of men workers are in either category. It follows, of course, that the average yearly income of full-time female workers is about $4,150; male workers $7,200. Only 3 percent of the women make more than $10,000 a year as compared to 23 percent of the men.

In the mid-1950s, full-time women workers averaged 64 percent of what men were earning.

By the late '60s it had slipped to 58 percent.

In 1940, women held 45 percent of all technical and professional jobs. [In 1969,] the figure was 37 percent.

In higher education, women slipped from 26 percent of faculty positions in 1920 to 22 percent in 1964.

It was in this climate that Betty Friedan, who would later found the National Organization for Women, wrote *The Feminine Mystique*. Essentially the message was that women had been sold a bill of goods -- not just for the benefit of men, but for the benefit of American industry as well. Industry stood to profit by women staying at home to consume.

March, 1971: Upward Bound

One of the things about being young is that those who are not so young ask, with tiring recurrence, "What do you want to be when you grow up?" And I, too, cannot resist the temptation ... especially to the girls in this audience: "What do you want to be when you grow up?"

Nurse, teacher, wife, mother? Why not doctor, scientist, architect, executive? Because you are a woman?

The lack of, or modest goals of young women is one of the things women's liberation is all about.

What is women's liberation? It is not easy to find a simple definition. Because it covers a sex rather than a race, ethnic groups, religion or some other segment of society, women's liberation is a very broad-based movement. Women are an oppressed majority in this country. They are 51 percent of the population, but only 1 percent of the nation's engineers, 7 percent of its doctors, 2 percent of the business executives. Only 3 percent in the U.S. Congress are women.

Today there are more than 1,000 state laws that discriminate against women. In one state, women have no legal guarantee that they will be lodged in a hotel room while traveling by themselves. In another state, a woman's clothes legally belong to her husband. In Kansas, we still have a law that a woman may be excused from jury duty merely by stating she is a woman. Of course, the clincher is that the only right guaranteed to a woman by the U.S. Constitution is the right to vote.

October, 1973: Wichita Downtown Optimists

Once you have squeezed the toothpaste out of the tube, there is virtually no way to get it back in. Similarly, it is a curious thing about the human condition: Once we have had a revelation, once our eyes have been opened, once we have lost our innocence, there is no going back.

This is what has happened to women. And this is why the women's movement – popularly and unfortunately referred to as "women's lib" – is not just a passing fad. Since the early days of this decade, this has been a subject at once topical, controversial and, for some, even laughable. Just the other day a coworker walked up to me and handed me a slip of paper. This is what is said:

> Salesman: May I show you a brochure?
> Customer: No, I don't wear them anymore. I'm for women's lib.

Such sniggering has been commonplace in the media and in some conversations when women's liberation has come up. Let me say that whether or not we will have so-called "women's liberation" is not a debatable subject. Whether or not all people will achieve the freedom they desire is perhaps debatable, but the very existence of the movement is not. It is growing rather than retrenching.

In our state legislature, women fared the best they have in years with the election of five women, one of them representing Sedgwick County. Four women ran in the primary here. A lengthy article in *Parade* magazine outlined the growing public and judicial support for a woman on the Supreme Court.

A recent issue of *Business Week* published a story about a young woman who is getting the last laugh on some of the country's largest employers. She has filed lawsuits against 32 companies because, as a graduating college senior, they would not interview her. She claims they violated the 1964 Civil Rights Act, because they interviewed only men for the executive training and sales jobs.

Women are now also letting the government and lending institutions know they don't like discriminatory practices in credit. In response to this growing militancy, a number of major stores, credit card companies and banks say they are changing their credit policies, and some creditors are actively pursuing women's business. The irony of the whole matter is that women are the major consumers. We spend most of the money and most advertising is aimed at the female consumer.

1970s: Audience Unknown

Today's magazines, newspapers, radio programs and television reports are filled with the topic of the "women's liberation movement," "women's revolution" and "women in revolt." Some think it is *the* revolution. A writer in *Playboy* – everybody's getting into the act – has described this as a phenomenon and reports it is now more powerful, revolutionary, morally justifiable and, at times, more ridiculous than any previous wave of feminist movement.

Many of you have seen reports of women burning bras, picketing the Miss America contest, fighting to take ROTC courses and breaking barriers at the racetracks. The women may appear kooky. But let's face it; they are the advance scouts of a forward moving army of women who are pressing for more rights.

Mid-1970s: Wichita Oil Secretaries

Just recently I read a letter in Dear Abby's column from a mother who was so distressed over the birth of her second girl baby that she felt only resentment toward the child. She almost couldn't bring herself to feed this tiny infant, simply because the parents had wanted a boy. Nor did she want to have sexual relations with the father for fear a third girl would be born.

And why did they want a boy? Even without knowing these particular people, we know the answer: Boys are considered the progenitors of our society, and because we find that men are more valued in terms of their contributions and women are somehow less. These kinds of cultural attitudes are what women's liberation, from one end of the country to the other, is trying to get at.

And allowing for all nature's differences and the myths and notions about men's work and women's work, it is clear that the great majority of the world's work can be done by both men and women. What do we want? We want to liberate men as well as women.

Life Changes
Nita Mark

Growing up as a girl in the 1940s and '50s, I somehow just knew what was acceptable behavior for a girl. Even though I was a tomboy and mostly played sports with the boys, I knew that when I got to junior high, I would have to turn in my sneakers for nice flats and high heels. Of course, we already had to wear dresses to school. I don't believe I ever heard the words *lesbian* or *gay* or even *homosexual*, yet somehow I knew that same-sex relationships had negative connotations and definite physical boundaries. So, I did the "afternoon teas" with my girl friends and went "steady" with five boys in the 7th grade.

During the rest of junior high and high school, I dated rarely and put up with the fact that even though I had made plans to go to a movie or do something with a girl friend, boys came first. If my girl friend was asked out on a date, we both knew the date took precedence, and our plans were canceled without question. I ran around with a group of 20 or 30 girls. Toward the end of my junior year, a friend arranged a blind date for me with a friend of her boyfriend; we double-dated. My date was two years older, nice, and he obviously liked me. We dated throughout my senior year and got engaged at my senior prom. A little over a year later, we married. That's the way things were for most of us in the late '50s. I knew my role and didn't really question it.

I call the '60s my pregnant decade. I had children in 1962, 1965 and 1969, as close as I could get to the average of 2.3 children. I considered myself normal. I was not thrilled with my sex life, but then none of my friends were either, and we mostly didn't talk about sex much. I went to church, quit working when I became pregnant, raised my children, cleaned the house and bowled for fun.

I was testing myself as a little bit of a rebel, but it only took the form of having natural childbirth and breast-feeding my children when few others were. My activism was as a group leader in La Leche League. I loved John Kennedy and his brother, Bobby. I also picketed against high meat prices at my local market. I supported Independent John Anderson for president. Pretty wild stuff, eh?

My activism at that time also took the form of being secretary of one of my bowling leagues and as a member of the board of directors of the local Women's Bowling Assn. There I met a fascinating woman. We instantly hit it off and began going to restaurants and talking for hours after the meetings and tournaments. Previously, I had been attracted to a couple of my friends but innately knew the "rules" and kept within the acceptable boundaries of behavior without too much questioning.

However, with this particular woman, I wanted more. I'll never forget the electric charge I felt when our little fingers touched on an armrest. We very gradually deepened our relationship. At one point she said to me, "We need to talk about what we are feeling." I responded that I didn't want to talk about "it," because "it" might go away. I just wanted to let it happen. Of course, we did have to talk. After some time, we decided that we wouldn't be able to see each other anymore, except at bowling functions. The responsibility of our husbands and six children, and the possibility of two broken marriages weighed heavily upon us. I went along with that decision for three weeks, and then I became suicidal and decided that everyone would be better off without me. I wrote my good-bye letters and made my plans to do the deed the next night.

For some reason, the next morning, my husband went through my purse before leaving for work. He found my letters and called my friend. When I got up, the two of them were sitting in the living room waiting for me. I knew I was in big trouble. I let them talk me into admitting myself to a hospital psych ward and ended up staying there for several weeks. Patients had to participate in occupational and recreational therapy before they were allowed to go home. I made a leather hair barrette for my friend. When I was in the hospital, my husband told my parents about my sexual identity problems. They couldn't accept it and didn't come to see me during my time in the hospital. My psychiatrist then decided that my husband should be admitted to check him out. I think the doctor wanted to see how I would function without him.

I found that I could handle the kids and be on my own. I became determined that I must get a divorce to be true to myself. My friend/partner told me that she wouldn't/ couldn't divorce, so I knew I was on my own. I was determined to do it anyway. I felt like I could no longer lead a double life, live a lie.

In the early '70s it wasn't easy to get a divorce. My husband believed I would be a bad influence on the children, and he threatened to expose me to the court if I didn't give him custody. I knew if a judge were told I was a lesbian, he would definitely give my husband full custody so I acquiesced. I even had to have a woman from my church testify for me that he would be a good custodial parent. He was very much a home-body. I was just returning to the workforce and entering Wichita State University to finally get my college education, so it seemed like it probably would be best for the kids if he had custody. You see, I still believed the conventional wisdom that said I was a deviant. So began my new life. My friend/partner and I continued our relationship, but she didn't move in with me for more than a year. It was another year after that before she finally got a divorce.

I did get a job and enrolled in WSU to get a degree in business administration with an emphasis in accounting. I ended up working full time and going to school for 10 years, mostly at night. I proudly graduated summa cum laude.

One of the first classes I took was Women In Society, taught by Dr. Carol Konek. Carol and that class changed my life. I developed self-confidence. I became a feminist. I met and learned about so many wonderful, intelligent, accomplished women, all of whom I found simply amazing. I was so lucky that WSU had one of the first women's studies programs in the country. I enrolled in every class titled Women in ... The entire faculty of the department helped me to grow and to appreciate women and their accomplishments.

I also met other lesbians; what a relief that was! I snuck away from work one day to attend a lecture by Kate Millett, author of *Sexual Politics*. A woman sitting next to me had flyers on her lap concerning an initial meeting of a Lesbian Rap Group. I asked her for a flyer and spoke to Kate Millett after the lecture. She told me there would be a gathering at Dorothy Walters' home that evening. I immediately got directions to

Dorothy's house. That evening, there were heel tracks from my house to Dorothy's house, because my partner wasn't that happy about meeting with "those people." I had a great time and, thus, began my life as a lesbian activist. Being "out" made sense to me as I was finally proud of who I was.

We started the Lesbian Rap Group with women from the university. We had 50 lesbians at the first meeting and were euphoric. From that experience, some of us felt the need to explore ourselves even more deeply and formed a consciousness-raising group of 10 women who greatly influenced me. Following the insights learned and the confidence gained from that group, we got involved in a mixed group of political gay men and lesbians called the Homophile Alliance of Sedgwick County. From that came our battle to add sexual orientation to the Wichita Civil Rights Ordinance. We succeeded in getting the ordinance passed, but then the religious right (or wrong as I prefer to call them) began petitioning for our hard-earned civil rights to be put to a vote of the people of Wichita. They easily acquired more than enough signatures on their petitions, mostly in their fundamentalist churches.

Wichita was one of the first few cities to pass such an ordinance and was mentioned in the movie *Milk*. I was so naïve that I thought we would win the vote, just because it was so "right." After all, everyone I knew (except my family) was for it. We worked hard, held fundraisers, made speeches and tried our best to uphold the ordinance. At that time, most of us were also very active in the Women's Political Caucus, NOW and the Women's Equality Coalition. The feminist community was very supportive of our efforts, and we were very appreciative. However, we lost by a vote of 5-to-1, almost exactly the same as their fundraising advantage. The defeat was hard to take. Several of my activist friends moved away. However, my children, friends and history were here, so I stayed.

I continued to be involved in sexual politics. I served as president of the mixed Wichita Business and Professional League, was a founding mother of The Lesbian Celebration, worked briefly with a group called Project 2000 that was attempting to pass another civil rights ordinance and wrote a column for *The Liberty Press*. Later, I became a member of the Women's Studies Community Council, serving 12 years on the board, and I worked diligently on the conception and construction of the Plaza of Heroines at WSU.

As my health deteriorated and I had to quit working for a living, my life has changed again. I moved to the suburbs to be near my son and grandchildren. Most of my activism is now confined to the Muscular Sclerosis Society and the Peggy Bowman Second Chance Fund. My friends and family are now even more important to my life. Sometimes I almost feel I have come half circle with my life (I obviously couldn't come full circle).

I'm now a little less confrontational, a little calmer, a little less angry and frustrated, but always a political junkie, a proud feminist and proud lesbian. And I'm very happy that things have changed so dramatically since the '50s, and that I was able to participate in and be a part of the change brought about by the '70s. My life came out just as it should. If I had realized my lesbianism in my teens, I would not have my three children and grandchildren, whom I adore. Living to see President Obama take the oath of office makes me very hopeful for the future of girls, women and lesbians in this country.

Teaching Women to Be Assertive

Nan Morgan Porter

My children have a hard time believing that there was a time when my friends and I hesitated to express our thoughts.

I went back to school in 1969 to stop being "just a housewife" and to become a clinical psychologist. It was an exhilarating time to be a student. There were civil rights issues, anti-war rallies, as well as women's rights issues. In the beginning, I was not interested in feminism. I had decided that only I really knew what I needed and what was right for me, and I didn't want to replace male authority figures with female authority figures. Then Gloria Steinem came to town and spoke at Wichita State University. She talked about sisterhood and the importance of not looking down on any woman regardless of how she spent her life. She talked about the importance of inclusion and cooperation, rather than authority. Suddenly I realized that I was a feminist. I just hadn't known it. There were many other important thoughts, but those were the principles that made sense to me.

One of the skills I acquired in school at that time was assertiveness. I had gone to a workshop in Topeka, followed it up with more training and then passed it on by running assertiveness training workshops in the counseling center at Wichita State. Like many women, I prefaced most of my statements with either "I'm sorry but" or "excuse me" without realizing how timorous or apologetic I sounded, not to mention insincere.

My favorite techniques were empathic assertion and a strategy called DESC. Both were most useful in resolving difficulties. In empathetic assertion, you state your position and acknowledge the other person's position in the same sentence. For example, "I know you want a new car, but I want to keep reducing our debt." This sentence opens negotiations respecting both positions.

The DESC is a four-step process in which you do the following:
1. Describe the issue specifically.
2. Express briefly how you feel.
3. Specify what you want to happen.
4. Explain the real life consequences if it does or doesn't happen.

I liked this process because it helped me express what I wanted and how it could happen. Both these techniques eliminated blaming and name-calling. I also found that it was easier for women of my generation to ask for what they wanted when they showed empathy for others. Changing that kind of speech habit is relatively easy. Most of us who were returning students had lots of valuable life experience, and those who learned to be assertive were not shy about sharing it. So speaking assertively rather than passively or aggressively was a great skill to have.

My three daughters have grown up to be assertive women. Even as children, they did not fear expressing themselves. It is difficult to remember living in a time when it was not okay for women to speak up and say what was on their minds.

A Conversation

Andrea Ramsay

I attended the International Women's Year conference. I remember a spirited conversation with a woman picketing on the sidewalk with a sign that read: "Don't send my daughter to war."

We both had a son and a daughter, and I asked her if she was willing to see her son go and her daughter to stay home.

She said, "Yes." It wasn't an attitude of 'at least protect one of them' – just that she thought it was okay for men and not for women to go to war. I could not separate my feelings about my son and my daughter in that way. For me, it was either okay for both or not okay for both, but not different based upon gender.

Afterword

It was with dedication and hard work that Wichita State University, one of the first women's study centers in the country, became one of the most important centers from which education and activism pulsated throughout the city. Other places of female energy included: a group of West Side Methodist women who wanted to be catalysts for women's rights in their church; the YWCA and three friends who had an idea for an employment program that helped displaced homemakers; a group of women artists who wanted a gallery to exhibit their work; women who started a feminist book store; a Junior League member who was determined all women should have a place to get birth control information and services; and female physical education teachers who had it with all the money and status going to male athletes. All those women and more radiated out into the community, like the spokes of a wheel, until there were hundreds and hundreds of others who were energized and politicized and who made history by improving the status of women.

The aforementioned WSU Center for Women Studies, a Planned Parenthood chapter, safe places for victims of domestic violence, a rape counseling center, Big Sisters and several other programs are still part of the legacy of the 1970s. Other organizations that were so successful they no longer are needed include: The Wichita Commission on the Status of Women (that, among many other things, put together a talent bank of women qualified to serve on the up-to-then almost totally male city committees and boards) and the local women's political caucus who lobbied local and state officials and who encouraged and supported women candidates.

An untitled poem read by the poet on the Capitol steps in Topeka on April 9, 1989
Carol Brunner Rutledge: 1938-2004

Well, look where we are again
    Where my mother stood, I stand again
    Where my grandmother stood, I stand again
There is nowhere else to be.

It has been such a very long time since we first started.
We now have anniversaries and memories and aging goals.
    In the great tradition of our Kansas mothers,
    we talked about and marched about and taught about
    and sometimes cried about what is right and what is fair.

It has been such good company.
We remember those who, at the beginning of enlightenment,
	made their statement for all women to come.
And those who marched the nation's streets we remember.
And those who braved the devastation of loneliness, we remember.
And those who broke under the strain, we remember without condemnation …

Powerful women with a powerful message.

Well, look where we are again
	Where my mother stood, I stand again
	Where my grandmother stood, I stand again
It is the only place to be.

It has been the only place since the first human dominated another.
	It was the only place for women of the prairie
	in the wagons, in the dugouts, soil and sun
	and unmarked graves …

It was the only place for farm women of the depression,
	dirt and wind and hunger and hopelessness …
	And for all the women since, who made it to power,
	in the Senate and the House, and the governing of our lives …

And for all the women since, in the corners of their kitchens, in the boardrooms
and bedrooms and the birth rooms of this nation …
And for all the women since …

We now become healers.
We will bring back the connectedness, which was broken long ago,
	long before we were here – broken by men and women
	who did not value each other.

In the great tradition of Mother Earth, we will heal the wounds
	and enable the growth of woman and man to that day
	when in the blazing light of knowledge, we stand
	side by side as equals.

We will lay aside the bitterness we inherited
that became our grounding for so long, and it will be hard.
We will work toward a land inhabited by women and men
who treat each other with respect and honor.

And we will do it with understanding.
And we will do it with love.

We will make whole the broken parts of our lives
      to become what we were rightfully intended to be at birth.
We will do it in spite of still-arrogant and wrong males.
We will do it in spite of the sad, sick, female right.
And somehow, we will learn to care for them.
Until the world has learned the meaning of equality.

We will do this for our daughters and our granddaughters.
We will do this for our sons and our grandsons.
We will do this for ourselves.

Well, look where we are again
      Where my mother stood, I stand again.
      Where my grandmother stood, I stand again

It's time to finish this race.

About the Contributors

Alexander, Beth I teach and practice at Michigan State University, although the majority of my work is as University Physician, the chief public health officer for the U (surgeon general). I plan for and manage H1N1, meningitis outbreaks, malaria on study abroad trips, etc. This is as much fun as tennis and gardening. I lived, trained and practiced in Wichita from 1971-1989, where I raised my children, practiced medicine and was sustained and encouraged by many women friends and co-conspirators.

Anderson, Anna R. I graduated from Wichita State University with a B.A. and M.A. in English Literature. I taught freshman composition, first as a graduate assistant and then as a lecturer. I am married to Christopher Shank. We have a daughter, Maria Moore, a grandchild, Heston, and a son, George Anderson. I am retired from a career in international banking.

Anderson, Marietta I believe people deserve to be treated fairly and have participated in social movements to achieve that goal. I have been active in free speech causes and in securing equal rights for workers, minorities and women, and have helped elect people to office who hold this same core belief.

Bagby, Sarah I was born in Iowa and raised in Kansas. I own Watermark Bookstore & Cafe. As such, I meet myriad people: readers, authors and friends needing nourishment of mind and body. I am married to Eric Cale, and we are proud of our daughter, Louise.

Baresch, Ruby In the '70s I was in a poetry workshop and co-edited, with James Meacham and Mardy Murphy, a small poetry magazine. My work was published in little magazines and elsewhere. Since then I have written mostly film reviews, but am now retired and again writing poetry and fiction.

Bennett, Lana Elaine The beauty I find on this globe astounds me; the innumerable ways people of all persuasions destroy and exclude astonish me; the courage of even more amazes me. The Mystery I embrace and the love of my family, along with the help I've received from women here in Wichita, give me hope.

Billings, Dorothy K. I am a professor of anthropology at Wichita State University. I studied anthropology at the University of Wisconsin-Madison (B.A., 1955); Auckland College, New Zealand; Columbia University (A.B.D., 1964); and the University of Sydney, Australia (Ph.D., 1972). My field research is Papua, New Guinea, and focuses on art, religion, values and sustainable development.

Bonavia, Emily I was born and raised in Wichita, where all the women are strong. My first heroine was Amelia Earhart, whose biography I read in the fourth grade. I have never lacked for female role models.

Bonwell, Gloria When I graduated from college at age 20, my grandmother said, "A pity you never married." I taught in Europe where, at age 28, I met my husband of 53 years. I have been an active community volunteer and a rehabilitation counselor. I am a grandmother of nine.

Bowman, Peggy I am a former biology teacher, Vista volunteer, lobbyist and health care administrator. Currently, I am a happy, retired lesbian with two children and four grandchildren and director of the Peggy Bowman Second Chance Fund which helps Kansas women with abortion funding.

Broadfoot, Elma I've worked in communications 40 years, in community organizing and consulting 20 years, and was the first popularly elected woman mayor of Wichita. My most challenging and fulfilling experience was as a caregiver to my grandson, who is now 8 years old and cancer free. He and my two-year-old granddaughter keep my 60-something muscles flexible, my imagination alive and my heart open.

Browning, Peg Roberts I graduated from KU in 1943 and received an M.A. in Philosophy in 1976. For three semesters, I team-taught Philosophy of Feminism at WSU with Dr. Deborah Soles. I was appointed to the Wichita Commission on Status of Women and served five years; I was president in 1982. From 1983-86, I served on the Kansas State Commission on Child Support.

Cole, Joan Brussat I came to Wichita in 1974 and, shortly thereafter, began serving on a number of city boards and commissions and private non-profit boards. In 1993, I was elected to the City Council where I served 8 years. My years of volunteer work with the Mental Health Association and Breakthrough led to employment as marketing director of a private psychiatric hospital in Wichita. After spending nine years on the Arts Council, I was appointed to the Kansas Arts Commission and served three years until Governor Brownback eliminated its funding. Currently, I am serving my 12th year on the Wichita Downtown Development Corporation.

Conlee, Mary Ellen I spent the first 30 years of life calling New England home before settling in Wichita in 1970. Two great sons filled my days in the '70s, and then on to my 30-year career as a lobbyist culminating in owning the Conlee Consulting Group, Inc.

Conley, Carolyn Patton I graduated from Wichita State University in 1966 and 1967 with two degrees in accounting. I have been a self-employed CPA since my son was born in 1978 and an active member of the community since the early 1970s.

Crocker, Elvira Valenzuela I am a long-time newspaper journalist and public relations practitioner. I retired from the National Education Association in Washington,

D.C., in 2000. I worked for newspapers in Garden City, Dodge City, Emporia and Wichita, and for the U.S. Department of Education. I now reside in Wichita where I freelance.

Davis, Janice Gary My entire career has involved working with young people. I have been a classroom teacher and administrator in both public and private educational institutions, and a central office administrator. I have also served as chief professional officer of the Boys and Girls Clubs of South Central Kansas. I am now retired.

Dilsaver, Donna My life has been lived within 25 miles of my birthplace, Oatville, KS, giving me good reason to have enjoyed visiting 21 countries, some returned to three times. My career in Wichita is chronicled in my autobiography, *An American Woman's Zest for Living*.

Docking, Jill S. I married into a Kansas political family. My husband's father and grandfather were both governors of the state. My husband was a lieutenant governor. I am a financial advisor. Tom and I have a son, daughter and two granddaughters.

Fife, Natasha Matson I am an assistant professor emeritus. During my 39 years at WSU, I held the following positions: instructor, women's physical education; assistant professor, Department of Physical Education; women's athletic director; and interim chair of the Department of Physical Education.

Foulston, Nola Tedesco My Italian parents were first generation Americans. In 1968, I left home in New York City and came west to attend college. Since 1977, I have practiced law in Wichita, and since 1989, I've served as district attorney for the 18th Judicial District. I am married to Steve, and we have a son, Andrew.

Gebert, Linda Bell I have three children, five grandchildren and a loving partner of 25 years. I've worked as a volunteer director, technical illustrator, graphic designer, silversmith and enameling teacher. In the 1970s, my studio morphed into Free To Be, a feminist bookstore and gallery. I also served on the Association of Volunteer Administrators, *Equal Time*, NOW and Rape Center boards.

Grabill, Jolene M. A photographer and garden designer, I've lived in the same stone house in Kansas for 19 years. I'm a fan of all things that open: flowers, pretty packages and young minds. I easily forget how old I am when in the company of someone whose age doesn't involve two numbers. In recent years I have learned to surrender my voice to the power of an image strong enough to speak for itself.

Gray, Brenda J. I am a Wichita native who has been working in the communications field as a marketing/public relations professional for more than 20 years. I am passionate for causes that positively impact the lives of women and children of color. I am the wife of Stephen, the mother of Brianne and Taj and the Nana of Raven and Brendon.

Green, Correne I worked at McConnell Air Force Base from 1989-2005. I'm anti-violence, anti-guns and antiwar. I adjusted to my job slowly, but after I became an EEO counselor, I felt more at home. I served on the Mid-America All-Indian Center board from 2006 to 2008. In 2008, Gov. Kathleen Sebelius appointed me to the Kansas Civil Service Commission.

Gregory, Melissa I was Secretary of Appointments for Kansas Gov. Mark Parkinson and held that position for former Gov. Kathleen Sebelius, as well. I also served on the executive staffs of Dan Glickman, former U.S. Secretary of Agriculture and former U.S. Congressman. I am married to Jim, and we have four adult children and one grandchild.

Gump, Marilynn Proud great-granddaughter of Alfretta, who refused to marry until she saved enough money to buy a dictionary; granddaughter of Fannie, who taught me poems; daughter of Edith and Bob, committed lifelong learners; sister of Linda, R.J. and Susan, adventurers, travelers, readers. I have worked as journalist, theater manager, registered nurse and now creative writer.

Hansen, Maxine Duncan Maxine was born in 1923 in a small town in Missouri. At the end of World War II, she married and moved to Chicago and later to the suburb of Glen Ellyn where her three children grew up. In 1975, she moved to Wichita.

Harp, Marilyn I am the executive director of Kansas Legal Services, Inc., the statewide provider of legal services for low-income persons. I graduated from the University of Kansas School of Law in 1979.

Harren, Mary McDonough I was born in Wichita to a St. Louis teacher and an Irish farmer. When Mother died, my siblings and I were raised by our father. I was greatly influenced by the Sisters of Charity who instilled a questioning of authority – especially in a patriarchal church. After my husband died in 1980, I followed the example of my father and raised my children by myself. I have three lovely granddaughters – my Three Graces.

Hicks, Liz I am a community pharmacist, feminist activist and Wichita Broadway Singer. I have written and produced programs on women's history, especially Kansans, and performed re-enactments. I have not yet succeeded in getting us an Equal Rights Amendment, although my daughter, Felicia, still believes I can.

Honeyman, Bonnie Bing My husband of 26 years, Dick Honeyman, and I live in an old house in Wichita's Riverside. I have two stepchildren and three step-granddaughters. I'm now a journalist. I became a writer thanks to some very dear people at *The Wichita Eagle*: the late Diane Lewis, Fran Kentling and the person who taught me how to write, Jon Roe.

Johnston, Colleen Kelly I write – letters to the editor, complaints to public officials, fiction, poetry and essays. As a progressive-liberal egalitarian woman, I make it my responsibility to be a citizen activist for women and all those discriminated against for any reason. My husband, James P. Johnston, shares that responsibility. We have six children who grew up as activists for many causes.

Johnston, Kerry I am a lifelong Kansan. I earned a bachelor's degree in advertising and public relations from Wichita State University. While employed as a communications specialist by day, I write poetry and fiction on the side. I am married with three children and two grandchildren.

Kennedy, Elizabeth "Liz" After growing up and living on the East Coast, my husband and I and our two children moved to Wichita in 1976. After a career in the arts and humanities with Wichita nonprofit organizations, I now telecommute and write about children's books for About.com, which is part of the New York Times Co.

Kentling, Fran I graduated from Wichita State and worked most of my career as an editor at *The Wichita Eagle*. Retired, I'm on the board of Crime Stoppers, the Sheriff's Civil Service Board and a volunteer with the Wichita Winefest's Walkabout, a fundraiser for Guadalupe Clinic. I am the mother of two and grandmother of seven.

Kingsbury, Pamela D. I graduated from the Wichita public school system and received a Ph.D. in art history at the University of Chicago. As an architectural historian, I have served on the Wichita and the Kansas preservation boards and have worked on architectural projects throughout Kansas.

Konek, Carol I think of myself as a compliant-subversive. I am now retired and a widow who is raising two peace-making grandsons, Dylan and Damon, and a great-grandson, Ryder. I also conduct a weekly reading group for feminist fiction and another group for women writing autobiographies and memoirs.

Lewis, Diane C. Diane was an early advocate for women's rights. A WSU graduate, she worked in both public relations and journalism. Her friends remember her as a lover of good wines, a gourmet cook, a theater and visual art enthusiast, and a world traveler. Diane was the first person to receive the Wichita Presswoman's Scholarship.

Mark, Nita I've worked as a company comptroller, nonprofit organization business manager and healthcare administrator. I'm a recipient of the Lifetime Achievement Award from GALA, a gay and lesbian organization. Now retired, I volunteer for Multiple Sclerosis organizations. I thoroughly enjoy my children and three delightful grandchildren.

Markley, Joyce My passion is playwriting. I have a WSU elementary education degree; am founder and president of Signature Exploratory Theatre & Arts, Inc.; and support NPR and many Wichita arts organizations. I am a member of the Dramatists Guild of America, Kansas Writer's Assosiation, the KPTS Signal Society and am a past member of WSU's Fine Arts Advisory Board.

Messner, Ruth Ann I was a co-founder and co-managing editor of Equal Time, a '70s feminist newspaper. I have a B.A. from Wichita State. In the mid '80s, I was the project/regional director for the National Health Screening Council and a board director of The *Wichitan* magazine. In 1983, I became owner/publisher. After completing graduate studies, I taught at Butler County Community College.

Mork, Victoria I married young, saved my husband from the Vietnam War draft with our son, but divorced later. I have two degrees from WSU, a B.F.A and a M.P.A. I organized for McCarthy and believed in LBJ's Great Society. I worked at SRS for 16 years; later I held positions with nonprofit and other government organizations. I currently work for the Kansas Commission on Peace Officers' Standards and Training.

murphy, mardy I moved back to Wichita in 1972 to be a graduate fellow in the WSU School of Business and Economics and to pursue an MFA in creative writing. I wrote poetry and, with others, was instrumental in operating several business ventures including Free To Be Bookstore and *Equal Time* newspaper.

Nelson, Susan I'm 79 years old, a native Kansan, retired English teacher and a person who still lives in the family home because the children like to come home to it. Currently I do volunteer teaching and attend a book, a Scrabble and a bridge club. I am supporting an abandoned cat as a result of blackmail.

Niernberger, Trix During the 1970s, I participated in Kansans for the ERA, Kansas Pro-Choice Action League, Wichita YWCA board of directors, Kansas Women's Political Caucus, abortion clinic defense and the campaign to retain the Wichita gay rights city ordinance. I have directed several nonprofit organizations and now write in upstate New York.

Paris, Myrna I grew up in Wichita and attended Southeast and WSU before moving to Pittsburgh in 1976. During a professional singing/acting career, I performed in many regional theaters and finally made it to New York. I also teach private students and have taught voice at WSU, Juilliard, Carnegie-Mellon and University of Indiana (Bloomington). I am married to author Barry Paris with two grown children.

Porter, Nan Morgan I am a retired psychotherapist and a member of the state Crime Victims Compensation Board. In the 1970s, I was a Metropolitan Area Planning commissioner and served on several boards, including Wichita Art Museum, Sister Cities, Planned Parenthood and Kansas State Network. I have four children – Ty, Beccy, Melissa and Amy, and five grandchildren – Jelani, Chloe, Jaryd, Benjamin and Stevie.

Pott, Katie I'm a native Kansan and a Wichitan since 1946. I graduated from Wichita East High in 1953 and the University of Kansas in 1957 with B.A. in history. I'm married to Tom, have two children and three grand kids. I worked part-time at WSU from 1975 to 1993 in summer session, university communications, admissions and the registrar's office. All were very enjoyable experiences!

Pottorff, Jo Ann After eight years on the Wichita School Board, I made the decision to run for the Kansas Legislature. I have been in the legislature for 27 years and have the distinction of being the longest serving woman in the legislature. I also sell real estate with J.P. Weigand.

Puntch, Robyn B. I recently retired from a 27-year career in fundraising. After spending 12 years working for various Wichita not-for-profits, I served as a major-gift fundraiser for UCLA and the California Institute of Technology.

Rachel I am a 79-year-old and active in the community. I returned to Wichita after Jack's death. Jeff grew up to be a productive and creative person, described by his wife as a gentle and lovely person. He did not reject his father outright, but recognized him as a troubled individual. For that I am grateful.

Ramsay, Andrea I am a practicing attorney in Wichita. My law degree is from the University of Kansas. I have had three children, one of whom is still living. I also have five grandchildren and four great- grandchildren.

Randle, Texanita My involvement in the women's movement coincided with my job as a USD 259 Family and Consumer Science teacher. Before I retired, I directed the South High Child Development Center, which provided child care for infants so their mothers could continue with their high school education. I am married to Bill Randle, and we have two sons and two grandchildren.

Reed, Ann T. I was reared on a Kansas farm and graduated from WSU in the '70s. My work history includes three years with the WSU Alumni Association and 16 years with Via Christi-St Joseph in Human Resources. After an MS diagnosis, I remain at home on disability and continue with limited volunteer opportunities.

Richards, Betty I am a painter turned jewelry designer and author of a book, *Ardis Heights*. I am a member of the National league of American Pen Women and a group of artists known as From the Studio. I have been a wife for 59 years and am mother of four children and grandmother of fourteen grandchildren and seven great-grandchildren.

Richards, Jane Anne I am a teacher, counselor, explorer. I have an M.A. in liberal studies from Valparaiso University and an education specialist degree from Wichita State University. I am still questioning; still searching; still experiencing moments of grace and peace.

Richards, Ruth E. As a volunteer, I always ended up doing either public relations or fundraising. So, in 1989, I turned my 26 years of volunteer activities into my first job with the Girl Scouts in Tulsa. I went on to work for the Oklahoma Nature Conservancy, The American Lung Association and Legal Aid of Oklahoma. I am now partially retired.

Roberts, Connie Bohannon I'm thankful for my education: B.S., KU; master's, UMKC; sabbatical year, WSU. Among my happy memories – I am co-founder of the Creede Repertory Theater, co-producer of Gifts & Girls and Gifts & Peace (conferences and cable), director of "Every Color Crew" and "I-Thou" players. For 30 years, I loved learning from my students in the public schools.

Roe, Myrne My husband is Jon; our son is Matt. They are the somebodies I love most in this world. Women, who helped me, more than they will ever know, through the bad days of my depression hell in 1973 are Sally Kitch, Carol Konek, Karla Langton, Connie Morris and Nan Porter. I thank them for caring.

Rosales, Carmen I am a businesswoman and a restaurateur, a mother of five daughters, a proud grandmother of four, a marathon runner and a brain aneurism survivor (who had a less than 2 percent chance of surviving). Most important, I am a cradle Catholic and very devout in my faith.

Ross, Novelene G. I am fortunate to have been loved and mentored by numerous strong, wise women, beginning with my mother, and by a dear husband who taught me how to honor and fight for civil rights. In 2000, I retired from a 27-year career at the Wichita Art Museum, where I had held the positions of curator of education, acting director and curator of collections.

Russell, Carolyn S. I am a PR counselor, business owner, photographer and traveler. I've worked in corporate communication for Fortune 100 companies, sold encyclopedias and cars, was a radio news reporter and anchor, a nurse and Army photographer, medic, journalist and broadcaster. I am now producing fine art prints of my photography, past and present.

Rutledge, Carol Brunner In her mid and later years, Carol identified herself as a writer. Newspapers had other terms for Carol – community activist, would-be politician, preservationist or historian. Women of history were her passion, especially women of Kansas. No one could see her one-woman performance of *I Am Kansas Woman* without coming away with renewed admiration for the contributions of women, nor fail to be convinced of not doing enough to right the injustices still remaining.

Simmons, Margaret I am a liberal feminist Democrat. Since the 1960s, I have tried to convert my views into action. I served on high-profile community boards, volunteered for campaigns, ran for office, became a cofounder of Women's Equality Coalition and worked as a campaign coordinator for then Congressman Dan Glickman. Now retired, I still want Democratic women to run for office and win.

Skeen, Anita I am currently professor in the Residential College in the Arts and Humanities at Michigan State University, where I am the arts coordinator for the college and director of The Center for Poetry. Before going to Michigan State in 1990, I was for 18 years on the faculty of the English department and MFA program at Wichita State University, where I taught creative writing, literature and women's studies. I have authored four volumes of poetry: *Each Hand a Map*; *Portraits*; *Outside the Fold, Outside the Frame*; *The Resurrection of the Animals*; and co-authored with poet Jane Taylor, *When We Say Shelter*. My most recent collection of poems, *Never the Whole Story*, has been selected for publication by Michigan State University Press.

Skinner, Margot Brown I was born in Chicago in 1935 and moved to Wichita in 1940. I attended the University of Colorado and graduated from the University of California-Berkeley with a B.A. in political science. My daughter, Mary, lives in New York City. My interest in political science continues (maybe not the science, but definitely the politics). I have volunteered with Planned Parenthood, the Wichita Art Museum and Friends of the Library.

Starkel, Lee Goodman While working in the Women's Studies Department, I received my undergraduate degree in August 1980 and my master's degree in liberal studies in December 1981, combining women's studies, minority studies and business administration. From 1981-2003, I helped coordinate the Women Writing Series, establish the Women's Studies Community Council Advisory Board and create the WSU Plaza of Heroines.

Stephan, Lynn Kincheloe I was one of the first women in Kansas to run an advertising agency. My creative work won regional and national awards and turned record profits for our clients. After receiving my M.A.L.S. at Wichita State, I volunteered for philanthropic organizations, including KPTS, The Kansas Humane Society and WSU. I am a freelance writer, married to Don Stephan and have three stepchildren and eight grandchildren.

Sweet, Donna E. I am professor of internal medicine at the University of Kansas School of Medicine-Wichita and graduated from KUSM-W, where I also completed my residency training. I see both general medicine and HIV/AIDS patients in my practice. In addition, I lecture nationally and internationally on AIDS issues, as well as health care reform

Van Gieson, Fern Merrifield As a feminist, I've been a butterfly and a worker bee, focus sometimes giving way to broadening concerns or the personal. I see myself as having been a sharer in strategies and actions toward changing attitudes and policies. At 82, I term myself a fallen-away activist. I needed a push forward and looking back seems to be providing it.

Vines, Peg I am one of 12 children and raised seven of my own (who well recall my loud soapbox days). I'm now retired from ad writing, but never from working for social justice and urging my 13 grandkids to keep up the tradition.

Vliet, Marni I received my B.A. and master's degree in education, with emphasis on health, from Wichita State. Now retired as president and CEO of the Kansas Health Foundation, a private philanthropy dedicated to improving the health of all Kansas, I am a strategic consultant to not-for-profit and for-profit organizations across Kansas and the country.

Wahto, Diane In 1963, I read *The Feminine Mystique,* while I rocked my third baby to sleep. By 1974, I was a single mother and a high school journalism teacher. I became active in the NEA because of its advocacy for teacher rights as well as women's rights. I read my poetry at the Salina Humanities Council April poetry reading series, where I received the New Voice Award. I'm working on compiling a book of my thirty-five years of poetry.

Walters Ph.D., Dorothy The Chapters of My Life as a Maverick: 1. Graduate School in American and English literature – Breaking the Stereotypes. 2. I am a what? – Becoming a lesbian before it was popular. 3. Women's Studies at WSU – Take that, you old fogies. We are going to change things. 4. Spontaneous Kundalini Awakening – The Ultimate Connection with the Divine Feminine. See www.kundalinisplendor. blogspot.com 5. Publications – two books in my seventies: *Marrow of Flame* (poetry); *Unmasking the Rose* (spiritual autobiography); one book in my eighties: *A Cloth of Fine Gold* (poetry) and another book of poems on the way.

Welsbacher, Anne I am a writer living in Wichita. My play, *Pardon My Dust,* premiered in 2009 at Wichita's Center for the Arts theatre. My mother, Betty Welsbacher, died in 2008. Her colleague and our family friend, Eunice (Euny) Boardman died in 2009.

Wilshusen, Kris In 1977, I graduated from the University of Northern Colorado with a major in special education and a minor in women's studies. I served as executive director, Planned Parenthood of Kansas, from 1991 to 1998. I also served as executive director of the Wichita Sexual Assault Center from 1988 to 1991.

Wright, Margalee Pilkington I think of myself as a circle-maker, a community builder, one who brings people together to serve the common good. It was my privilege to serve the people of Wichita as mayor and the people of Kansas as a member of the Kansas Corporation Commission. Wichita has always been my home.

Zadoka, Priscilla I have two grown children: Phil is a teacher in Lexington, KY, and Sheila is a mother and a returning college student pursuing a degree in criminal justice in Wichita. My two children have given me five grandsons who are the joy of my life

Acknowledgments

Thank you to all the women who participated in this anthology as writers, interviewers and supporters. Without you, of course, there would be no book.

My special thanks go to Sarah Bagby whose expertise and considerable assistance made publication possible. Also thanks to Fran Kentling and Kate Goad for proofreading copy. Linda Gebert went the extra mile to help find photos and write essays to fill in issue gaps not covered by someone else. In addition to Linda, I would like to mention the other women on staff at *Equal Time*: Mardy Binter Murphy, Ruth Ann Messner, Sherry Eslick Buettgenback, the late Glendora Johnson and Carol Dannar McEwen. Anita Skeen wrote a wonderful introduction.

I appreciate my writing group – Margalee Wright, Linda Gebert, Betty Richards, Alta Brock, Emily Bonavia, Jane Richards, Diane Wato, Marilynn Gump and Colleen Johnston – who were the first to urge me to proceed with this book.

To my husband of 54 years, Jon Roe: I appreciate you for critiquing, proofing, handholding and telling me to "knock it off" when I worked too hard and got too overwrought. And thank you, Donovan Rutledge, for going through many boxes of your late wife Carol's, writings so that her poem could be included in the anthology.

Finally, to all the Wichita feminists in the 1970s, too many of whom are now deceased: Thank you for making positive differences in the lives of today's women and men, for gender equality for one truly yields equality for both.

About the Editor

Photograph by Jon Roe

Myrne Roe is a former teacher, congressional staff director, university public relations administrator, editorial writer and nationally syndicated columnist. Her columns about her struggles with chronic, clinical depression won several awards from public health and mental health organizations.

Now retired, she has published a poetry chapbook, *Ironing out the Wrinkles*. Her poems have been published in regional publications, and have won awards from Kansas Writers Association, *Byline Magazine*, Kansas Voices, Heartland Authors and the Winfield (KS) Arts and Humanities Council.

She also compiled and edited *Under Hope's Roof*, which chronicles the lives of 14 homeless people. Published by Inter-Faith Ministries Wichita, book sales benefited IFM's homeless and housing services.

She has been married to Jon for 52 years; they have an adult son, Matt.

Photo Index

Exploring Feminism, Page 1
Left to Right: Dr. Carol Konek, Dr. Dorothy K. Walters and Dr. Sally Kitch,
Center for Women's Studies faculty at Wichita State University, 1983.

Redefining Women's Work, Page 37
Ruth Luzzati, the only women being sworn into the Kansas State legislature in 1973.

Challenging Financial Status Quo, Page 87
Pharmacist Liz Hicks at work, circa 1970.

Removing Sexism from the Curriculum, Page 103
Wichita State University's women's basketball team at Henry Levitt Arena,
January 1978. Photo by Kathy Ivy.

Struggling for Equality as Women and Minorities, Page 133
Carmen Rosales and her baby at Easter, 1974.

Finding a Feminist Faith, Page 149
Photograph from Anita Bryant protest, December 1977. Photo credit: *Equal Time*

Pursuing Heath Care for Women, Page 163
Marni Vliet with her two daughters, Sasha and Whitney Vliet, and Scarlett Higgins,
1977. Photo by Trish Higgins

Organizing for Political Clouth, Page 179
The Women's Equality Coalition meeting at YWCA, November 1977.
Photo credit: *Equal Time*

Embracing Our Artistic Gifts, Page 217
The first WomenArt/WomenFair, 1978. Photo credit: *Equal Time*

Facing Crimes of Violence Against Women, Page 231
Peg Vines at work in the 1970s. She was instrumental in starting the Women's Crisis
Center.

Speaking Up and Speaking Out, Page 251
Colleen Kelly Johnston speaking at a NOW rally at the State Capitol.

General Index

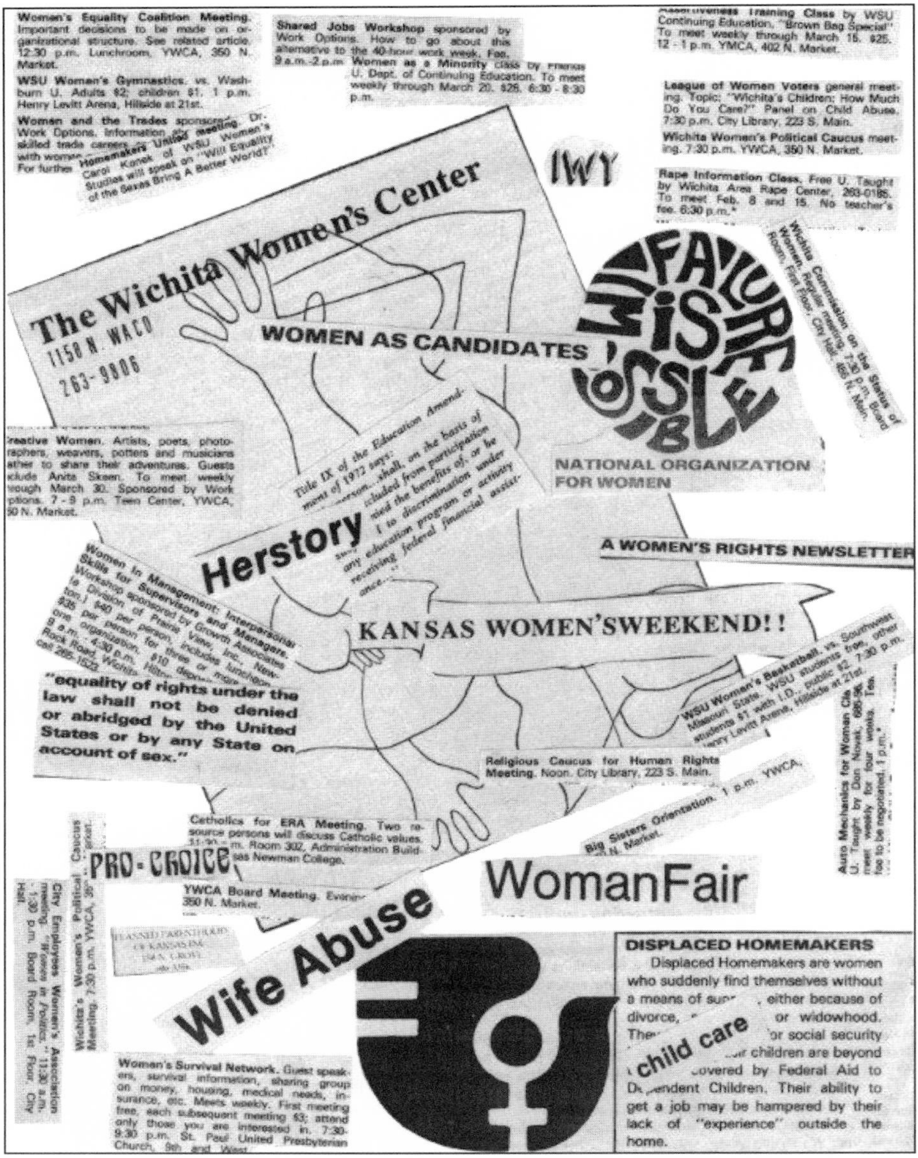
Women's Equality Coalition Meeting. Important decisions to be made on organizational structure. See related article. 12:30 p.m. Lunchroom, YWCA, 350 N. Market.
WSU Women's Gymnastics vs. Washburn U. Adults $2; children $1. 1 p.m. Henry Levitt Arena, Hillside at 21st.
Shared Jobs Workshop sponsored by Work Options. How to go about this alternative to the 40-hour work week. Fee. 9 a.m.-2 p.m.
Women as a Minority class by Friends U. Dept. of Continuing Education. To meet weekly through March 20. $26. 6:30 - 8:30 p.m.
Continuing Education, "Brown Bag Special." To meet weekly through March 15. $25. 12 - 1 p.m. YMCA, 402 N. Market.
League of Women Voters general meeting. Topic: "Wichita's Children: How Much Do You Care?" Panel on Child Abuse. 7:30 p.m. City Library, 223 S. Main.
Wichita Women's Political Caucus meeting. 7:30 p.m. YWCA, 350 N. Market.
Rape Information Class. Free U. Taught by Wichita Area Rape Center, 263-0185. To meet Feb. 8 and 15. No teacher's fee. 6:30 p.m.
Homemakers United meeting. Carol Konek of WSU Women's Studies will speak on "Will Equality of the Sexes Bring A Better World?"
IWY
The Wichita Women's Center
1158 N. WACO
263-9806
WOMEN AS CANDIDATES
FAILURE IS IMPOSSIBLE
NATIONAL ORGANIZATION FOR WOMEN
Wichita Commission on the Status of Women. Regular meeting. 7:30 p.m. Board Room, First Floor, City Hall, 455 N. Main.
Title IX of the Education Amendments of 1972 says: "No person...shall, on the basis of sex, be excluded from participation in, be denied the benefits of, or be subjected to discrimination under any education program or activity receiving federal financial assistance."
Herstory
A WOMEN'S RIGHTS NEWSLETTER
KANSAS WOMEN'SWEEKEND!!
"equality of rights under the law shall not be denied or abridged by the United States or by any State on account of sex."
WSU Women's Basketball vs. Southwest Missouri State. WSU students free, other students $1 with I.D., public $2. 7:30 p.m. Henry Levitt Arena, Hillside at 21st.
Religious Caucus for Human Rights Meeting. Noon. City Library, 223 S. Main.
Big Sisters Orientation. 1 p.m. YWCA.
Auto Mechanics for Women Class. Free U. Taught by Don Novak. To meet weekly for four weeks. Fee to be negotiated. 1 p.m.
Catholics for ERA Meeting. Two resource persons will discuss Catholic values. Room 302, Administration Building, Kansas Newman College.
PRO-CHOICE
YWCA Board Meeting. 350 N. Market.
WomanFair
Wife Abuse
City Employees Women's Association meeting. "Women in Politics." 11:30 a.m.-1:30 p.m. Board Room, 1st Floor, City Hall.
Wichita Women's Political Caucus Meeting. 7:30 p.m. YWCA, 350 N. Market.
Women's Survival Network. Guest speakers, survival information, sharing group on money, housing, medical needs, insurance, etc. Meets weekly. First meeting free, each subsequent meeting $3; attend only those you are interested in. 7:30-9:30 p.m. St. Paul United Presbyterian Church, 9th and West.
child care
DISPLACED HOMEMAKERS
Displaced Homemakers are women who suddenly find themselves without a means of support, either because of divorce, or widowhood. or social security children are beyond covered by Federal Aid to Dependent Children. Their ability to get a job may be hampered by their lack of "experience" outside the home.

Collage by Myrne Roe